To. Lurline,

I do hope that you will find this journey educational as you take this "Walk With Me"

R. h Carter
27th. May 2022

WALK WITH ME

WALK WITH ME

AN AUTOBIOGRAPHY

COLLIN LEROY CARTER

First published in Great Britain by Hansib Publications in 2017

Hansib Publications Limited
P.O. Box 226, Hertford, SG14 3WY

info@hansibpublications.com
www.hansibpublications.com

Reprinted 2018

ISBN 978-1-910553-82-4

A CIP catalogue record for this book
is available from the British Library

Front cover photo of Glendairy Prison Gully, Barbados, and
back cover photo, courtesy of Annette Ione Smith

Design & Production by Hansib Publications Ltd
Cover design concept by Jonathan Lewis

Printed in Great Britain

Dedication

It is said that, "no man is an island," but Mable Matilda Carter repeatedly told her five sons that she was, "the only man" in her home.

Hence, this book is dedicated to the late great Mable Matilda Carter, my mother, my mentor and my island

I would also like to dedicate this book to all of my Ancestors, on whose shoulders I stand.

To my wife, my brothers, my children, my grandchildren and great-grandchildren.

ACKNOWLEDGEMENTS

I am deeply indebted to the people who helped me to make my dream of publishing this book a reality. I am especially grateful to:

My brother, Rudolph Carter, a "Griot" in the true sense of the word. Thank you for filling in the missing pieces of our family's history.

My dear friend, Arif Ali, of Hansib Publications. Thank you for dropping everything at a moment's notice to publish *Walk With Me*.

My friends and acquaintances who, on hearing that I had commenced this "walk", gave me much encouragement and made it known that they would be anxiously awaiting their own personally signed copy of this book.

My researcher, Annette Ione Smith, author of *Etched* and *Rend*. I met Annette whilst she was in Barbados doing research on one of her own books, but she graciously decided that mine was the greater cause! I am indebted to her for her sterling research work and her assistance in getting the idea of the book committed to paper.

For all those whose names are not mentioned here, but who have assisted in whichever way, I thank you ALL.

CONTENTS

BOOK IV
1960-1970: Her Majesty's Subject

BOOK V
1970-1980: Self-Sufficiency

BOOK VI
1980-1990: Planning and Planting

BOOK VII
1990-2000: A True Pan-Africanist

BOOK VIII
2000-2014: Still Pressing On

BOOK IX
Historical Reflections and Tributes

FOREWORD

An engaging and insightful look at growing up in Barbados in the 1940s and 1950s through the keyhole of one man's experiences, this first book is part historical text, part 'coming of age' story, part Pan-Africanist manual. This publication speaks to many themes that easily resonate to persons of Afro-Caribbean descent, and indeed any person who wishes an insider's view into the origins and realities of working class Caribbean persons of that generation.

'Walk with Me' looks back across three generations, but each era is presented via the lens of the writer, a 'self-made' man who over a period of time and character-shaping experiences has come to a greater understanding of self, purpose and his unique place in Caribbean diasporic history. In telling his story he has touched on many themes: the persistent legacy of slavery and plantation life; the institution of matriarch lead homes; the commitment to family; the importance of pride, self- respect and personal discipline; the need of hard work and sacrifice towards accomplishing major goals; and self confidence in pursuing business opportunities towards self and community empowerment.

Each aspect of this document has the potential to be an entire volume in itself and the reader is soon aware that for all that is shared so much more can be written. The activities and day to day life of any people has always been central to the culture of that nation. It is the ordinary folk who undertake their day-to-day practices utilising considerable indigenous knowledge daily in their food preparation, funerary traditions, etc. Mable Carter, by far the greatest influence in Collin Carter's life, actively used her culinary and vending skills to carve a livelihood for her family and with her grassroots entrepreneurship contributed to the national economy by this very act of expressing her native culture. There can be no doubt about the value of this too often overlooked contribution. Esteemed Barbadian academic and writer George Lamming[1] refers to the labour of our working class folk as that of intellectuals. He states:

> *"The word intellectual may be applied to all forms of labour which could not possibly be done without some exercise of the mind ... the fisherman and the farmer may be regarded as cultural and intellectual workers in their own right. Social practise has provided them with a considerable body of knowledge and a capacity to make discriminating judgements in their daily work."*

It is in recognition of such consistent contribution to Barbados at the community and national level that give us much cause to celebrate our cultural workers in the widest sense. Without a doubt it was his mother's entrepreneurial spirit and determined self-reliance that shaped Collin's confidence in stepping into the world of work and his eventual self-employment and investment in several business ventures. His mother's and indeed his intellectual work has been the basis of her and subsequently his success in the face of enormous challenges.

This book therefore recognizes and salutes the sterling efforts of the entrepreneurial working class whose work and commitment over generations has demonstrated the model of self-reliance as being a true expression of Independence. Professor Woodville Marshall[2] has noted that in a Post-Emancipation society, it was the working class that:

> *"... initiated the conversion of those plantation territories into modern societies. In a variety of ways they attempted to build local self-generating communities. They founded villages and markets... they clamoured for extension of educational facilities, for improvements in communication and markets; they started the local co-operative movement... Peasant development was emancipation in action."*

So in celebration of our common history, we celebrate our entrepreneurs in recognition of the key roles that they have played and continue to play in asserting a national identity, feeding the nation, demonstrating self-determination and maintaining a national marketplace.

It is also notable that following the path of members of such influential groups as the Caribbean Artists Movement, it is within the diaspora that much of the growing of awareness of the common struggle and history that unites the region is discovered and the need for social and political agitation for change is developed. It is the act of travelling to the 'centre' of the colonial system that the truth about the system is clearly seen and the myths of the system as taught and perpetuated within the colonies challenged. Collin's journey, is then instructive to those who may have not had the privilege of that 'line of sight' in not only understanding the experiences that shaped him but the relevance of his knowledge gained to all of us members of these societies and their diasporas.

The Community has always been important as a core of cultural and economic development, even if too often remaining unexploited. In travelling to the UK Collin's understanding of community embraced a wider diaspora, but his approach remained true to the source: It is within the traditions of each space and the resources of that environment that the innate creativity of our people can be harnessed for its expression and development. This is the lesson that his personal journey clearly shows us and the context within which his invitation to 'Walk with Me' must be taken.

Andrea Wells
**Chief Cultural Officer, National Cultural Foundation, Barbados,
September 2017**

1. George Lamming, *Coming, Coming Home: Conversations II*, House of Nehesi Publishers, 2000
2. Woodville Marshall, *Notes on Peasant Development in the West Indies since 1838*, 1968

BOOK I

Sesa wo Suban
"I change or transform my life"

Transformation

CHAPTER 1

With this ring, I thee wed

"Marriage is like a groundnut; you have to crack it to see what's inside." GHANAIAN PROVERB

It was Saturday, August 31, 1895. This day was of no particular historical importance to the rest of the world but for me, Collin Leroy Carter, it was a day of major importance. It was the day my grandfather, James Thomas Carter, would wed my grandmother, Delcina Franklin. However, according to records at the Barbados National Archives she was, on her wedding day, Delcina Carter which, if the records were correct, would suggest that she would walk into the church a 'Carter' before her wedding and would walk out with the same surname (Carter) after her wedding.

At first I speculated as to why they both had the same surname. I wondered if there was any relation or kinship existing between my grandparents; however, upon further delving, I am of the convinced mind that my grandparents were not related. It's my firm belief that because neither could read nor write, they were unaware that their marriage certificate had listed both of them with the same surname before marriage, and so this mistake would, years later, cause some confusion in my mind as to my grandmother's maiden name.

This "naming mistake" could very well be a coincidence, or perhaps just indifference on the part of the official responsible for recording the respective details, which is why they ended up with the same last names on their marriage certificate as recorded in the Barbados Archives. To the best of my knowledge marriages between close kin would have been such a taboo for them (and would have left future generations marred by this stigma) that it's something I'm sure that not enough love would have existed for them to mar their children and future generations with this burden. It was their inability to read and write; They were probably this first generation of so called 'Free Slaves'; at six or seven years old they would most likely be working in a third-class gang (children) in the fields, thus contributing to the financial help their parents would have thought necessary.

On further delving I found my late mother's birth certificate, which clearly showed that my grandmother's maiden name was Franklin. How my grandmother happened to have her maiden name recorded as Carter isn't relevant. Suffice to say they were married. In my imagination, my grandfather was 'sharo'[1]. For his "big day" he would have worn whatever were his "best clothes", be they begged or borrowed. The man I am today would want to imagine that he would be standing there at the altar dressed in a dapper suit, clean white shirt, perhaps a tie and shoes which would have been highly polished as he waited on the woman he had chosen to make his wife – my grandmother – to walk down the aisle to him in a flowing wedding dress, freshly cut flowers in her hands, a tulle veil shielding her shy eyes.

However, that is fanciful thinking. Common sense would dictate that, given the times and conditions of the day, it would have been nothing like that. That type of dress was reserved for the plantocracy[2] Nonetheless, whatever my grandfather wore that day someone in his family (perhaps an aunt, a sister or even his wife-to-be) would have seen to it that it was clean and creased. My grandmother would have been 'decked' as well, even if her dress (begged or borrowed) was made from bleached flour bags and trimmed perhaps with a bit of lace.

It is true that slavery, or the forced enslavement of Africans and their descendants, was considered to be over from the effective date of August 1, 1838. However, the conditioning (or 'seasoning'[3] as it was called) remained. So, on reflection, I can only speculate as to whether or not my grandparents would have preferred to "jump the broom"[4] (as they would have done if their ancestors had not been kidnapped, chained and brought to Barbados) is something that I can only imagine. I also don't know if they would have looked upon it as something the "slaves" did because they weren't afforded the opportunity to marry in a church as they, my grandparents, were preparing to do. None of that bore any real importance. What was of paramount importance was that they were about to be married.

Times and things had changed a little, to such a point that they are preparing to be married in a church by a white Rector who probably didn't care one way or another about the persons before him. He probably saw them as he saw all the others who had come before him: just another two "niggers", resplendent in their now perfectly "enslaved" minds, an imposed and accepted idea of finery. Whatever the circumstances or the thinking they are standing before him to be joined, by him, in holy matrimony.

The time of the wedding is not known to me. What is known is that the wedding took place at St Luke's Anglican Church. In those days the Rector or Reverend George B. Taylor, a white man, officiated. Neither set of parents for the bride or groom were present as these two were wed. According to the copy of their marriage certificate from St Luke's Anglican Church (which is available at the National Archives in; Barbados), both my grandmother's and grandfather's parents were deceased. The marriage certificate gives my grandfather's age as 28 years and states that he was a labourer. It also shows that there were two witnesses to this union. When they got married my grandparents were still living on Brighton Plantation in the parish of St George, so I will take certain liberties that he was in actual fact a "field hand" on that plantation, rather than the more pleasant-sounding "labourer".

I remember my grandfather wearing collarless shirts, in retrospect I believe that those were the hand me downs from the planter. I was about six years when I met him; I was taken to spend a day or two in the holiday with my grandfather, who at that time was married to his second wife after the passing of my grandmother in the 1920s. I recall clearly my grandfather holding my hand walking through the district very proudly with his last grandson, his daughter's last boy, walking by his side. He usually kept two or three sweets in his pocket which he would dole out to me one after the other, I can also remember him giving me three or so spoonfuls of port wine in a small glass followed by the words "you drink that boy, it would help get the rid of the worms."

Knowing my grandfather's age, I did some very simple arithmetic. My grandfather was born in 1867, some thirty-three years after slaves were supposedly emancipated in Barbados. Those thirty-three years (which for most people equals a generation) meant that all my great-grandparents were enslaved and perhaps born on that very plantation where my grandparents were preparing to return as husband and wife. I will never know if this was something that either of them was thinking about on that August day; it was after-all their wedding day.

However, what is clearly known is that this church wedding would not have been a privilege afforded my great-grandparents or great-great-grandparents prior to or during the four-to-six years following the Slavery Abolition Act of 1833[5] when the British were so graciously manumitting/freeing the slaves. I use the term "manumitting/freeing" in its most loose sense, since technically emancipation for the slaves in Barbados and those territories under British rule didn't really occur on 1 August 1834 but took a further six years before the true physical shackles of the enslaved would ultimately be broken.

The Slavery Abolition Act of 1833 made provision that the British plantocracy would be 'compensated' for the loss of the slaves they 'owned'. This compensation was to come in the form of a division of £20 million (in 1833 this amounted to 5 per cent of the government's GDP[6]). The names listed in the returns for slave compensation indicate that slave ownership was spread over many hundreds of British families including Henry Phillpotts (the then Bishop of Exeter) who was paid £12,700 for 665 slaves in the West Indies. One such British family received £40,000 pounds for the 665 slaves that they 'owned' at the time: that equates to £19.0977 per slave. If you can imagine, a human being valued/appraised for £19.00. It is no wonder that the Black man has had to struggle and some, today, even continue to struggle, not just with worth but self-worth.

Consider that these Black men, women and children were violently stolen and forcedly enslaved, but the slave owners were the ones who were more than adequately compensated. This exploitation of those that had been forcefully enslaved continued under the guise of an "apprenticeship". An apprentice could be any slave over the age of six years. Despite the Act of 1833, emancipation/freedom would be delayed; doled out based on the slaves' 'occupation' while enslaved. House slaves/negroes/niggers and the crafts worker would become fully emancipated four years and so could look forward to their so-called full physical freedom on 1 August 1838. The field hands/negroes/niggers had to wait another two years (1840) before full freedom would be theirs.

Whilst everyone waited for this freedom they had to work from sun-up to sun-down to 'pay' for the land on which their chattel houses stood. Should they work over 40 hours then they would be compensated for the time over forty hours. Here again the slave master benefited, as he did not have the added expense of feeding, clothing, or 'maintaining' the health of the 'free' slaves.

My grandparents, as well as my mother, were supposed to be born as 'free slaves'. But how can one be free and also enslaved at the same time? One needs to ponder on this contradiction. According to Dr Harold A.A. Gibbs in the book, *Recrystallisation Into The New-Age Black Man* my grandparents could well have been direct descendants of African Royalty, who were faultless in finding themselves trapped, shackled, kidnapped and taken to anywhere in the world. Enslaved and placed under conditions that had no resemblance to their Royal Statehood, with little or no hope of having it restored to them. Gibbs states that the term 'free slave' is said to be the term used by so-called educated Blacks. I agree with him that, "…we are still a people without dignity, wealth, and a distinct culture of our own as we once had."

Whilst a law was passed to abolish slavery, the law did not free our minds or change or mindset. I would argue that one hundred and eighty four years after the supposed legal end of our physical enslavement, many are still mentally enslaved with the 'seasoning' of our forefathers. This is not a uniquely modern-day predicament: *African History at the Tower of London* (written and compiled by Harry Cumberbatch, Sidney Millen, Philip Morgan and Fabian Tompsett) tells the story of George Laurens: "A Slave Who Refused His Freedom."

George was the property of Henry Laurens, was best known for being an American political leader during that country's Revolutionary War. He was also a prosperous merchant and slave trader. Laurens was accused of treason by the British authorities and, when he was imprisoned at the Tower of London in September 1780, George was imprisoned with him. Henry Laurens was released in December 1781 and, together with George, travelled to France where he played a pivotal role in the Treaty of Paris which led to the end of the American Revolutionary War. On their arrival in Philadelphia Laurens offered George his freedom but George refused. He preferred to remain a slave on his master's plantation. Upon Henry Lauren's death, George assumed his surname and was bequeathed one hundred and twenty dollars.

George was not unique in his desire to remain a slave. During the centuries of slavery in the United States, there were indeed freed Black people, who had been freed by their 'masters', or who had acquired enough money to 'buy' their freedom. But many slaves did not want to be free, because they felt 'secure' in their bondage. There was the certainty that Massa would brutalise them and sell their children, but they knew that in return for this brutality, they would be clothed, housed and fed. To their minds, the degradations of slavery seemed to far outweigh an uncertain future as a free person.

It is downright folly to think that the enslavers and their vampires are ever going to part with any of the wealth, power and position they have gorged themselves on for 400 years, or stand idly by and watch the Black man devise a system that will bring us real freedom. Even though fifty-five years had passed since slaves were finally granted their so-called 'freedom' my grandparents were illiterate. When the wedding was over and it was time for them to sign the register, both would acknowledge their union by placing an 'X' where their signatures should have been. Perhaps like so many children of slaves or children born on plantations, at reaching the age of six or seven they were put out to the field to earn their keep to help their parents pay rent for the land on which their chattel house stood. In my grandparents' case, that land was owned by a planter by the name of Conrad Pile. Years earlier, Conrad Pile had donated to the Anglican Church the land on which St Luke's Church was built. St Luke's was considered a "church of ease", which meant such churches were constructed to accommodate those persons who could not get to their local parish church. In the case of my grandparents that inaccessible or "further away church" would have been St George's Parish Church. This definition of "ease" had nothing to do with Blacks. The "ease" was for whites who would not have to travel far to their church of ease. Let's not forget that they used the same Christianity to further enslave the minds of Africans.

There is no record or any living witnesses to say what happened after my grandparents were married. Would they have gathered at their home, or the home of a family member or friend, and have a celebration? I don't know. What I do know is that from their union six children were born: Gerald, Lillian, Mable Matilda, Edna, Dora, and Berry. Some forty-two years after Mable Matilda Carter born on 5 May 1898, I would be born to her: her fifth son and her last child. I would follow Lemuel, Rudolph, Victor and Carl. Unlike my mother and her siblings, each one of us would have a different father. My eldest brother Lemuel was born on the same Brighton Plantation: after my mother left the country to work and live in town[7] he stayed with and was raised by my grandparents. My mother would never know what was like to walk down a church aisle with (or without) a bouquet of flowers, never look up to see a man waiting for her to make her his wife. She would become a mother five times but never would she marry, and never be a wife.

I always used to call myself "May Carter's Good Time Child" or, sometimes jokingly, say that I am the product of a good time: not so much my mother's good time but my father's. I had no idea when I said that how very true the latter part of that statement was. Once the truth of that statement came home to roost I then had to take a different look at my father, Aubrey Alleyne, a man whom I never had an opportunity to know because he never acknowledged me or my existence. This different look has evolved into abject indifference to a point where I can honestly say that after all these years, I bear him no animosity. By not acknowledging me, by ignoring my existence, what he did back then is no different to what some of the descendants of the enslaved are doing today. When some men directly and indirectly continue to make women pregnant and then deny or abandon the products of their 'good times', they are acting like Aubrey Alleyne. According to Dr Joy DeGruy Ph.D, author of *Post Traumatic Slave Syndrome: America's Legacy of Enduring Injury and Healing (PTSS)* this kind of behaviour is synonymous with 'Post Traumatic Slave Syndrome'[8].

This denial and abandonment of the by-products of their good times further perpetuates that vicious cycle, when enslaved men were used as breeding studs for the economic advancement of their enslavers. Before they were enslaved, these men would certainly not have considered breeding/mating with their beloved Queens without any emotional connection. However, these men were now 'seasoned slaves' given no more consideration than a basic farm animal. In this respect, they were expected to reproduce in much the same way. Massa wanted more chattels and so they robotically produced. This mindless, emotionless copulating had not only damaged the psyche of these once strong-willed and bodied men, but also the by-products of these couplings: their children. These well-seasoned men did not see children as their future generations. They simply saw children to whom they had no emotional connection, so they could easily walk away from "Massa's chattel". Their 'real' fathers had nothing to do with them. After all, they were Massa's property and he was responsible for feeding, clothing and "rearing/seasoning" them. They had done what was expected of them: copulate, reproduce, end of the story. Or was it?

This ability to dismiss and abandon their children is a direct correlation of this emasculation of African men during slavery. It affected my father and a great many like him. Although he (and others like him) was more than a bit removed from physical slavery, the scars of mental and emotional enslavement remained. To him, and sad though it was my mother, a beautiful, strong and loving woman, was just like the enslaved women who were used by the enslavers to breed and sometimes abandon their children. To him, she was just a wench to copulate with and move on. She was just someone with whom he could have a good time. He didn't care that his "good-time wench" was about to produce a child. When the product of that good time arrived, it had no emotional impact on him. I could almost imagine him looking around for his "Massa" to let him know that he, Aubrey Alleyne, was indeed a good buck, a good house nigger. He had done like all the other 'breeding bucks', he had added to Massa's chattel and produced a son.

Here is where Aubrey Alleyne should have conferred with my mother. Had he done so he would have known that she was no wench. She shouldn't have been characterised as anyone's 'good time'. She was a hardworking woman and doing all that she could to earn a living for herself and her children.

With the exception of Lemuel, we all lived in Carrington Village, St Michael. My mother earned a living by being a hawker[9] on Tweedside Road, which was about three minutes away from where we lived. This close proximity to her home and her boys afforded her a degree of comfort: if she needed to, she could get home in a hurry to her boys. This short distance to her home also meant that my brother Rudolph (my second oldest brother) wouldn't have far to go in the dark when he went to meet her in the evenings to walk home with her.

The spot[10] my mother found also assured her that she would be safe from nonsense; not that she could not or would not have defended herself should it have been necessary. The spot was in front of my Godfather's rum shop. I understand from Rudolph that it was here that my mother met my father. I do not know how long it was from introduction to friendship. What I have learned is that he was a chauffeur for white people in Pine Hill, which was near Government

House[11]. It was also five to ten minutes' walk away from where she sold her goods.

During the time they met Black people didn't live in that part of St Michael. The Pine Hill area was where the white people lived and sent their children to schools such as St Winifred's School. It was an accepted practice that no Black children were allowed to attend St Winifred's, even though some of these Black children might have been equally as bright (and in some cases brighter).

In the Pine Hill area, Belmont Road was "the great divide". On one side of Belmont Road, white people lived in areas which included Belleville, Pine Hill and (a bit further afield) Strathclyde, Graham Hall, Navy Gardens and Highgate Gardens/Park. Black people lived on the other side of Belmont Road in areas like Carrington Village (where my mother, brothers and I lived) Peterkin, Black Rock and Bank Hall and other such related areas. The biggest example of "the great divide" was the Strathclyde Road. The Black people on one side of this divide serviced the needs of the whites on the other side. They worked as maids, cooks, butlers, chauffeurs, gardeners, laundry women and nursemaids. Unless they had a note from their employers, these (Black) employees could be arrested if they were caught in these areas "after hours". Considering these racial conditions in Barbados of yesteryear, one could be forgiven for asking "if Prime Minister Hendrik Verwoerd, the father of South African apartheid, was a South African or a Barbadian?"

I'm not sure what thoughts (if any) my mother would have had about this as she went about her daily task of setting up her tray in her 'spot', selling her goods and at night taking her tray up and walking home with my brother Rudolph. I'm not 100 per cent certain what was on my mother's tray but she was a baker so it's easy to guess that there were breads of varying sizes, textures and taste. She was very gifted when it came to making anything that involved flour, sugar and baking powder. Some of her specialties were sweet (coconut) bread, turnovers, cassava, corn and coconut pone and "top hats". Top hats were her own creation: they looked like a Jamaican patty but were filled with sweet coconut spiced with cinnamon and nutmeg. Given how hard she had to work to make all these baked goods, there is a very good likelihood that my mother might not have had romance on her mind when Aubrey Alleyne started coming around her 'spot'.

FOOTNOTES

1. Old Bajan (Barbadian) slang word for being well dressed.
2. Planters (former slave owners) that were so-called aristocrats.
3. Slaves were tortured for the purpose of "breaking" them and conditioning them to their new lot in life. Owners and their overseers immediately sought to obliterate the identities of their newly acquired slaves, break their wills and sever any bonds with the past. They forced Africans to adapt to new working and living conditions, to learn a new language and adopt new customs. This 'seasoning' process could last two or three years.
4. This is an African ceremony dating back to the 1600s: the bride and groom signify their entrance into a new life and their creation of a new family by symbolically "sweeping away" their former single lives, problems and concerns, and jumping over the broom to enter upon a new adventure as husband and wife.
5. An 1833 Act of the Parliament of the United Kingdom which abolished slavery throughout the British Empire (with the exceptions "of the Territories in the Possession of the East India Company", Ceylon, (now Sri Lanka) and Saint Helena; the exceptions were eliminated in 1843.
6. https://en.wikipedia.org/wiki/Slavery_Abolition_Act_1833.
7. "Town" refers to Bridgetown, the capital of Barbados, located in the parish of St Michael.
8. Post Traumatic Slave Syndrome describes a set of behaviours, beliefs and actions associated with or related to multi-generational trauma experienced by African Americans. These include (but are not limited to) undiagnosed and untreated Post Traumatic Stress Disorder (PTSD) in enslaved Africans and their descendants. DeGruy argues that the syndrome continues because children whose parents suffer from PTSS are often indoctrinated into the same behaviours. She contends that PTSS is not a disorder that can simply be treated and remedied clinically, but also requires profound social change in individuals, as well as in institutions that continue to perpetuate inequality and injustice toward the descendants of enslaved Africans.
9. A hawker is a vendor of merchandise that can be easily transported; they sell inexpensive items, handicrafts or food items. Whether stationary or mobile, they often advertise by loud street cries or chants, and conduct banter with customers, so to attract attention and enhance sales.
10. The area (sometimes called a "patch") from where a hawker will sell on a regular basis.
11. The official residence and office of the Governor-General of Barbados.

BOOK II

1940 – 1950
The Weight of the World

Adindra symbol, Asase Ye Duru

"The Earth has weight"
Symbol of providence and the Divinity of Mother Earth

Djembe drum, African musical instrument
All Africans answer the call of the Djembe

CHAPTER 2

Almost the weight of the world

"Though the cheetah is fierce it does not devour its cubs" ETHIOPIAN PROVERB

There were many things I knew about Mable Matilda Carter and I learned many more on this journey. Some of the things I knew about her in childhood changed as I grew older. As a child I might have felt she was at time too stern, strict, tough or even hard on my brothers and me. I also knew without being told that she worked hard, and often had to work harder because, as she so often said, she was "the man" in her house.

Now that I'm older I know what she really was. Mable Matilda Carter was a disciplinarian. She was resilient, dedicated and self-determining. She was all these things because life had taught her many lessons. Many were hard but all of them were valuable. Life had not dealt Mable Carter the same hand it had dealt other women. Yes, it dealt her the child-making hand, but what it didn't deal her was the man-staying hand. None of the men in her life were present by the time I came along. Whether or not she intended it to be this way, one thing was clear: we were all her children. That was our absolute. What wasn't absolute was our fathers. All five of her sons had a different father. Whilst she knew who each son's father was, we didn't. Saying it so bluntly might seem harsh but it was the truth. She faced and accepted her truths, and it's my thinking that all of this might have contributed to her resolve to be the 'man' in her house.

With this determining spirit she set out to make sure that her sons would be different; they would be unlike their fathers. They would be the kind of men that wouldn't shirk responsibilities. When presented with challenges, they would look these challenges squarely in the face and deal with them accordingly. The one way she could achieve this end was by being the strict disciplinarian. She was going to be the mirror that we looked in and, with that knowledge, she made sure that the toughest parts of her shone through. And in that respect, my mother was the best example of a man that I knew. That is not to say that my mother did not display any emotions but her main focus was to show us how to be men and how to behave. As far as my mother was concerned, there was a time and place for everything. When she drew the line it was drawn in granite and everyone (her sons, our friends, her friends, and neighbours) respected her boundaries. Mable Carter didn't stand for foolishness, nor did she have time for it.

The extent of her strength never really dawned on me until 2012. As I do when I'm home in Barbados I visited my brother Rudolph and, as we so often did, we started to reminisce about Mammy and her baking especially her cassava pone! Until that moment I hadn't given much thought as to how all those bags of cassava made it into the house. As a child I gave no consideration to the fact that bags of cassava had to come into the house first before they went back out as bread, flour, or cassava pone. Had I known then (or understood) what I was about to learn, one of those baked goods would not have gone down as quickly and as greedily as they did.

As the man of her house, the responsibility of getting all those bags of cassava rested not only on my mother's shoulders...but also on her head. But "rested" is not the best descriptive word as there was no real rest involved. She had to carry the weight of almost 100 pounds (sometimes more) on her head, getting these extremely heavy bags home before she could work her magic with sugar, essence, dried fruit, flour, etc. and turn them all into money to keep her house afloat.

When Rudolph described the sound the filled crocus bags of cassava made when she got that 'hand' down with them, the sound of the solid thud on the floor which was followed by an aching groan from my mother as she was ever-so-temporarily relieved from her burden, I can truly say that the women of her era were the greatest. As a grown man, I grieved at the knowledge that my mother (and others like her) had to become 'beasts of burden' just to be able to provide for their families, that none of her sons' fathers were men enough to stay and help carry this load. When she put down that heavy flour bag, with that aching groan, she had gone from a beast of burden to the woman who had proven once again what it took to be the man of her house: strength and gumption

I guess that this is where I got both my physical and emotional strength: I too had to draw on my own physical strength when I eventually held jobs where lifting heavy objects was required and expected. As a shipping agent I lifted barrels filled with household effects, machinery and plant equipment. My circumstances and jobs may have changed but there was one thing that remained constant: lifting. Even now; my job as an Undertaker requires lifting, albeit not as much as in years past. All of these things had significant weight but I'm sure none of them weighed as much as the endless bags of cassava Mammy had to lift to ensure the survival of herself and her sons. The irony was not lost on me when I had to draw on that same strength whilst lifting heavy bags of cement to help build my homes in Barbados. Here I was now, the man in my own house and, just like Mammy did, I lifted.

Mammy may not have had a good deal of 'formal' education, but she had a good head for business. She not only knew how much work (and supplies) would have been required to feed her children but also how much would be needed to turn a profit. Mammy's 'client base' was made up of Blacks who came for themselves and those who came on behalf of their white employers. She would have done her homework and knew what people wanted, what sold most often on which day of the week, who bought what and when. She wouldn't have wasted time putting something on her tray that didn't earn her household money. Whilst we would have been happy with any 'excess' that she would have to bring back home for us to eat, Mammy would not. Sitting around and watching us eat away the profits was not why she went to bed late and rose early.

Mammy had a special 'cry' to draw her customers. As her breads were freshly baked (and I can attest they were quite delicious!) in a lilting sing-song voice she would call out, "Hot and sweeeeeeeeeeet! Hot and sweeeeeeeeeeet!" My mother didn't use a brawling, garish cry; her own unique 'cry' was all she needed to say to get her customers' attention. She was a bit dramatic and theatrical; I would even say that her tone was a bit sultry, even 'promising' as she cried "Hot and sweeeeeeeeeeet! Hot and sweeeeeeeeeeet!" And the cry worked, as she boasted about the fact that she had regular customers.

I don't know if my father was one of my mother's customers before him and my mother 'got friendly'. What I do know (from my brother Rudolph) is that my father made regular visits from the Government House area where he worked to Tweedside Road: he was friendly with some of the other chauffeurs and maids who bought goods in the area. In fact he often accompanied a maid who also worked for the same employer as he did; perhaps he used this maid as a 'wing man' (so to speak) as a way of getting close to some of the other hawkers and, eventually, my mother.

Aubrey Alleyne was a good-looking man with a strong build; perhaps, to my mother's thinking, a strong build might also have meant a strong character. She was a physically and mentally strong woman, so perhaps she may have felt she discerned similar strengths in him. I am sure that after much consideration, and especially in light of the past failed relationships which had resulted in four sons, she weighed up the chances she would be taking in letting this man into her and her four son's lives and allowed herself to 'take up'[1] with him. I'm convinced that, because of this long consideration, he mattered.

This relationship between him and my mother eventually deepened to the point where, Mammy, who had not allowed any man to come to her home after Carl's father had left, allowed him to visit her at her home in Carrington Village on evenings after she came home from selling. Rudolph (who was about thirteen at the time) said that he would go and meet my mother every evening at 9.00 pm and they would walk home together, she carrying the tray and he the bench.

By the time my mother got home from work, Rudolph would have taken care of Victor and Carl, so all she had to do was get ready and make herself presentable for my father's visit. According to Rudolph, my father visited often. Then he stopped coming around. As time would reveal, my mother had become pregnant and I can only assume that once she told him she was pregnant he stopped visiting. Whatever long-lasting relationship she had hoped for with this man had come to an end. He'd had his good time and he never came back. My mother was left alone not only with a child growing in her belly but perhaps with great sadness and disappointment growing in her heart.

Whatever feelings my mother had for my father must have dissipated over the nine months I grew in her belly. If she were enamoured of him, those feelings lost their glow and lustre when he left her, alone and pregnant, to continue carrying heavy burdens and selling as if 'nothing' had happened. I don't know if he continued to frequent the Tweedside Road area and, if he did, if he continued to act as if nothing had transpired between them. Perhaps he avoided the area altogether and just allowed the maid (the 'wing man') to go to the hawker women to get what was needed for their white employer.

Whether or not he came, or the maid came, it had to be all very difficult for Mammy because she had to go on as if nothing had happened. I say as if 'nothing' had happened because (as I found out from my brother Rudolph in September 2011) my mother never told anyone she was pregnant again. According to Rudolph, Mammy "had a bit of size", so I'm sure that, for as long as her pregnancy didn't show, more than a degree of embarrassment influenced her decision. Mammy wanted to avoid the ridicule and gossip of her neighbours, some of which, I'm sure, would have been scathing, unkind and hurtful. Here she was, unmarried and having four other children…and now pregnant again.

In fact, my mother hid her pregnancy so well that not even my brother Rudolph knew! On the night my mother 'took in'[2] she called Rudolph and told him to go call Ms Waith (the midwife). She dispensed him with no other information, other than to say to Ms Waith that she was ill. Rudolph said that our mother said to him, "Doll (her pet name for him), go and get Mrs Waith for me. Tell her I'm sick and to come now."

Mable Matilda Carter

Rudolph said he didn't question my mother as to why she needed a midwife. He simply went. He remembered it was night-time and my mother had woken him from sleeping. When he got to Mrs Waith's house he woke her. He said that she asked in a very sleepy voice, "Who, who is that?" and he said, "It's me, Doll. Mammy sent me. She ask you to come now. She's sick." Mrs Waith said to Rudolph, "Go and tell your mother that I say to do what she knows to do. I'll be there." Rudolph left and went back to my mother. He said when he walked through the door he heard the sound of a child crying and it was only then that he'd figured out what the chauffer and his mother were doing. When Rudolph said this he smiled a sheepish smile, as if it was a thought that he shouldn't have had.

Soon after he returned home, Mrs Waith arrived behind him. She went in to see about my mother and the crying child – me. She said to my mother, "May Carter, what foolishness you doing? Look at this boy. You could have killed him. Look, the cord is wrapped around his neck. You out there carrying on like you strong and lifting all those things and you know better."

My mother said to her "Stop talking and help me with this boy."

So, on 1 November 1940, "this boy" as my mother called me that night, came into this world. I would become a man, the man that my father Aubrey Alleyne would never be. If he was still alive, the man that I am now would look at Aubrey Alleyne, this man who, so many years ago, saw the strong, upstanding, courageous woman that was Mable Matilda Carter and, like a fool, mistook her as just a 'good time'. I would show him what I, Collin Leroy Carter, his 'good time child', had achieved, which far exceeded what his master and mistress hoped for themselves and even what he had hoped for himself. I would look him firmly and squarely in the eyes and I would have said to him: "Come. Walk with Me."

FOOTNOTES

1. 'Take up' is a Barbadian colloquialism for starting a relationship.
2. 'Take in' is a Barbadian colloquialism for going into labour.

CHAPTER 3

School days and life at St Giles

"Patience is the key which solves all problems"
SUDANESE PROVERB

It's 1941 and all over Europe a European/Caucasian tribal war is raging: Hitler's Germany, Mussolini's Italy and the rest of the Europe are deciding who is and isn't worthy of living. Billions are spent on guns and bombs and even plough shears are being melted down to make armaments. Several other wars are being raged in Barbados. None of these wars will ever dot the pages of history books, nor will they be talked about on the radio. Other than for the players involved, these wars are non-existent.

However, the outcome of these wars will impact not only my life, but that of my mother and brothers. What are these internal wars that are raging and where are they taking place? They are taking place in Carrington village and many other villages across Barbados. The major players are Mable Matilda Carter and Collin L. Carter and the many others like us. My part in my war won't start for another three years but while I wait for my call to the proverbial front line Mable Carter is strategising and looking at ways to deploy, not her troops, but her limited resources. By this time my eldest brother Lemuel is no longer living with us, but she does still have four sons to prepare for the world and it's a battle she doesn't intend to lose.

Her war, along with Europe's, rages on; decisions made in Europe are affecting and impacting on millions of lives. Some of these decisions will ultimately affect Barbados, but none of the decision-makers are thinking of my pristine, white sandy beach, sun-drenched island that's only a dot on their maps (if it even appears at all). But the size of our island did not matter. England (the so called Mother country) was now at war and Barbados (little England) was right in there fighting for mother. Many young men from across the entire Caribbean, including the late Errol W. Barrow, Barbados' very first Prime Minister (and the Father of Independence) served and some gave their lives fighting for some cause that had nothing to do with African people or their descendants.

On 11 September 1942 the impact of this war was fully realised by everyone on the island when a German U-514 Aufferen (a U-boat) torpedoed the Canadian-owned merchant vessel called the Cornwallis in the Bridgetown port. People living in and around my village testified to the sound of the explosion when the Cornwallis was hit.

There is someone though who, even if she wanted to, doesn't have time to pay attention to the Cornwallis or any other event. That someone is my mother, Mable Carter. Just before their war got started Mable Carter had raged a war of her own: in this case, motherhood for fifth time. That last child is beginning to get on her nerves. That child of course is me and I've grown along with the war. The 'skirmishes' included the escalating hardships and the rationing of food items based on allocation of food vouchers. Now, at age of four, my war begins. My war cry was always the same, "I want to go to school with Victor and Carl!"

I'm sure that at first my mother ignored my cry and chalked it up to a little boy's whining. My insistent cries persisted and that was where another war began. Mammy's attempts to ignore the pleading and crying of her last boy to go to school with his two older brothers continued for as long as her nerves could take my pleading. My cry was always the same: "I want to go to school with Victor and Carl too." I wanted to be with them, to be where they were all day at this magical special place called 'school'. I wanted to be at this place that required special clothing, a slate with which to make letters and numbers and then, with a dry or wet cloth, wipe it clean again. I had no idea what school really was, but in my imagination it was an exciting place where my brothers went all day, leaving me alone to amuse myself until they returned with exciting stories of things that happened at this place called school.

Finally "May's Last Boy" wore her down with my insistent cries each morning when she readied and sent my two older brothers off to school. I'd irritated my mother so much that when I was four years old she asked the head teacher of the school if he would take me: because of the siblings connection (I had three older brothers going there and one had just left) the headmaster, Mr Cumberbatch, did not perceive that I would be a problem. So he accepted me at age four. My first day of primary school at St Giles came six months earlier that it did for most children on the island. The regular starting age was five but I was May Carter's last boy. That may not have meant anything to anyone else on the island but to Mable Carter it held a special place. So, accepted, off to school I went.

I'd won my battle *and* my war. I was the happiest boy in Barbados, I was on my way to St Giles Boys School. Mammy also won her war, as she was able to get me off her nerves and return a semblance of peace to her house.

Mammy did like all other mothers on their child's first day at school: she took me to school. However, I had the edge on a lot of other children, in that I had two older siblings at school and so, after that first morning, I was in their regimental care. Watching my mother walk away from the school gate, I did not experience that feeling of fear, dread or perhaps abandonment some of the other children may have felt. For many children, the experience of starting school for the first time was extremely traumatic: the bustle and jostle of the boys, the temporary loss of their mothers or guardians and let's not forget the fear and terror of the pit toilets! For me, however, my first day was exciting. I did not need any guiding, emotionally-laced counselling from teachers, nor did I have any "first day of school" jitters. I was at school with my two older brothers. I was exactly where I wanted to be.

I was dressed like all the other children: a khaki short pants, a short-sleeved khaki shirt, my new school socks and school pumps, a bag for my slate and most importantly my two bigger brothers. All I was thinking about is that I was now like my brothers. I had arrived for my first day at the magical place where I was transformed from "May's Last Boy" (as I was affectionately called by my mother's friends and neighbours who usually would have forgotten my name but knew my place in my family's lineage!) to Collin, who was now a student in Lower Primer at St Giles Boys' School (affectionately known as the College on the Hill.)

Our teachers took great interest in the education and general welfare of the children. I can clearly remember my first week at school. It was learning from day one. Lessons first began for me in Class "Lower Primer" and Miss Inniss (later to become Mrs Carrington) was my very first teacher. The days were divided into what would now be called "the 3 Rs": reading, writing and counting (arithmetic), with a short recess and lunch period. We were taught to recognise the letters of the alphabet, properly pronounce and give the phonetic sound of each letter and to identify each letter with the use of a noun. e.g. "A" is for apple; "A" gives the sound of Ah. "B" is for bat; "B" gives the sound bah. "C" is for cat; "C" gives the sound cah. This was done in a flowing, rhythmical method. From this method we were later taught how to construct and pronounce words.

For counting, adding and subtraction we were introduced to an instrument we called a Ball Frame. In other parts of the world it was called an Abacus. On this instrument we were taught to count and to perform calculations. With the use of a slate and pencil we were taught penmanship (the art of producing good handwriting) starting with the formation of letters using a double lined method.

I smile now as I recall the song all children recited as we 'hurried' our slates to dry. After we'd recorded our work and it was time to clean the slate, the class monitor would come around and using a Limacol[1] bottle filled with water, he would put some water on the slate and we would then use our hands to wipe off the work that was no longer needed so we could be ready for our next lesson.

While the slate was wet we would set the slate on one corner and spin it, carefully, like a spinning top. As we were spinning it we would sing: "Monkey, monkey dry my slate; when I marry I'll give you a piece of cake." We would repeat this until the slate was dry. I'm sure none of Barbados' famed Green monkeys ever got that promise fulfilled: I certainly didn't keep my end of the bargain but the monkeys now get their revenge by raiding my gardens and taking what they want: mangoes, five fingers bananas (carambola) and any other edible goods they can get their hands (or paws!) on.

By the end of the second year at school we were expected to be able to write well, spell, count, know at least some of the times tables (multiplication) and a degree of calculations. Apart from the Ball Frame or Abacus, each boy was expected to carry to school a box of matchsticks which we used to assist with counting, doing calculations, making and identifying shapes and objects.

Whilst in London towards the end of 2012, I was listening to a particular story on the evening news: statistics were being discussed regarding how school children world-wide were doing academically. It was said that Asian countries were holding the top five places, the performance of English school children ranked somewhere in the mid-twenties in reading, math and the sciences. The pupils at one prestigious English school were doing exceptionally well and a

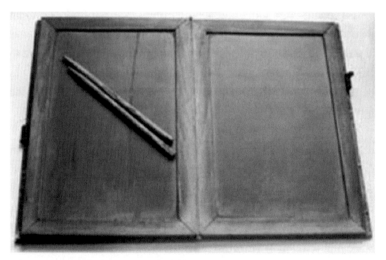

Writing slate

teacher was asked what method was used to teach the children. This teacher explained that she was using a teaching model that was being used in Singapore: the pupils were requested to bring to school a hundred drinking straws as an introductory method to counting, adding, and subtracting. I was truly amazed to learn that some seventy years after I was taught this method at St Giles (my "College on the Hill") it was now being reprised and children being taught this method were excelling.

This made me reminisce, not so much on the use of the matchsticks, but the method we (students and parents alike) went about amassing our matchsticks. Once a parent (mostly a mother) understood that her child needed matchsticks to take to school, not another matchstick was discarded. There was no such thing as electric ignition stoves so all mothers (Mammy included) used matches to light kerosene burners, wood or charcoal fires in the yard; these fires were used to cook our food, boil our water, etc. If enough matchsticks couldn't be collected at home, then we created a type of 'litter patrol' and made sure that not one matchstick, discarded by a smoker, had enough time to litter our streets. Immediately upon being 'spied' it was gathered and added to the collection.

By year three I was eight years old and was introduced to the exercise book, pen and ink. The school supplied the ink and each desk had provisions for about six ceramic inkwells. We used what was called a 'common pen' which was just a pen nib pushed into a nib holder on a stick. To write, the nib of the pen would be lightly dipped into the ink; any excess ink would be discarded on the opening of the inkwell and you would then write. It was not long before every boy mastered the art of writing with the common pen, even though at times it could be messy. Blotting paper or pieces of chalk were used to eradicate any excess ink. Lead pencils (black leads) were also in common usage. The ball point pen came in later years.

On the last day at the end of each term, we did what was called 'scraping': using a sharp piece of glass, we scraped ink marks from our desks and benches, then sand-papered them.

"Instructions in youth are like engravings in stone."

MOROCCAN PROVERB

My school days were relatively happy ones. In those days St Giles School was heavily overly subscribed and was considered the ivy league of Primary/Elementary schools in Barbados, followed closely by Wesley Hall Boys' School. I guess at any time there were in excess of 700 children ranging from approximately five to fourteen years and for this large number of students there were about twenty teachers. There were about sixteen male teachers and four female teachers – I can still remember the names of all or most of them. The teachers taught every subject which included: English, Math, Geography, British History, Metalwork, Woodwork, General Biology, Basic Art and Religious Education. In addition to the regular classes, there were also extra-curricular activities: Boy Scouts, Sports, Music, Gymnastics and Gardening. Some of the 'regular' teachers would also teach the extra-curricular activities.

Learning was considered a no-nonsense business and a privilege. You were there to learn and, depending on the circumstances, this was accomplished with or without the application of a leather strap or a cane to your back, hands, legs, or backside by the teacher. Corporal punishment was the standard method of 'control' employed in getting the students (not just at St Giles but at all schools in Barbados) to 'behave.' Corporal punishment was accepted by students, parents and of course by the teachers. Subject to the nature of the transgression, getting a beating at school most often meant getting *another* beating at home.

The logic behind this is now comical to me. The teacher would beat you for misbehaving in class, on the street, or on the school grounds. Often times you could be assured that your parent was going to be made aware of your errant ways. Some teachers may have been close or nearby neighbours, and no boy wanted the teacher to tell on him. Telling on you meant another beating followed by the threat, "Don't let me have to come up to that school for you!"

If your parent had to "come up at that school" for you it mean a public flogging for all your peers and teachers to see. No words can describe that shame, that mortification. The boys would tease you unmercifully. You would hear things like, "He muddah beat he in front of de whole school." or "He muddah mek he cry in front de whole school." Some teachers were always quick to dispense a beating. One in particular was Mr Greenidge who taught the 3rd Class. His beatings were both regular and sadistic. His deft application of his straps was enough to make boys dread his class. However, since one had to 'go through' that clas avoiding him or his leather strap was a fantasy soon dispensed with. The only (or best) hope was to get in and out of Mr Greenidge's class without becoming his whipping boy.

It's only fair to say that Mr Greenidge wasn't the only teacher who regularly applied his strap to an errant boy: many of the teachers had 'names' for their straps and most of the boys knew these 'names' only too well. Usually, the reference was made in the form of a threat. For the majority of boys, the implied or veiled threat of retrieving the named strap was enough to bring them in line.

The male teachers saw to it that no boy at St Giles ever lacked for a positive male role model or mentor.. Discipline and learning were the order of the day, and it was strictly imposed. This discipline started the minute you were on the school's grounds and extended to your behaviour at school, at home or when you were out playing in the neighbourhood.

Our school day started at 8.45 am and ended at 3.00 pm. As with everything else there was order. We were expected, upon arrival to school, to line up in the schoolyard for what was referred to as "Inspection." During 'Inspection' you had to show your teeth and fingernails, which were supposed to be clean, and your hair was expected to be neatly combed. No one wanted to fail inspection, because this meant that the 'infraction' had to be corrected immediately and you could only go to your classroom when you were deemed clean enough to do so. Failing inspection meant you were sent to the nearest tap in the schoolyard to clean them.

The unkempt hair got a somewhat different treatment: if it wasn't properly combed (or appeared not to be combed at all) one of the bigger boys would be assigned to comb the miscreant's hair. The school generously provided the comb, usually a wide tooth one with a handle. These combs were seemingly indestructible and usually made of the kind of plastic that could withstand any knot or kink that was in any boy's hair. Having your hair combed by an older boy was unto itself another form of punishment, as that boy had no sympathy for you and probably less desire to comb your hair. Plus, some part of him might well be annoyed at the fact that you had dared come to school with your hair unkempt.

This would not have been the gentle type of hair-combing one would expect if you were at home. There would be lots of rough tugging, pulling, shoving and conking (hitting) you in the head. The 'comber' would either hold you in a semi-head-lock, a thinly veiled or outright choke hold, or take his fingers and apply such pressure to your head that you would feel faint.

It didn't matter how you felt once the 'comber' was done, as long you now looked presentable, didn't wander too far from your line of your classmates and that, when the other boys were marching into the school hall for prayers, you were in your spot. Not walking a straight line gave the teachers even more freedom to liberally apply their named leather strap to your behind or legs right there in the schoolyard.

Assembly included morning prayers: from my recollection they followed the Anglican Church ritualistic format: a hymn or two sung from the Ancient and Modern Hymnal, and a bible reading related to the respective Anglican Christian season. For example, during Lent a Lenten hymn was sung and an example of the scripture readings would be the temptations of Jesus by Satan.

At the end of prayers we were expected to march from the Assembly Hall to our respective classrooms like good Christian soldiers, while singing some English folk song such as: 'Do you know John Peel?' (an old English hunting song) or 'What Shall We do With the Drunken Sailor?' (an old English drinking song). You could say our poor little brains were 'assaulted' as we were forced to assimilate these English traditions and learn these pub songs which in 'good ole England' were sung by the inebriated or the soon to be inebriated. When the songs were not English pub/folk songs then we were bombarded with hymns and songs from the Anglican Hymnal.

One needs to remember that the British have always been a very "religious people". They transplanted scores of Christian denominations to Barbados. The white settlers were Anglicans and this, by force, became the religious faith of most Afrikan Barbadians. On Thursday afternoons an Anglican priest came to St Giles to teach Religious Knowledge (as it was then called) to the senior boys. I vividly remember the Reverend O.C. Haynes, Priest in Charge of St Barnabas Church, in Two Mile Hill, riding his bicycle to St Giles on Thursday afternoon to administer this function.

The school children's daily diet was supplemented with a plastic glass of milk and two biscuits during the morning sessions. The senior boys (those between the ages of 12 and 14 years) were delegated on a daily rotation basis to prepare the milk with an exact portion of powder milk mixed with water and sugar. Lunchtime was from 12:00 noon to 1:00 pm and because we lived about twenty minutes' walk away from St Giles it was convenient for me to go home for lunch. But this was timed to the very second: twenty minutes home, twenty minutes to eat, and twenty minutes to get back to school.

There were days when I had soup for lunch. So picture it if you can: twenty minutes in the midday sun, walking over hot tar roads (and sometime barefoot), twenty minutes sweating over a hot bowl of soup. The sweating might have started before I sat down to the soup because a teacher might have kept you back a few minutes to finish something before letting you out for lunch. Those few minutes delay meant that, as the smallest of May Carter's boys, my two older brothers Victor and Carl would almost drag me home. I would have to walk and run to keep up, or at best stop them from dragging me home. Should I lag behind I would hear, "He gine mek we late!" I would do my best to keep up as I didn't want the responsibility of making them late. Even if I wanted to, I couldn't complain about how fast they were walking, how difficult it was for me to keep up, or that I didn't particularly like being dragged. Not one complaint ever passed my lips as I wanted to avoid the slaps that would come across my head (and almost seemingly out of nowhere) if I had.

Lunch time could get ever more stressful if we got home on one of those 'soup' days only to hear Mammy say, "The pot not quite ready; give me five minutes." Those would be the longest five minutes ever. Once Mammy was done we would gobble off the hot soup (now you understand where the sweating comes in) and then; having lost ten minutes out of the lunch hour (five with the teacher and five waiting on Mammy) it would be even more tugging, dragging, running, chastisement at my inability to keep up and me, mostly running at this point as I tried to keep up and not get slapped. Again, let's not forget that hot blazing sun. Either way, by the time we made it back, we would be sweating like labourers on a plantation's cane field.

No thought would be given to the almost softened tar; well, not at this time. There would be time to appreciate this softened tar; just not while we were rushing back. When our thoughts turned to the soften tar it would be when we were needed to make a cricket ball. Necessity, being the mother of invention, had taught us how to fashion a ball for cricket out of the soften tar and sand.

MAKING A TAR CRICKET BALL

1. 1 bottle cap or sharp stick, old spoon, old knife or anything you can get your hands on that would dig up the softened tar.
2. Secure the tar from the road UNDETECTED. This was the most important part and it had to be done deftly because you didn't want an adult seeing you. They'd shout out something like "Stop digging up the road!" Or "Stop mashing up the road, I gine tell yuh muddah that I see you digging up the road." Getting caught meant that you won't get a ball to play cricket (and may well take a beating for "digging up the road.")
3. Roll the tar ball in the sand and set it aside to cool.
4. Once it cooled you had the perfect cricket ball.

There was another (and equally as important) step involved in creating this cricket ball: getting your hands clean of all the tar. This would best be accomplished by 'acquiring' (stealing) some of your mother's treasured kerosene oil to remove the tar. Again, this usually had to be done without your mother's knowledge! If you were caught anytime you could well get two beatings: one for 'digging up the 'people's road' and the second for being 'stupid enough' to waste her precious kerosene.

The Christmas season also offered to us the opportunity to make tar balls without stress. In those days, Christmas hams were imported and came covered with a tarred outer protection; we also used this tar to make balls.

MEALS FOR THE NEEDY

The state also provided a hot meal for needy children who had to journey to and from Queens Park which was further away from St Giles. The boys who went to Queens Park were usually given a 15 minutes leeway for returning to school late after lunch. Back then, almost every section of Barbadian society was negatively class conscious, so these children were referred to as "Park Food Boys", even by those who were just as destitute.

The big day in our school year was Prize Giving Day. This was held at the end of the academic year (around early July) when most of the boys from classes 5, 6, and 7 would be involved in the annual school play or choir, Scouts performance or gymnastics display. Prizes were awarded for various achievements e.g. Head Boy of the Year, Excellent Work, Sports Champion, Keenest Scout, Highest Academic Achievements, Gardening, etc. The school Sports Day was another big day for the school and this consisted of track and field and bicycle races.

The school plays were generally based on literary works, usually from Dickens. Shakespeare's *Merchant of Venice*, *Hamlet*, *Oliver Twist*, *As You Like It* or *Macbeth*. The female teachers were the producers, directors, costume designers, make-up artists. Senior boys also were involved, assisting with stage management, props, etc, for this great occasion. The dress rehearsal was performed the day before Prize Giving, thus permitting all the younger children below class Five to be the audience. On the day of the show, the senior boys were invited and they came in their numbers wearing their fineries. Leading up to the day, the teachers made sure that the boys had every nook and cranny cleaned; even the gardens were in top shape. Days before the event, the school lawns were out of bounds in order to permit the grass to grow. On the day of the show, there would be the indoor performance which featured the school choir singing a selection of songs, followed by the school play and the Prize Giving. We would then move outdoors for scout activities and gymnastics were performed on the lawn.

I was never an 'A' student, but rather one of just above average academic ability. I got on exceptionally well with all my teachers and the other boys alike. I don't remember being involved in any more than two fights during my ten years at St Giles; of course I had two bigger brothers at the school which automatically meant that if anyone picked a fight with me they were also picking a fight with my siblings. That old saying "Touch one; touch all!" springs to mind! As time passed one then another of my brothers left the school but that didn't make me an easier target; by the time both of my elder brothers had left St Giles, I was more than able to hold my own.

During this time I became interested in the Boys Scouts activities. I started occasionally watching them, albeit from a distance and, I guess you could say, with a longing eye. Mr Vere Murray, the Scout Master, took notice of my distant observations, but I continued to watch from a distance because I knew in my heart that my mother would object to me joining the Boy Scouts. It wasn't that she objected to the organisation per se, but such activities would take me away from the things at home that she had for me to do. The other objection she had to me joining the Boy Scouts would have been the cost of the uniform. I know I would have to tread very carefully if I ever acquired enough guts to approach her about my interest.

Mr Murray eventually asked me if I wanted to join. I did but I was also smart enough to put him in the line of Mammy's fire. I told him yes but he would have to personally ask my mother. As Deane's Village was on his route to or from school he said it wouldn't have been a problem. As expected, he did ask my mother if I could join the scouts and true to May Carter's form, she promptly told him that she had a lot of scouting for me to do. It was at this point that my brother Rudolph interjected and begged her to let me join. Sandwiched between Rudolph and the Scout Master my mother was the judge and jury. The Scout Master and my brother were the lawyers for me (the defendant). Suffice to say for the first time I saw my mother giving in, but not easily.

Her permission was given with many stipulations: "Scouts or no scouts you will do every task and errand I give you to do." For me this was a challenge that I knew I was going to accept as I so badly wanted to be a Scout. In my excitement I hadn't noticed that she had raised her hand above and over my head. In a well-timed stealth move (which would be the envy of any army today) she activated the invisible bomb she'd been holding. Her dream-shattering bomb was the utterance of this sentence: "I will not be paying for the clothes because I have better things to do with the money!"

My heart sunk a little with that remark but I decided that whilst I might be the only scout without a uniform, a scout I was going to be! Even without the uniform I took to scouting like a metaphorical duck to water. It didn't take me long to understand that the Scouts at St Giles were expected to be exemplary examples to the other students and in everything in which we were engaged. The teaching staff and the community at large expected us to be positive role models, both for the other boys at St Giles and in the wider community, and we worked assiduously to live up to those expectations. I made it my personal goal to never fall short, on any level, of this expectation. I was, after all, a St Giles Boy Scout.

As much I took on the role of being a keen scout it never left my head that although I *felt* like a St Giles Boy Scout, outwardly I didn't quite fit the bill, because I was without the requisite uniform. I knew Mammy wasn't going to change her mind about paying for it. I also knew that if I wanted this much needed uniform, I would have to find a way to acquire it myself. So I decided I would buy my own uniform. It's not that I had money at my disposal for such a venture. I would have to save it. I went about it the only way that I knew how, by making a 'puzzling tin' (which today would be called a 'piggybank'). At that time every boy and girl knew what it was for and, more importantly, how to make one.

MAKING A PUZZLING TIN

1. Secure a tin can or a wooden box: any type with a removable lid/top would do.
2. Secure the cover tightly using a hammer (or whatever is available) to bang this cover into place so that no one can easily pry the cover off (that is in fact your security device – even from yourself.)
3. Using a knife to cut a hole through the top to make a slender opening. This should be just wide and long enough for the entry of coins.

I was now on my way to 'independent saving'. I understood the level of sacrifice that it would take to save for my scout uniform but it was very important for me to do this. I accepted that there would be many things I would have to do without (or as my mother would say, "I had to cut my eye against.") This meant that I would see things that I wanted but make a decision to do without them. I did errands for neighbours such as bringing water, going to the shop, making kites and washing my brother Rudolph's bicycle. I saved every cent I got from these chores so that I could get my scout uniform. This sustained effort on my part got the attention of my older brother Rudolph and he assisted in the purchase of my first scout uniform.

With the purchase of my uniform I was, in my heart, now fully a St Giles Boy Scout. My outside had finally caught up with my inside. On reflection I can see how adhering to the Boy Scouts Laws in principle have served me throughout my life. Looking at the Scouts Laws I can honestly say that I've never forgotten them. Most of them have become an inherent part of who I am and how I conduct myself today.

Collin with members of his Scout troop

THE MEANING OF THE SCOUT LAWS
https://meritbadge.org/wiki/index.php/Scout_Law

1. A Scout is *Trustworthy*.
2. A Scout tells the truth. He is honest, and he keeps his promises. People can depend on him.
3. A Scout is *Loyal*.
4. A Scout is true to his family, friends, Scout leaders, school and nation.
5. A Scout is *Helpful*.
6. A Scout cares about other people. He willingly volunteers to help others without expecting payment or reward.
7. A Scout is *Friendly*.
8. A Scout is a friend to all He is a brother to other Scouts. He offers his friendship to people of all races and nations, and respects them even if their beliefs and customs are different from his own.
9. A Scout is *Courteous*.

10. A Scout is polite to everyone regardless of age or position. He knows that using good manners makes it easier for people to get along.

11. A Scout is *Kind*.

12. A Scout knows there is strength in being gentle. He treats others as he wants to be treated. Without good reason, he does not harm or kill any living thing.

13. A Scout is *Obedient*.

14. A Scout follows the rules of his family, school, and troop. He obeys the laws of his community and country. If he thinks these rules and laws are unfair, he tries to have them changed in an orderly manner rather than disobeying them.

15. A Scout is *Cheerful*.

16. A Scout looks for the bright side of life. He cheerfully does tasks that come his way. He tries to make others happy.

17. A Scout is *Thrifty*.

18. A Scout works to pay his way and to help others. He saves for unforeseen needs. He protects and conserves natural resources. He carefully uses time and property.

19. A Scout is *Brave*.

20. A Scout can face danger even if he is afraid. He has the courage to stand for what he thinks is right even if others laugh at or threaten him.

21. A Scout is *Clean*.

22. A Scout keeps his body and mind fit and clean. He goes around with those who believe in living by these same ideals. He helps keep his home and community clean.

23. A Scout is *Reverent*.

24. A Scout is reverent toward God. He is faithful in his religious duties. He respects the beliefs of others.

FOOTNOTES

1. Limacol is a liquid blend of aromatic compounds used to instantly refresh and reinvigorate, developed in the British Caribbean in the 1920s – specifically in the then colony of British Guiana (now Guyana) and manufactured by the British company, Bookers.
2. Going into labour.

CHAPTER 4

School vacation

"Wisdom does not come overnight."
SOMALI PROVERB

Like all school children everywhere I looked forward to school vacation. The school year was broken up so that there were three vacations: Christmas, Easter and, of course, Summer – the end of school year. This may have been the longest school break but for me it wasn't the most exciting. To me, the most exciting of the vacations was Christmas. Christmas vacation signified 'feasting and abundance'. It might not have been 'abundance' the way abundance is thought of today, but back when I was growing up (and even until I left the Barbados) Christmas was synonymous with abundance, fun, laughter, more freedom, family and friends.

The days leading up to Christmas were exciting. Everyone was in the true spirit of Christmas. The closer it came to Christmas the more excited we became. There wasn't going to be endless gifts to give/ exchange or open, but there was going to be those special things we loved. Mammy, the baker's baker, saw to it that we had those special sweet treats. She not only baked for her household, but for other people as well. Mammy was always the entrepreneur: if and where there was an extra dollar to be made, she was going to make it. It wasn't exploitation or greed: it was business. She had a skill and so she utilised them at every turn to bring additional money into the house. We weren't staying small, we were growing and so any extra earning was welcomed.

Like all the other women on the island, Mammy spruced up the house. New curtains (or freshly washed and pressed ones) were hung; floors and furniture were scrubbed, polished and varnished. Every nook, cranny, plate, glass, and jug sparkled. The mattresses were filled with freshly cut and dried Kus Kus[1] grass. Everything in and about the home had to be in a pristine state. As a further example of English brainwashing, it was customary to sprinkle white sand or white marl around the house to emulate snow.

Mammy might not have been able to paint the house every Christmas, but she did what she could. There was the requisite oilskin tablecloth, which wasn't really cloth at all: it was a kind of plastic. Almost every woman on the island used this cloth to cover the dining table. On Christmas morning there was the 5.00 am Christmas Morning Church service, then off to Queens Park where the Royal Barbados Police Band[2] would entertain the crowd with a variety of seasonal and popular songs. The people in Queen's Park would also provide a 'fashion show' of sorts, as it was customary to attend Queen's Park in all one's finery. Men dressed in their best suits, women were resplendent in their dresses, hats and bonnets. In earlier years various choirs would go through the villages singing Christmas carols. Sometimes villages or districts would combine their choirs; they were led by 'Star Bearer' (a member carrying a large star made from wood or cardboard and covered with coloured translucent paper). The choirs would receive Christmas treats and money in consideration; some also competed in singing competitions for prizes.

After we had our fill of Christmas morning in Queens Park we then headed home to have our bellies filled. We had chocolate tea: again, this wasn't the kind of 'drinking chocolate' children have nowadays. This 'chocolate tea' was very special. Mammy made this chocolate from scratch, as did all mothers on the island. She would parch cocoa beans by heating sea sand in an iron pot. Once the sand was hot she added the beans. Once the beans were parched she would take them out and, using a mill or sometimes two flint stones, she would grind the beans. This ground the cocoa into a paste which was rolled into cocoa sticks or balls and left to dehydrate. When required, the cocoa stick/ball was added to boiling water and cinnamon sticks. When it had reached 'perfection', Mammy then added sugar and milk … aahhh… HEAVEN! This cup of heaven was at the top of our Christmas breakfast menu and like everywhere else on the island it was referred to as Chocolate Tea[3]. We also looked forward to the rest of our Christmas breakfast: Cassava pone[4], ham, saltbread[5]. To me, these were the clouds that made up the perfect heavenly morning.

Lunch followed several hours later. While we waited for the rest of the Christmas Day feast to continue Mammy would send us off to neighbouring homes in the village, especially close relatives and friends of hers, with parcels of Christmas goodies. When it was lunchtime we hurried home and Mammy didn't disappoint. The smell of the roasting meats and baking goods coming from all over the village called you and made your belly gnaw at itself! Awaiting us was roast pork: spiced and seasoned with dried thyme and other herbs, scallions (or green seasoning as we called it), chives, onion, hot peppers (so hot it was like some hell fire sitting on the tip of your tongue!) salt all blended together and stuffed into tiny perfectly placed holes; a roast fowl (similarly seasoned), dove green pigeon peas and rice, jug jug[6], pork dripping gravy and a selection of salads: lettuce, tomatoes, cucumber. Then we had ample portions of mauby, sorrel, or ginger beer to wash this down. Bellies full, we rested and waited. What were we waiting on? Great Cake (cake made with fruit that had been soaked in rum for months!) and pudding (what is known today as 'pound' or 'plain' cake).

Boxing Day was equally as exciting. Like the whole of Barbados, we were waiting to welcome Mother Sally, the Tuk Band and the Bank Holiday Bear.[8] Again, this activity draws its original art form from African culture. In the absence of radios and television sets, we were creative. We had to be.

FOOTNOTES

1. Kus Kus (or cuscus) grass is soft, curly, pleasant smelling grass (Vetiveria zizanioides) native to most tropical regions. It has a variety of uses: stuffing mattresses and cushions, making mats, purses, hats, baskets and fans.
2. The Royal Barbados Police Band was founded in 1835 and is one of the oldest police bands in the world.
3. Barbadians of a certain age call most hot drinks "tea": Coffee "tea", cocoa (hot chocolate) "tea", Milo "tea", or tea "tea".
4. Pone is a sweet treat made from cassava root blended with grated coconut, eggs, sugar, shortening, raisins, milk, vanilla essence, orange peel and mixed spices.
5. Salt bread is a traditional Barbadian soft roll.
6. Jug-Jug is traditional Christmas dish in Barbados. There are a number of theories as to its origins: some say it is African in origin (as it was initially made from what is known in Barbados as 'guinea corn'); other theories is that the dish is a corruption of the Scottish dish haggis, or that it was a creative result of a poor Barbadian stuck with peas, corn and meat. 'Jug' (as it's called) consists mostly of pigeon peas, meat (normally leftover ham, beef, pork or lamb) spices, onion, salt and stock.
7. Mauby is made from the bark of the Mauby tree, boiled with cinnamon, orange peel, nutmeg and cloves, and sweetened to taste. It is rather a unique flavour, with a bitter after taste. Sorrel is made from the petals of the sorrel plant: dark red in colour and a little sour, with a raspberry-like flavour.
8. A Tuk Band is a Barbadian musical ensemble, which plays tuk or rukatuk music. It is accompanied by characters that are African in origin. African tribes used costumed figures to represent elements such as fertility, witch doctors, and describing routes of commercial transportation, as well as having survived difficult times. In the Tuk Band the regular costumed figures are Shaggy Bear (who is sometimes called the Bank Holiday Bear), the Donkey Man, Mother Sally, a masked man dressed up like a woman with an exaggerated behind, and the Stiltman. Shaggy Bear is said to represent an African witch doctor figure, who gained a reputation as the Bank Holiday Bear because he always shows up on island Bank Holidays. The Donkey Cart was an important means of transportation in the past, and the Donkey Man is representative of the island transportation that was used by the locals. Mother Sally represents the female fertility, and with an exaggerated back end.

BOOK III

1950 – 1960
Raging Her Own War

Adinkra symbol, Onyankopon adom nti biribiara beye yie

"By God's grace, all will be well"
(Symbol of hope, providence, faith)

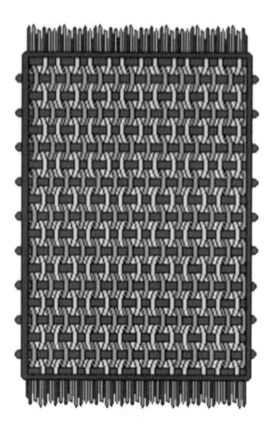

Kwanzaa symbol, Mkeka (The Mat)
Symbolic of our tradition and history
And therefore the foundation on which we build

CHAPTER 5

A place called Carrington Village

*"Between true friends even water drunk together
is sweet enough"* ZIMBABWEAN PROVERB

When I was a small boy, Barbados in the 1940s and 1950s was large,
yet small as compared to the Barbados I know today. As a child my
exploration and view of Barbados were limited to the occasional
church excursion. These outings afford me the opportunity to see
places in Barbados that my mother, because of our circumstances
couldn't afford to take me. The Barbados I knew then was also
colourful: not in the way the houses were painted (for those that could
afford paint) but it was the hum of the neighbours and the
neighbourhood that kept it colourful. Nowadays it'd be called the
'atmosphere' or the 'vibe'. When I was growing up, my neighbourhood
lacked many things that we expect to have today, things we take for
granted. No child today could envisage a house without electricity,
running water, gas, radio, internet, satellite TV, mobile phone, or a
thousand and one different things and gadgets to plug in. Everything
but an automated Mum and Dad. Nor do most of them have even the
slightest idea what it means to be raised by a village.

Carrington Village, where I grew up, was more than just a village.
It was a pulsing, thriving neighbourhood where every adult was
respected (and some feared) not for the reasons that children fear
adults these days. Back then, every child in the neighbourhood knew

that these adults wouldn't think twice about either chastising them if they were seen acting foolishly, or misbehaving. They didn't hold their tongues or feared to let you know that they'd seen you acting the fool, or doing what you knew was unacceptable. You also knew without them saying that they were going to 'tell on you.' "Telling" on you meant a scolding or a beating. A beating could commence just on the strength of what an adult said (or thought) they saw you doing; heard (or thought) they heard you saying. Most of us loved adults but within the confines of how a child could 'dislike' an adult we did, particularly those who just had to find something to complain about.

No game went without someone finding something to shout at you about, threaten to tell your mother (father; if you had one) or just take matters into their own hands. There would be no arguments from your parent either. In addition to complaining or telling on you, older folk had other ways of keeping you in order to make you behave. The use of scary stories was one such 'tool'. As with any child, we had our long list of fears: not necessarily the monster under the bed or in the closet (so many of us didn't have a bed for the monster to go under, and most of us didn't know what a closet was or that it existed!) If a closet was something to hold clothes…well, as far as we knew, the thing that held clothes was a wardrobe or a 'press' and a 'closet' was actually a 'water closet' or toilet (in my village It was the outhouse!)

I'm sure that the grown-ups knew that these stories were going to scare us into behaving. Take for instance the story of the Bakoo, or Bakou Man. This was an especially fearful creature, even though he was of miniature stature (standing no more than four inches). He was like a genie (in that he granted the wishes of his owner) but unlike the genie he also had 'wishes' that had to be fulfilled. If they were not, then all hell broke lose and he showed you who was boss. If my memory serves me correctly (and here I ask that my feet not be held to the flame), the Bakoo/Bakou man became 'yours' if you first acquired the 'egg' from the special enchanted hen that laid it. You then had to hatch the egg by keeping it under your armpit until it was ready to be hatched. Once it was hatched you had your very own Bakoo Man.

This Bakoo Man could fulfil any wish of the owner – no matter what the wish was. He could only be seen by its owner, and so he could wreak havoc and go unseen. Failure to 'feed' the Bakoo could then mean that you had a tormentor for life – that is, if he didn't beat you to death! But should you survive the beating the Bakoo Man was yours.

We also had other boogie men: 'conward', 'duppie', and 'hag'. Each one in a child's mind was worse than the other. 'Conward' was an evil spirit that made a woman look pregnant but she never gave birth. Like the Bakoo, this pregnancy wreaked havoc in a person's life. The Conward was oftentimes not the desire of the woman that carried it, but rather it was a spell or curse that was cast on her. This was believed to be done through Obeah. The woman, not wanting this ghost child, would seek out the assistance of an Obeah man or woman but sometimes to no avail. The pregnancy of course was not normal and then never producing a child it was usually a torment in the 'mother's life. Conward would communicate with the people around. When a priest went to find out where Conward came from, the spirit told the priest that his name was Conward and he came from Trinidad.

Every child feared duppies[1] and I was no exception. To many people a duppy is simply the ghost of a departed loved one, but in the true meaning of the word a duppy is a malevolent spirit or ghost. A child could love you dearly while you lived but once you died and became a duppy all the love that child had for you turns to fear. It's ironic that I am a Funeral Director and don't give much thought to duppies now, but believe me when I say that this fear has remained with some people even to this day. I would bet that if you offered someone that I grew up with £3,000 to collect a body, but stipulated that they must go through a funeral home or a graveyard to collect it, I am sure the money would remain uncollected. The fear of duppies 'getting them' would be the deterrent. Yet, at the age of three, my grandson doesn't have this fear; his relationship with the dearly departed is different. He hasn't been taught to fear the dead, so he is not affected in the same way as children who have had the Caribbean experience of yesteryear.

Added to this list of day and night creatures to fear is the hag. I'm not sure if she was more fearsome than the others, but because she wasn't particular about her prey, we might have feared her the most. She was the only one purported to feast on your blood. It was said that hags took off their skin when they went about their haunting. They did this by flying through the air as a ball of fire. The hags needed to protect their skins and keep them cool while they were out of them so they hid them under water barrels; apparently they loved the cold. However, if a person came across a hag's skin all they had to do was sprinkle it with salt and pepper; when the hag returned and put the skin back on it would burn them. The hag would then sing a song to their skin which went something like this: "Skin, skin, skin you don't know me now?" According to legend, if a hag was caught skin-less in daylight, it would burn

We may not have any 'mod cons', but we could entertain ourselves. We played football ... but please don't think we went out and *bought* a football. Oh no. And here I have to smile when I think back on those days. Playing football wasn't easily accomplished, because first of all we needed to acquire the much needed football. It wasn't as easy as requesting or borrowing one and we certainly didn't go out and buy one. Ingenuity was required, which often meant making one. So our football was either an old felt hat stuffed with anything: an old shirt sewn together to keep the stuffing inside or, if we were lucky, a pig's bladder. If we were lucky enough to acquire a pig's bladder there would be a 'delay' in the game, which would be 'called' because our football would need time to cure. Our future football had first to be inflated and this was done by getting a papaw shank, inserting it into the pig's bladder and blowing the bladder up to the required stiffness. The downside of this was the risk of blistering your lip from the 'milk' that was secreted by the freshly cut papaw shank, but once this was done it was securely tied (so that air wouldn't escape) and then placed out of harm's way to dry. Once dried, the game reconvened. Now that didn't mean that we didn't play football whilst waiting for the bladder to dry: remember there was always the old stuffed hat.

In addition to football, we used our creativity and imagination to create our toys. Even the game of cricket experienced more than a degree of our ingenuity. With football we only needed a ball, but with cricket we needed the bat, ball, wickets and shin pads. All of these items were made by us; our bats were fashioned from pieces of wood or coconut tree branches. We also used an assortment of buckets, cans, stones, wood or sticks to assemble our wickets. And cricket was not just played during daylight hours; if we were fortunate to get one of Barbados' beautiful full moons, then all games were possible.

We played Hide and Seek, Tradesman, Doctor, Whip and Judge. A group of ten children would play pretend court. The particular 'titles' were written and put into a hat. Each person would put their hand in the hat and pull a word. You had names like: Accused, Whip, the Judge, the Doctor, Stop, etc. To start the game someone would ask who is the honourable judge of this court. If you'd pulled the 'judge' name, then you'd say that you were the judge. The judge would then be asked who he was judging. The 'judge' would call a name; if he/she guessed incorrectly then they would say wrongly judged. The correct defendant was called out. The case was called. The 'crime' was brought before the court. The deeds were described. Then a punishment was decided. Once the punishment was assigned the defendant was examined by a doctor who then stated the defendant's fitness for punishment. Once the fitness was determined then the number of lashes would be determined. If you were lucky, you had a friend who would call 'stop' so that you were spared the full punishment. However, if you didn't have a friend to call stop then a fight could commence because that person might be hit too hard by the whip.

CHAPTER 6

The move

"A child who is to be successful is not reared exclusively on a bed of down. " AKAN PEOPLE

With the exception of my grandfather, all the other men in my mother's life (including my father) had gone. Mable Matilda Carter was now a woman who had five sons to raise, without the help of a man. So, as soon as she could after my birth she returned to her life as she knew it: baking sweetbreads, pone, top hats and anything she could create and sell that would bring a penny into her house and take care of her sons. But even with her most arduous efforts we were poor. Very poor. I understand poverty now, but as a child neither the word nor its meaning existed. I had no idea we were very poor, as most of the people and children I knew sailed in the same boat. As children, we were happy and always found ways to keep ourselves content, doing one thing or another, playing games, etc.

My first awakening of how very poor we were came when I was about eight years old and coincided with my entrance to Class Two and being taught by my second male teacher, Mr Ignatius Byer, at St Giles. Mammy rented the small parcel of land in Carrington Village on which her chattel house (our home) stood. Our near-destitute condition was brought into sharp focus, for me, by the landlady and her husband, the landlord. As far as they were concerned, they considered my brother, Victor, to be their 'houseboy' and they made no secret about this. One day, whilst on his way to work, the landlord saw Victor and told him that his wife wanted him to wash their car. It was accepted in today's society that children are expected to take the initiative, and even make their own decisions. But this kind of behaviour would have been inconceivable in the 1940s and even more so in Mable Carter's house. Being both mother and father to us, Mammy made it clear that NOTHING was done in her house, or concerning her sons, without her say-so. Everyone who knew Mable Carter accepted this. That is not to say that we did not on occasion try to 'act independently', but this didn't happen too often as we knew such actions would be at our own peril. Being one of Mable Carter's sons, Victor knew better than to just stop what he was doing and go and wash this woman's car, so he went to Mammy to find out if he could indeed undertake this. Mammy told him that he could, but only when he'd finished doing the chores that she had set for him.

Without question or objection Victor stayed and finished his chores. When he was done, he then went to the landlady to tell her he was able to wash the car. The landlady either didn't really know May Carter, or had either a moment of temporary insanity, or she forgot to whom she was speaking. She spoke to Victor harshly and promptly sent him back to Mammy with a 'message'. "Go and tell mother that I don't need you anymore! You didn't come when I needed you, which was right away, so go back home to your mother!"

Now, one would have thought that this woman (who knew May Carter well enough) would have given that message deeper thought and would have seen the error in her judgment; she would have exercised good common sense and 'let it go'. But the landlady was intent on reminding my brother and the rest of us (especially Mammy) that we needed her, hence the message and its tone. In doing so, she lit the short fuse to the keg of dynamite known as May Carter.

No sooner had Victor duly delivered the message than Mammy, sparks flying from every crease and crevice of her 'keg', discharged her maternal and righteous indignation at the landlady. As far as Mammy was concerned, the landlady was out of order. Mammy told her: "Victor was doing something for me and I told him he could come and wash your car once he was done helping me! Now if you knew you wanted a child to do what you wanted and when you wanted, then you should have done what you know women do and let your husband give you one!"

Having discharged her full load my mother didn't wait for the landlady to reply. She would not have cared if the landlady *did* have a reply. She just stormed away; she had said her piece and there was no reason to wait around to see the impact. Her words had been delivered with a marksman's accuracy and the velocity of a mother defending her young and Mammy didn't care about the damage that her words may have caused.

The landlady complained to her husband as the "mitigating gall" of May Carter and later that day the landlord came to Mammy. Like his wife, he 'temporarily forgot' that Mable Carter was this serious protector of her brood. Outfitted in layers of insanity, a fake manly bravado, laced to the top of his stiff button-down shirt and waistcoat, angry at my mother for making small measure and dispensing of his temporarily insane wife, he presented what he hoped to be a formidable front. This tightly-laced angry man with his faux gallantry 'stepped' to Mable Carter to defend his wife's honour because, in his opinion, in speaking her mind and in the tone used, my mother had insulted his wife.

For this 'affront' my mother would be put 'on warning': should she be late with the rent or even miss a month, she would have to move her chattel house off his land. To Mable Carter this meant she would have to take up her already falling apart house and set it, with its sparse contents, somewhere else.

As she had done since we first moved to Quaker's Road, Carrington Village, my mother continued to faithfully pay her rent on time. This timely behaviour annoyed the landlord and one day, for no apparent reason other than the fact that he could, he gave my mother notice. She would have to move off his land.

So move she did. Mammy was strong and determined and took these values to search for somewhere else to move her house. She rented a piece of land three quarters of a mile away in Deane's Village, St Michael, and made arrangements to move her house.

On the day the house was taken down my mother did the unexpected. I say it was unexpected because, let's not forget, she was moving because a woman had felt insulted and a man, feeling he had to defend his wife's honour, had angrily told Mammy to take her house off his property. Despite the fact that the day had to be very difficult for her, she cleaned up the house spotlessly. She took those things that were too broken and she filled in the outhouse (outdoor toilet) pit. Since we were going to need the outhouse structure to place over the new pit that had also been taken down to be moved to the new location. After my mother had filled in the pit she covered it with dirt and then said to the landlord: "You see that I clean up your place. I'm clean so I'm leaving it clean."

That was the last conversation for years that my mother had with the landlord. We later found out that the landlord was sorry, because he didn't really mean for my mother to move her house. When he'd told her to move he'd wanted her to beg him to let her stay on his land with her five sons. But he *really* didn't know Mable Carter. My mother had pride. He would never have lived long enough to hear Mable Carter beg him (or anyone else) for anything.

No one realised what poor condition the house was in until it was taken down to be moved to Deane's Village. The carpenters had dismantled the house, loaded it on the lorry and transported it to Deane's Village, but it was only when they tried to re-assemble it that they discovered what really poor shape the house was in. The carpenters couldn't put it back together again. It's not that they suddenly lost their skills or that the house was so complex in its design that it baffled them. Our house was simply too old. The carpenters were like the King's men with Humpty Dumpty: despite their every effort, they were fighting a losing battle trying to put it back together again. Just like Humpty Dumpty, our house stayed piled on the ground – a different kind of fragile. This was the roof over our heads, it was safety from the elements, it was the place where we were safe; our family home. The fragile, old pieces of lumber piled on the ground weren't just pieces of wood... they were the fabric of our lives. The scattered lumber was now just useless pieces of wood.

Unable to re-assemble Mammy's house, the main carpenter pitched a tent for us so that we would all have shelter for the night. None of her sons minded, but I'm sure it bothered Mammy that she didn't have a solid house for her sons. We lived under that tent until Mammy was able to get lumber to build us a new house. Mammy couldn't afford the lumber on her own, but the head carpenter, Mr Sealy, had a relationship with a lumber company in Bridgetown and so made arrangements for Mammy to have credit. Thanks to his kindness (and perhaps feeling sorry for a woman with her five sons sleeping under a tarp) the lumber company allowed Mammy to get enough material to build us a new house. It wasn't the Taj Mahal but it was home. Once again, Mable Carter had come through for her sons. She provided a home for her boys. She was indeed the man of her house.

CHAPTER 7

The standpipe

"Water is colourless and tasteless but you can live on it longer than eating food" AFRICAN PROVERB

Another feature that also made Carrington Village intriguing was the one place where the paths of the whole neighbourhood – young and old, man and woman, boy and girl – met and crossed. That was the standpipe[1]. None of the individual homes had piped water, so everyone had to 'bring' water. These days, indoor running water is taken for granted, but in those days this meant making a trek from your house to the nearest standpipe or well. During the 1940s and 1950s, this well was on Stephenson's Road in Delamere Land, off Belmont Road.

The water that was drawn from this well wasn't for consumption but was for household chores: feeding the animals, cleaning the house, washing flour bags and clothes. Although there was chlorine bleach (or "EC" as it was called) it had to be purchased by the pint and you had to carry your own bottle to the EC factory to get it. The factory was situated opposite the old Town Hall in Bridgetown. If a woman had some EC she used it, but it would be far-fetched to think she would make a special trip to Bridgetown just to purchase a pint of EC.

So the women did what they had to do to keep the whites white or to aid in the bleaching of flour bags. Flour bags were the order of the day; they were made of coarse cotton and were treasures for the village women of the island. Once the merchant's stamp was bleached out they had a multiplicity of purposes: properly bleached, a woman could use them get clothing for herself and her family, make household items such as pillow cases, sheets, or kitchen towels.

The process of bleaching the flour bags was an art form and many village women perfected this art. My mother Mable Carter was no exception. The flour bags would be begged for or purchased from a local shop owner, then washed in large galvanised[2] or wooden tubs. The wooden tubs were made by a local cooper; he was the person who would make barrels that would have been made for the storage or export of rum or molasses. The cooper would then cut the barrels in half, allowing the women to have two wash-tubs.

A woman/mother/wife could be seen in the backyard of her house on wash-day, with her wash tub filled with water, her washboard (called a jucking board), piles of dirty clothes and blue or yellow soap. On the ground beside her would be another galvanised or wooden tub filled with water; into this she would drop the clothes to be rinsed or bleached. With the washing done, the clothes were spread out on the bleaching ground, which was usually a parcel of land set aside for just this purpose. It was covered with grass (I know, you wouldn't imagine that grass, rocks and white/soon to be white clothes would go together but, as I said before, bleaching clothes was an art!)

The items to be bleached would be spread on the grass; rocks were placed on the corners to stop them blowing away. Then the clothes were sprinkled with water which was repeated several times. The sun was the bleaching agent. Each time the sun dried the clothes, they were sprinkled again. It was that process of wetting and drying (and perhaps the grass) that bleached the clothes. Sometimes it took several days to complete this process, but in the end the women had achieved the set-upon goal – a perfectly white piece of cotton; all signs of the merchant's stamp gone. The bag was now fit for purpose. In Mable Carter's house one of these bleached flour bags was set aside to cover the buckets of water that she used for drinking, cooking, and general household consumption.

You made as many trips to the standpipe as was necessary to fill a barrel. I never drew water from the well but, like everyone else, I went to the standpipe. In some cases the standpipe was a three-sided cement structure fitted with a faucet from which water was available. "The pipe" (as it was commonly known) was one of the communal centres in most villages.

Going to the pipe for water was not an option; it was what everyone did in our village. Although there were men who did bring water, in most cases the task of fetching was relegated to the women and children. That is unless that man was Cuba. For lack of better words, Cuba had a 'water business'. When fetching water, no one wanted to be in line behind Cuba as it was normally a monumental wait. Cuba had a water barrel/drum and brought water for other people. He would come to the pipe, attach his hose which he then inserted in his barrel, which he carried on a cart. Needless to say the barrel took a long time to fill!

No one really thought twice about the men not bringing water was just that the women and children fetched most of the water. That's the way it was and the way it continued. The task of getting water required a lot of strength to lift the buckets of water from the pipe and then carry them to your house. At the stand pipe the neighbourhood women talked about all and everything. I use the word "talk" loosely, because the talking was mostly gossip, either about goings-on in our neighbourhood or about anything that was going on the island. In addition to the gossip and friendly banter, the pipe played a vital role in the budding love affairs of the young or the young at heart. If a boy started to like a girl or vice versa, arrangements could be made to meet 'at the pipe'.

It was not uncommon to have fights break out as well. A fight could start if someone wanted to jump the line intending to fill their bucket out of turn. That brazen act would not be tolerated between women in the same age group, or from one youth to another, but if it were an adult to a child you simply moved out of the way and let the adult get the water. She would probably have said something like: "You boy, move out the way. You in got no way to go. I got to go home and cook." Or, "I got to go and finish my man's food." Or, "I got clothes waiting on the 'bleach'." There were times you showed displeasure but that was *all* you did. There was never any talking back. That adult felt that they could skip their turn in the line or to jump the queue. That was an unspoken rule and everyone understood it. However, other than that exception, everyone was expected to wait in line to get their water. You filled your galvanised bucket, pan/ tub or whatever receptacle you'd brought to carry your water in. Your turn was based on your time of arrival. Some of the women didn't mind the wait time, as it allowed them to engage in or get all the juicy gossip.

The pipe also played an integral part in the upkeep of your personal hygiene. Sometimes you went to the pipe to get your bath and, sometimes at night if you were playing outside, you were sent to the pipe to wash up. Bathing at night very rarely occurred, but the washing up could happen in the yard. You took a tin cup and used the outside general water to wash up. However, if the moon was bright you could be sent to the standpipe to have a wash-up before you could go to bed. This command to have a wash usually came in the form of a question. My mother would ask: "Collin did you wash your face and hands before coming in this house?" My answer usually trailed behind me as I scampered outside, either to the yard or to the pipe, to do the mandatory washing up.

A wash-up was just that: a wash-up. Most every child understood the term "wash your face and hands" as well as the fine techniques involved. A "washing face and hand" happened whilst you were fully clothed. You washed up to get rid of the dirt and dust accumulated during play or, as my mother often called it "horsing around." You washed your legs, arms and face. Sometimes took your left leg and used it to get rid of the dirt on the right foot by rubbing the sole of your foot across the top of the other and then you reversed the process. Or at times you simply used your hands to aid in the process. You then moved to your arms, then on to your face. You cupped your hands together and you washed your face or, if you were brave enough, you put your face under the running water and washed your face. All washing was done with speed; you just wanted to get the day's dirt and dust gone or at best to appear to your waiting mother that you'd complied with the night-time ablution.

Once you were done you didn't waste any time stepping out of the standpipe. Let's not fantasise about someone waiting at the pipe holding a towel for you. What was going to happen was a mad dash home. That homebound journey was no stroll nor did you waste time to talk to anyone. You ran home and by the time you ran home your feet, arms and face were dry, compliments of the night air. The amusing thing about the run home is that is usually undid the task of having just washed your feet since, like all the other children, I was bare foot.

The standpipe where I first started drawing water was located in Quakers Road, Carrington Village and that didn't change when we moved to Deane's Village. I might have just been a little boy, perhaps six or seven in Carrington Village but bringing water was expected of me. I didn't have as big a container as my brothers or the others that went to get water, but I brought water in what I was given and was expected to fill and carry a skillet. I carried this until, like all my brothers, I was big enough to carry a bucket or two.

Although not everything centred on bringing or getting water; a lot of what made life in my village different, and yet the same as any other village, were the characters that either lived there or came through. They either ended up at the standpipe or were talked about at the stand pipe. Once such person that both brought water and got talked about was a woman we all called 'English Pisser'.

'English Pisser' didn't have the required thick skin necessary to take the ribbing from the neighbourhood women. She didn't want the other women to know that she had to 'bring water', so she created a kind of 'ruse' so that she wouldn't be seen at the standpipe. But she failed to realise that she didn't have to go to those extraordinary measures, since it really wasn't a secret. She, like the rest of us, didn't have piped water in her house, so of course she had to 'bring water'.

It was alleged that English Pisser would wait until dark and then, with a valise (a small suitcase) packed with empty bottles, she went to the pipe. Pride made her fill her empty bottles, pack them in her valise and then make that solitary journey back to her home. Her pride overrode any fear that she may or may not have had of any possible danger that might be lurking in the dark. There were no streetlights to light her way, but none of that matter to English Pisser. She was able to get her water and keep her pride.

Of course, English Pisser wasn't really her name – I never knew what it was – but that didn't stop anyone from calling her that. It was a nickname and, like all other nicknames, it stuck. Some nicknames were used in the place of your real name; people may not have known, say, Gladys Braithwaite, but if Gladys Braithwaite's nickname was English Pisser, then people would know who she was! No one ever had the balls to look English Pisser in the face and call her that, but whenever the name 'English Pisser' was mentioned everyone knew who you were talking about.

Women like English Pisser were all part of what made living in my village spark with life. Bajans have little time for 'foolishness' and anytime someone was spotted acting 'poor great'[3] or she was called on it. The taunting didn't stop there; sometimes a friend could get you in trouble. When the boys wanted fun, they would figure that you didn't know a person had a particular colourful name like 'Rat-Attack-Sardines', or 'Duncan Dead Fowl' or 'Spirits', and would urge you to say the particular nickname when the individual was passing. They knew that it would irritate this individual and possibly get a reaction out of them; the now-aggravated person may even throw rocks at you.

Josephine was one such lady that got this treatment. When the children wanted to 'fret' her they would say, "Joe Joe suck muh toe." This would upset her and she would fret. Not all individuals reacted to this name-calling or saw it as teasing; some of them actually answered. One such individual was 'Two-Dicky'[4]. Two Dicky got his nickname as a result of a protrusion caused by an umbilical hernia.

These were just some of the colourful characters that dotted the canvas known as Carrington Village. In addition to mentioning these particular individuals, 'special mention' must also be given to the individuals below. Some were from Carrington Village and some were just well-known throughout Barbados.

Sharkey

Beanzie: Humba Humba Pokey water

Mice Coffee: it is alleged that he drank his coffee only to find a mouse
at the bottom of the cup

Jah Jah (local/village)

Angel (local/village)

Godfrey: A self-appointed preacher, who wore a morning tail coat and
attended all funerals at Westbury Cemetery and its environs

Dee Dee

Ding Ding: The first Barbadian with dread locks; he lived with a white
woman

Town Man and Town Woman: dean/emptied the pits of out-houses

Johnny Lady Bird: dean/emptied the pits of out-houses. He was also
a rose tree trimmer[5])

Ceeola-woman: She was mental (or what we called a mad woman)
She had two children round the age of 12 years of age. She walked
the road with the children on her back.

FOOTNOTES

1. A standpipe is a freestanding pipe fitted with a tap which is installed outdoors
to dispense water in areas which do not have a running water supply to the
buildings. In the Caribbean, standpipes were used as a communal water
supply for neighbourhoods and were often focal points of these
neighbourhoods.
2. A large tin tub used for washing clothes and bathing.
3. Giving yourself unwarranted airs and graces; behaving like you're better that
others who share your socio-economic circumstances.
4. 'Dicky' is Bajan slang for penis.
5. A cleaner of out-houses/pit toilets.

CHAPTER 8

Getting up and coming in

"Rising early makes the road short."
SENEGALESE PROVERB

Like most people living in the Caribbean, most Barbadians rose early and May Carter's household was no exception. I don't think this 'early rising' had anything to do with catching the 'early' worm (as told in many a myth and fairy tale.) I believe that this is as a result of ingrained/inherited coding in our DNA left over from slavery. We rise early; in many households most days start at the crack of dawn. Then and even today it's perceived to be pure laziness if a man, woman or child stays in bed till the sun is high in the sky.

Being in bed after the crack of dawn meant that you were either very ill or had, sometime during the night, lost you mind. In my mother's house it would be the former; she won't have tolerated any of her sons not being out of bed in good time. It simply was not going to happen in her house. So we got up and got dressed: we dressed in anything Mammy had allocated for playing in the village, which were easily identifiable by the occasional patch here and there.

Most people in Barbados awoke to the rays of the sun. In the Carrington Village/Deane's Village areas, we had a unique 'alarm bell': the ringing of the Glendairy Prison bell. The prison was no more than a quarter of a mile away: the bell was rung at 5.00 am to wake the prisoners and again at 8.30 pm to signal the end of their day. So, due to the prison's proximity to the villages everyone had an 'alarm clock' of sorts and responded to the bell.

Once we were up there was an accustomed rhythm of the day...unless it was a morning that a condemned prisoner was scheduled to be hung[1]. Most everyone knew the day when an execution was scheduled and sadly enough some people knew the executioner. The day before the execution he could be seen entering the prison, as he would have to spend the night there prior to the execution. Executions were carried out between 6 and 7 o'clock in the morning. We didn't watch the executions but heard the sound of the gallows at the moment of execution: the best way I can describe it is to say it sounded like a trip and a thud. We would go to the hill behind the prison perimeter wall: from there, we could see the external walls of the part of the prison that housed the gallows. From that vantage point we could see over the prison's perimeter wall and enough of that part of the prison yard.

The interruption of the sounds of the execution didn't stay with you all day. It had become common place and, since it was an accepted and accustomed practice, it was only a moment of reflection that someone had just died. Other than that, the morning continued uninterrupted. Adjacent to the prison's perimeter wall was a gully or dry riverbed. We played cricket and football in that gully. Part of the gully had some steps which we called Jacob's Ladder; people used these steps as a short-cut to the main road, Bridge Road to Station Hill.

Those of us who had animals (not pets: cows, sheep, goat, or pigs) or poultry tended them before going to school or work. The grazing animals were put out to pasture or any available spot of land that had grass. Poultry was fed and pens were cleaned. The pigs were another story. Most boys who had pigs had to clean and wash the pig pens before school. Sadly, the stench of pig excrement tended to linger; it stayed with you all day and (unfortunately!) announced to those in close proximity that you'd been cleaning out the pig pen. Needless to say, this would lead to the person being teased unmercifully.

All of these chores, including bringing water from the pipe and sweeping the yard, had to be done before you had breakfast or, as we called, it 'tea'. Having breakfast back then wasn't the same as breakfast today: it certainly didn't carry the same importance. There was no 'full English' of bacon, eggs, sausages, toast, beans, etc. It was just what the literal meaning of the word: a way to break the fast that your body went through as you slept. If you were Bajan it simply meant, "breaking the air out your stomach."

You could break the air out your stomach with a hot cup of tea (depending on your age it could be cocoa, bush tea, green tea or coffee). Very few people drank their tea without milk and sugar as was the British custom, but if you didn't have milk or sugar you drank it plain like that. You had a slice of bread, eggs, salt bread or crackers (perhaps spread with butter or jam) and you went to school. On the day Mammy had something else we got that something else: sweet bread, cassava pone, pudding (pound cake) or 'bakes' (a concoction of flour, sugar, assorted spices, cornmeal and water which were mixed together and deep fried in grease) but when she didn't you got your cup of tea and whatever she had which had no crime, stigma or shame attached to it. It was what it was and you were glad that you had what was given.

Just as children today relish the end of the school day, so too did we. In May Carter's house chores always had to be done before we could play. I know we played, but not the way other children did. That "let loose, gone wild, don't have an owner" kind of playing hardly ever happened; if it did some adult would most likely be keeping you in check. We also had better sense about Glendairy's Gully. That gully was many things for many boys, but what it seldom was for any of May Carter's boys was a place of enjoyment. I'm not saying that enjoyment couldn't be had in Glendairy's Gully, what I'm saying that doing any of the things the boys did in the gully was limited for any of May Carter's boys. We would have to take the chance when we could and hoped that no adult who knew our mother saw us. The end result would have been the same as if she'd seen us herself.

We often looked longingly as we watched the neighbourhood boys enjoying the Gully as it went through its many changes. In dry season it was a cricket or football field. When the rains came it was transformed, as if by magic, into a river where some of the neighbourhood boys fished (in a pond we called Bammow Pond) and swam to cool their bodies from that blazing Bajan sun. The river existed for only as long as it rained torrentially but when the rain stopped and the unrelenting sun had its own way, it wasn't long before it was transformed, to another playing field surrounding the back prison yard, filled with the sounds of playing boys. It was always young boys and young adult males – never females. I played in Glendairy Gully through both of these phases and, thanks to Mammy, never had to experience the sound of the children's laughter from inside Glendairy Prison.

Whether we were playing in the gully or any of the places in the neighbourhood where children played, there was one thing that was very clear. We were not expected to go far from home without the permission of parent(s). Nowadays parents have to worry about the safety of their children, but back then the world was a safer place and parents didn't worry about someone kidnapping your child from in front your house. Bajan children knew where their line was drawn when it came to playing outside. You played where your mother told you to play, you played with those children she said it was OK to play with and you played the places she told you to play. There wasn't anything like you playing where you felt like or with whom. Not if you wanted to ever see outside again … that day.

Going off on your own could result in many things; most of them could only be solved if you had a more vivid imagination than your mother, or if you could somehow manage to wander off from home and not encounter anyone who knew you or your mother. If you somehow managed to have a slip in memory as to where your play or boundary lines were drawn, took yourself over to someone else's boundary line and that person's parents noticed that you were outside your play 'area', then that parent became your parent and chastised you accordingly. You didn't have to wait to get home to discover your fate.

In Carrington Village and Deane's Village (and just about every other village in Barbados) the entire villages were involved in raising the child. You could find yourself being reprimanded by one of your friends' parents, and you knew that as soon as you got back home that parent was going let your mother know that you were seen, "behaving like if he mek himself. I ain't say nothing to him right there and then but I decided that once I saw you May I could let you know that Collin was out in front my house like if he ain't got no respect for somebody bigger than he."

That kind of complaint would seal your fate. A mother or village elder who was so distraught by your behaviour she couldn't hit you right there and then might very well get you limited to your immediate front yard-and no further. As she would say: "As far as my eyes could see you."

Either way, none of that would make a difference to my mother and other mothers in the Village. Even on moonlit nights every child knew when he or she was expected to come in. This was an unwritten rule but nevertheless, it was written in stone. Smaller children went to bed when chickens did and, as you got older, different things signalled different times for you to be inside where you lived, to be washed up and ready for bed. For the older children it was the sound of the Glendairy Prison bells: this meant it was 8.30 pm and all manner of foul, beast and children were expected to be inside by then. Qualifying as May Carter's Last Boy I was on my way in when the bell started and inside by the time the last of the rings sounded I was in bed!

FOOTNOTE

1. In March 2014, the government of Barbados announced plans to abolish the mandatory death sentence for murder. However, to date, this punishment is still on the statute books. The last hanging in Barbados took place in 1984.

CHAPTER 9

Going to Church: My Mother and King Jesus

"My beloved spoke to me and said to me, 'Arise, my darling, my beautiful one, come with me."
SONG OF SOLOMON 2:10

It was generally expected that every child should go to church; especially "Sunday School". We went every Sundays and, in my case, sometimes during the week. For those few children that did not go to Sunday school, no matter the denomination, the church came to them. I remember some of the holy rollers bringing Sunday school to the village in an open-air fashion hence it were difficult, if not impossible, for any child to escape church. If by some miracle you did not attend, then you and your mother were considered to be heading (and with great speed) for a head-on crash with hell.

I started attending the Pilgrim Holiness Church, followed by the New Testament Church of God (Pentecostal). Our Sunday school teacher taught us the need to be good boys and girls; failing which "the black bird would pick out our eyes."

My concept was of an old, white-bearded male God, sitting on some specifically-made chair, obscured by the clouds, spending his time writing all the deeds committed by everyone and woe betide you if you stole a drop of your mother's condensed milk, a pinch of sugar or a scale of salt fish. His punishment would be severe, hence you were forced as a child to love this old white man – God; because of the power he would employ to destroy you for any deed that went contrary to what you were told the bible expected you to do. Against this backdrop, without exception every home was bombarded with multiple images of this all-white, royal, Christian family: God, his son Jesus and his mother, the Virgin Mary.

All through childhood and beyond, images abounded with white angels, white disciples, white Roman soldiers … the list goes on ad infinitum. Just stop to ponder what such an up-bringing is designed to do to one's mental enslavement, thus producing a post traumatic slave syndrome on one's psyche. This was all dangerous stuff designed and employed to make us into the fools we were intended to remain up to this day. Living examples can be readily seen in the way we see hair care products (wigs and weaves), bleaching creams, plastic/cosmetic surgery. Look closely at our totally enslaved approach to religion which, whether we call ourselves Christian, Muslim, Hebrew Israelite (as given to us in the 17th century by new African people) was all designed and used by white people to mess with and control us for their acquisition of wealth, power and economic stability

My mother, affectionately known as May to her friends (or 'Miss May') went about the business of providing for her household and her five boys. Mammy never talked about the gossip or what she felt/ knew people were saying about her and her sons. Mammy understood that we were poor but encouraged us *never* should we show it. She would say: "You must have pride."

That being said, I am sure she knew (and was not surprised by the fact) that some of the people of our village thought she felt she was more important than she was. God knows that no one would think of my mother in the context of the virtuous woman of Proverbs 31: it speaks of the kind of woman that would make a man an excellent wife. In spite of having five sons with five different fathers, and the poverty which existed in our home, her domestic virtues abounded. A continual sunshine rested on our home. I'm sure my mother knew Proverbs 31 but I wouldn't venture to say whether or not she saw herself throughout the verses. Even though she might not have seen herself as a virtuous woman, she did however name her firstborn

Lemuel. This name Lemuel is the name of the King in Proverbs 31 whose mother, the Queen, had a vision which showed him how to identify a virtuous woman. Coincidence? I'll never know.

Just as the Queen admonished her son Lemuel not to take strong drink, so too did my mother. She didn't just tell Lemuel, she told all of us. Of course we heard her admonishment and as children we did not, but as we became men we did drink, but in moderation. We also never forgot her warning: "Man drunk or sober still mind your business." This meant that, whatever the circumstances, she always wanted us to be responsible for our actions and behaviour.

Lemuel left Barbados for Guyana in 1948; I was about 7 years old when he left. He returned to Barbados for the first time in 1955 for Barbados' Independence with his wife and two daughters. He spent three months and promised Mammy faithfully that he would visit at least every two years, a promise that up until the time of his death was never kept. After Mammy's diagnosis I felt it was necessary for me to meet my eldest sibling and his family whom I didn't know. In 1977, I journeyed to Guyana with Rudolph and Victor in search of him. The journey from Barbados to the hinterland of Guyana took plane, taxi, ferry and then a forty-mile taxi journey to Lemuel's home. We spent about a week together, I discussed Mammy's illness among other things and of course one could imagine we had about three decades of family history to discuss. Lemuel promised that he would return to Barbados for a visit. My next visit to Guyana was for his funeral in October 1985.

Like the women referred to in Proverbs 31, Mammy worked·tirelessly. The Proverbs 31 women dyed fabrics purple and sold them; Mammy prepared and dyed fabric (in her case, flour bags with Jiffy dye). She also had another skill: to take flour, sugar, coconut, cassava, ground corn, raisins, cinnamon, nutmeg, banana leaves and turn these ingredients into delicacies. She worked late into the night and was up before sunrise to provide for her household and others. She was strong – physically, mentally and spiritually – and was always ready to serve those less fortunate. She was considered fearless and spoke with wisdom.

It was the wisdom that came from being the mother of five sons but with no man in her life that led Mammy to make a life-altering decision. She wouldn't waste any more of her time or energy on men. She would find another way to fill that void left in her life by the men that had entered it. She married King Jesus. This marriage wasn't like the ones that the Catholic nuns entered into with Jesus because, as we understood it, those nuns were supposed to be chaste. In no way could my mother be considered as 'chaste' ... her five sons were proof of that.

I was glad for my mother. She didn't have to be chaste to marry King Jesus. She could go to him just as she was and he would accept her. Unlike men and women, King Jesus didn't judge. Everyone was welcome to join him in 'marriage'. My mother did so willingly. She entered into this holy alliance without the slightest fear of rejection. Finally, my mother had met her one true love and he would be hers until death, and even then in death she was assured a seat at his feet. This was a husband worthy of my mother and she would work hard to show her love and devotion to him.

But what did a marriage to King Jesus entail? I was about 8 years old when this marriage occurred, so I didn't fully understand that it had happened, but it impacted my life. Being my mother's last boy made me, in this marriage, the stepson of Jesus. As Jesus' stepson it meant that my mother and I had to go to his house, and often. My mother wasn't the only one who was married to Jeses; other women had experienced disappointment, hurt, pain and anguish at the hands of men and women, so they had all decided to marry the one who won't hurt, abuse or disappoint them ever. That someone was King Jesus. They were all willing to share him so my mother, like all the other women, came to show their devotion and admiration. They seldom came alone, as there was more often than not some son or daughter who didn't have a daddy and needed the one that would be proud to call them son or daughter.

Like all other stepchildren I had to go wherever and whenever my mother went to his house. That meant that each and every time the church door opened, we, the stepchildren, and all his wives, were there. My mother was a very devoted wife. She joined every organisation in his house to her devotion. In addition to all of these 'wifely' duties, my mother kept a steady and authoritative hand and 'hold' on her boys. The more devoted my mother became to the church, the more we understood what we could or couldn't do; what we could or couldn't get away with. And that was as close to 'nothing' as it could possibly get.

As one of May Carter's boys there was a certain expectancy, but as the step-son of Jesus this expectancy took on a new meaning. It now meant that even if we thought we could act up and do something so ridiculous as to embarrass May Carter, doing something that would anger your step-father, her husband King Jesus, well, that was another thing altogether. Not only that, but it was the kind of thing that could very well get you sitting at the foot of his throne long before May Carter arrived. None of us were in a hurry to get there.

So we accepted our 'lot'. Our lot meant that we were always under the scrutiny of the village that was helping to raise us and all the other village children. This "raising" of the child by the village meant that no child in could step out of line. Some of the other children came close to stepping on the line (and even got away with that) but that privilege wasn't afforded to any of May Carter's boys. We were expected to toe the line and toe it we did. My brothers and I stayed under the magnifying glass of every adult in Deane's Village. This constant scrutiny only happened because we were May Carter's boys and everyone knew Mammy didn't tolerate any nonsense.

In retrospect, my mother's parenting book was bible based: there were the Ten Commandments, the seven deadly sins and any rule or law that said, *"thou shall not... "* I am sure Mammy had her favourite parts from the book of Proverbs (especially the parts that talked about 'sparing the rod and spoiling the child' AND 'training up a child in the way he should go so that when he was old he won't depart from them') Mammy wasn't going to give you till you were old to see whether or not you were going to depart from her training. There were no roads with detour signs over them when it came to her discipline. Her road was straight and it was narrow. It didn't slope in any direction but if you acted the fool Mammy would have snatched that road right up and used it to beat some good sense right into you.

I'm also sure that Mammy did a lot of meditating and intercessory praying on our behalf to save us from hell's wrath. First, she put the fear of Mable Matilda Carter into us; when that was good and sunken in, she added the fear of our 'stepfather' and when *that* had sunken in as well she went on and added the fear of our 'Step-grandfather: The Fear of God. That fear (or its premise) worked on Rudolph, Carl and me to some degree (by this time my eldest brother Lemuel had migrated to British Guiana (Guyana). It may or may not have had some impact on Victor, but it didn't have the same impact on him that it did with us.

Mammy probably realised that Victor's head was hard, his ears didn't work quite as well or he'd simply 'pulled a Pharaoh' and decided to harden his heart against these fears. Either way, whatever his reasoning, Victor kept Mammy on her knees in prayer. I'm not sure if she went there so that she wouldn't have to send him to sit at the feet of his stepfather; perhaps she felt that if she spent that time working diligently doing all that she could, she would keep the hand cart that would take him to hell from being made.

Now Victor wasn't bad the way (not in the way it is understood today) but back in those days Victor was hip and wanted to be part of the "in" crowd. The in crowd didn't follow their mothers to King Jesus' house. They found other houses to go to and, to get in to those houses, a young 'cat' (such as Victor) had to look right. Looking right was important to Victor; so important, in fact, that he paid extra to the tailors to make him a pair of trousers in 36 hours to wear to his next dance. Victor could easily attend four dances some Saturday nights wearing the latest fashions!

CHAPTER 10

"Til de Doris or hearse comes and turn 'round'"

"Tell me, and I'll forget. Show me, and I may not remember. Involve me, and I'll understand."
NATIVE AMERICAN PROVERB

I smile now as I think on some of the things I've done in my childhood and in my young adult days that caused my mother to hold her head, take off a shoe and threaten to 'lick' off my head or some other threat of bodily harm. My mother had an endless arsenal of sayings, wits and wisdoms. She also had an equal amount of ways to threaten my brothers and me. To me, the most damning of all her threats was the one where she said she would either beat me until the hearse came and turned around. You got it. She was going to beat me until I was dead. If, however, my brothers and I were fighting (as all brothers do) she would say, "If you all don't stop that foolishness I gine beat you all and two vans coming here today; the hearse for you all and the Doris for me." The Doris was another word that people of my mother's generation used to describe a police van. The Doris might have been the make or model of the car, as it looked like a station wagon and had part wooden sides.

I can well imagine that there will be those individuals who might think that those threats made by my mother were akin to child abuse. The threats must be seen in their full context. It's not that I'm condoning child abuse on any level, but today's thinking can't be employed. If anything, we should remember that people of my mother's generation were not that far removed from slavery. This behaviour (threats as well as beatings) was a direct correlation to what they would have experienced on the plantation. People of my mother's generation (and those of her fore-parents) were taught that obedience was to be obtained by all and any means. We are a people that have suffered the worse kinds of atrocities by our enslavers, so we were taught that obedience had to be obtained from children, as no one wanted a child that didn't seem to know or understand the consequences of disobedience. It didn't matter what was used – belt, whip, stick, hand, shoe, or rope. Children were expected to be obedient and, if they were not, that obedience would be beaten into them.

Like so many boys my age, we sometimes tested our mothers and their religion. In their minds, being good Christians (and they all aspired to be) meant that they took Proverbs 13:24 rather seriously. No one was ever going to accuse them of hating their sons. Nope. The scripture said, "He who spareth the rod hateth his son but he that loveth him correcteth him betimes." So, with that scripture firmly planted in my mother's mind, she was going to make sure that she didn't spare the rod and end up with a lot of spoiled children who felt unloved. The women of my village were so hell-bent on making sure that we didn't become spoiled or felt unloved that if a serious beating had to commence (one that might end up involving a hearse and "The Doris) we were sent to pick our own whip. Now, to me, *that* was child abuse. How do you send the victim to secure his/her own whip, that it was going to end up being their one-way ticket to ride in the hearse and your ride in The Doris?

Now that we understand the thinking behind the threat, perhaps we can be a bit more sympathetic to my poor mother who had to make sure that she demonstrated that she loved us all just the way she was taught. But knowing deep in my heart that my mother was never going to carry out the threat didn't make it any the less mortifying, as I knew the difficulty involved in getting one or both of these vehicles to our house. If we employ modern thinking and the quick response time to get either a hearse or a police car it's almost funny, but taken in its full context it really wasn't funny. My mother and all mothers of my village knew what it meant for either a hearse or a police car or even ambulance to make its way in or out of our village or any other village in Barbados in those times

When my mother was making these threat times and things were very different. Imagine Barbados in the 1940s and 1950s. The little unpaved, dirt roads (or gaps as they were called) where we lived were our oasis. Both sides of the road were dotted with chattel houses sitting on roughly quarried stones, separated from each other with very narrow foot paths .A mother may have had to split her house spot to accommodate a shed for a grown child with their new families, and these sat almost dangerously close to the only accessible thoroughfare that took us out to the slightly wider roads. These thoroughfares were so narrow as to be almost inaccessible where pedestrians, the much envied bicycles, an occasional car, donkey cart and child taking either cow, sheep or goat out to graze, jostled each other for space, so they could get on with the task of daily living.

Because most of the gaps in my village were too small for two of anything to pass each other, we devised our own way of making this little strip of dirt work. We moved along this pathway like ants without getting in the way of the other. Someone (or something) would stop so the other could go by. So can you now clearly imagine the idea of anything making a U-turn in my gap was an impossible feat? Any driver wishing of turning around and going back the other way had to go to the top of the gap and turn around. Are you starting to get the picture?

CHAPTER 11

My first job as a Cash Boy

"You must act as if it's impossible to fail."
GHANAIAN PROVERB

June 1955 rolled around and found me, aged fourteen and a half years old, and finished school. I had not graduated in the way we understand graduations today but, according to the educational system in Barbados at the time, I had reached the age where the government was no longer compelled to either keep me in school or obligated to educate me beyond this age. I had to accept that no longer was I a student at my beloved St Giles, but I also understood that there weren't many options available to me or any other boy in my educational, economic and social status. I had to work.

Unable to pay for private lessons for me, and having a clear understanding of how things were in Barbados, Mammy made a decision. In Mammy's thinking (and because of her close relationship with God and the church) she knew how a 15-year-old boy, with time on his hands, could find much work to do in the devil's workshop. She was going to see to it that she, not the devil, would find work for me. My hands would neither be idle nor busy in his workshop. If I wanted to, I could find work in Satan's workshop, but it wouldn't be around her or while living in her house.

Two months earlier, during the Easter vacation, Mammy had taken me down to see Mr Browne, a neighbourhood mechanic. Mr Browne was well known as the 'Top-Notch' motor mechanic in or near our village. To Mammy, this level of expertise was all the more reason for her to speak to him about taking me on as an apprentice. She told him that I would be leaving St Giles in three months and she would appreciate it if he would take me on and teach me how to become a motor mechanic. When he agreed Mammy knew that she'd outwitted the devil. She'd found the work for me to do.

Mr Browne suggested to my mother that I start my apprenticeship during the two-week Easter Holiday and, once I was finished school, I would continue my training. People brought cars, vans and lorries from far and wide for him to repair. This steady stream of vehicles meant that there would always be something for me to learn. So, as suggested by Mr Browne, as soon as my Easter two-week school vacation started I 'reported' for my apprenticeship and very reluctantly kissed my two week Easter Holiday goodbye.

I wasn't quite sure what being an apprentice to a motor mechanic meant, but I knew for sure it won't involve any kite-making or flying. My two-week stint mainly involved unbolting car sumps/crankcases, draining the old oil from them and then washing them with gas/petrol. Unlike mechanics today we had no hoist, inspection pit nor proper jacks, and this job entailed lying on my back under the respective vehicle.

Mr Browne himself was a very likable man; however he liked to indulge in his liquor and his tipple of choice was rum and water. He also smoked, and his cigarettes were a constant companion. I must say here that at no time did he try or suggest that I join him in any of his indulgences. His common-law spouse, Miss Standard, was a "poor-white" woman who also smoked heavily, but to the boys in Deane's Village none of that mattered. What mattered was her treatment of us and Miss Standard was to us like a "nice big sister." My friends and I caught crabs using crab traps, snares of varying varieties or filling the crab holes with water to flush the crabs out. We used traps to catch birds; we usually caught wood doves. Mrs Standard enjoyed watching us while we joke and ribbed each other. She would provide us with matches to light a fire to cook any birds or crabs we caught. We could always depend on her to provide what we needed to get our boyhood treats prepared, since our mothers were not going to allow us to cook these 'treasures' in their pots. She was also the surrogate friend and mother to two girls: Shirley and Betty. Upon reflection I don't think Mrs Standard had any children of her own, which would probably explain her affinity to some of the neighbourhood children.

As the two weeks progressed I must admit that the prospect of becoming a mechanic filled me with dread and it had nothing to do with the work or working hard. What filled me with dread was the grease. I had images of this thick, dark mechanic grease covering me everywhere: on my clothes, matting my hair and keeping it clumped to my head. I saw my hands permanently greasy and worst of all my cuticles, marred with thick crude grease that I would never be able to wash off. Please bear in mind that back then we did not have gloves or the kind of chemical substances to remove grease like we do today. I heard the calls of 'grease monkey'. Those images bothered me and when Mammy mentioned getting two pairs of dungarees for me to work in I had to tell her the truth. That painful truth was that, as likeable as he was, I didn't want to work with Mr Browne. I didn't want to be a mechanic and I certainly didn't want to become a 'grease monkey'.

When I told Mammy that I didn't want to be a mechanic, she accepted my decision without argument. However, she did make a simple statement. She said: "You don't have to become a mechanic, but what you've got to do is get a job or a trade, or you won't get one grain of rice in my house." Mammy had laid down the law. We were at an impasse: I didn't want to be a mechanic but she wasn't about to have me or my idle hands in her house.

I would have been content learning any other trade: plumbing, carpentry, joinery or even gold smithying. I simply couldn't see myself covered from head to toe in grease for the rest of my life. Entertaining all of those thoughts were one thing, but the thought that most occupied my mind was this: "I want to eat and Mammy don't make joke. I have to get a job." I know that getting this job was not something I could do at my leisure but as soon as I left school. In the few days before school ended, I applied to a few department stores in the city (Bridgetown) asking if there were any vacancies for a Cash Boy.

My two days seeking employment paid off because I was able to procure a job as a Cash Boy. I started working the Monday after my last day at St Giles. My new job was in a big department store on Broad Street (the main shopping street in Bridgetown) I was one of the newest Cash Boys at George Sahaley's and I was proud. I was a wage earner.

Sahaley's was not as large as some of the other department stores, but it served the needs of those who needed to purchase fabric, shoes, shirts, and other sundries that would be utilised by tailors and seamstresses. Tailors and seamstresses were used by most Barbadians, since many could not afford the limited supply of ready-made clothing that was sold in the stores. The store also sold oilskin cloth/plastic which, as mentioned earlier, was primarily for Christmas table cloths.

So, what was my role as a Cash Boy? When the customer made a purchase they would hand over cash to the clerk (customer attendant). They in turn would write a receipt and then give the money and receipt to a Cash Boy (me, or one of the others) to take to the cashier. The cashier would record the purchase, then the Cash Boy would take a copy of that sales slip and any remaining change back to the customer. What I remember most was assisting the clerks with re-rolling the fabric after a customer had made a purchase. I would then wait for the familiar call of, "Cash! Caaaasssshhh!" The reply would be, "Boy!" That cry meant it was time for me, or one of the other boys, to go to the clerk, collect the sales slip and run over to the cashiers.

My wages then were $3.00 a week (approximately £1 at today's exchange rate) and it was given in a small brown sealed envelope. Upon receiving my first wage packet I was so excited I ripped it open. When I got home I showed Mammy my opened envelope and she said to me, "Why did you open it? From now on; when you get your pay packet you bring it to me." I had enough sense not to be powerful foolish and say something to her like, "Cause I work for it." That would have been certain death.

I guess Mammy was concerned that, as a young boy, the $3.00 in my hand might 'burn a hole in my pocket' (as the old people used to say). On my way home I had to pass three ice-cream parlours and I could very well be tempted to stop in and blow away a portion of my $3.00 on ice-cream, hamburger, milkshake, crackerjack popcorn or any of the things young people were excited about. This couldn't be risked, so I handed over my wage packet. Mammy kept two and a half out of the three dollars I was making and gave me fifty cents. This was the expected thing to do; she was still taking care of the house and fulfilling our needs to the best of her ability. Mammy was quite conservative in her spending, so you could find that in a week or two she would present you with a new shirt or pants.

I was doing all that I could to impress my new employer and prove to them that, in hiring me, they'd made the right decision. As a Cash Boy I didn't have a uniform and even in the intense Barbadian heat I wore short grey flannel pants. They were my Sunday school 'best' clothes as there wasn't any money to purchase material to have special shorts made for work. I also wore my Sunday school shirts and the only other things that were necessary were a pair of well-polished shoes and a tie.

CHAPTER 12

A 'newly minted' Cash Boy and a hurricane called Janet

"A person who says it cannot be done should not interrupt the man doing it." SWAZI PROVERB

On the morning of 22 September 1955, I'd been working as a Cash Boy for three months. Even though I'd heard that Hurricane Janet was due to hit Barbados, l did what I'd done every morning since starting to work at Sahaley; I dressed with meticulous care and headed to work. As I walked the twenty-minute walk I noticed that the sky was unusually overcast. There was a slight rain, but not enough to deter me from getting to work. I walked to work blissfully oblivious to the buzz of an impending hurricane. The only thing on my mind was getting to work promptly at 8.00 am

I was proud that despite the overcast skies, I'd pressed on to work and arrived on time. But when I got there the store managers asked me, "What are you doing here? Haven't you heard there's a hurricane coming? Go back home."

When asked if I hadn't heard I didn't want to answer, as I would have told her the truth. I'd not long started on the job and I wanted to create an excellent impression. We didn't have electricity or radios and therefore many of us had only heard by word-of-mouth of this impending hurricane. We did not have the kind of communication system that people take for granted today. There were very few telephones and they were few and far between. We mainly depended on government and business premises from which we could make phone calls. We may not have had a modern communication system, but messages did get to the recipient(s)! A phone call might have been transmitted to places like police stations in-outlying districts then one would request that whoever received the phone call sent a message by someone: bus drivers, conductors and the general public passed on messages and information orally.

Obviously there were no such things as mobile phones, the internet or even personal radios. However there was a radio distribution service which later became known as 'Rediffusion'. This service was transmitted from Bridgetown and consisted of just a speaker box within in the homes of those who could afford to pay the rental for this service. In 1955 most rural areas did could not receive this service because of the distance from the Bridgetown Transmitting Station. There was no street lighting, no paved roads or electricity in the village and in rural districts the infrastructure was almost non-existent. The majority of the island depended on kerosene lamps and stoves, open-air wood fires for cooking; therefore, the impact of a Category 4 hurricane with winds in excess of 120 miles per hour would naturally take its toll on the island's majority of chattel houses.

I'd never experienced a hurricane so I had no idea what the real effect would be. As I made the return trip to my home in Deane's Village I noticed that the store owners, who had been encouraged to board up their store windows were doing so, and with a great urgency. I slowed my walking pace as I watched the activity around me. The morning looked like none I'd ever seen before. The clouds were very dark and it was raining lightly, then the winds began to kick up. I noticed that the wind velocity was expeditiously attacking everyone's headdress. Caps, straw hats and even fedoras were no match for the wind. Suffice to say that a few hairpins were being uprooted causing a few of the ladies' hats, like boats bobbing in the Careenage, to lose their anchoring. If not for a carefully executed 'snatch and grab' these hats would have gone sailing on the increasing winds and would become just another one of the many stories that would be told in the years to come about what happened on the day that Hurricane Janet paid Barbados a visit.

Ordinarily, if I were going to take a bus home, I would have walked along Broad Street to Trafalgar Square, onto Bridge Street and into the bus stand to catch a route 21 bus. However, this morning everything seemed different and I had to see as much as I could. So I walked the entire journey home by way of Broad Street, entranced by the never-before sight of schooners doing a merry dance on the water of the Careenage. I also noticed that the tide was almost at the level of the road and these vessels were being tossed around like paper boats in a whirlpool. Everyone was making a hasty retreat out of the city.

I travelled by the way of St Michael's Row, Constitution Road, Halls Road, Harmony Hall and Hinds Bury Road. Everyone was now talking about the impending hurricane. By the time I reached home my brothers were hastily trying to secure the house by using long pieces of wood as props. Those of us who didn't have Rediffusion relied on getting the news from those that had this luxury. The verbal news travelled quickly as no one had ever experienced a hurricane and there was a sense of urgency to get the news to those who may have had family and friends in rural districts.

My mother, who was always thinking ahead, had finished cooking. I remember looking at the food and thinking that there was enough to feed an army (and perhaps a few angels, too!) Women across the island had been praying hard and asking God for deliverance from these troubled waters.

We were told where the official hurricane shelters were; unsure of what was in store for us (and the island as a whole) we left the house and went to the nearest shelter. Our shelter was situated at the corner of the village and was the home of pastor of the village church. Given that most of the chattel houses in our village were constructed of wood, this house was constructed of coral stones and cement and could, by all accounts, withstand the winds of a hurricane.

By midday we were witnessing what Hurricane Janet had in store for us. Outside trees swayed, bent, straightened and some, whose roots couldn't withstand the pressure of the wind, became uprooted. Utility poles were falling like matchsticks. Inside the house every adult was commenting and giving an opinion. There was a sombre tone: a certain amount of excitement mixed with a degree of fear and a potpourri of emotions. My mother, who had walked with her pot of food, was sharing food to those persons who had had to leave their homes without a chance to cook. There was a true community spirit within this house. It· was now a converted shelter, filled not with just the family that owned it, but with anyone seeking shelter from the ravages of the hurricane.

As a young man I found it relatively exciting. I had my mother and my brothers with me and so I felt safe where I was. Also I was getting a first-hand view and looking out the window and seeing sheets of galvanise sailing through the air, the uprooted trees and all the debris swirling around. To those who cared to listen, I was giving an eyewitness account of the goings-on outside. I also found it very exciting to watch the torrential rain as it seemingly fell from the sky "in buckets per drop" (as we would describe it).

This never-before-seen volume of rain that came with Hurricane Janet also flooded what were usually dry rivers and gullies. I was able to watch, with the enthusiasm of youth and from the safety of the window, as one of the rivers filled up, the rising water flooding the dry riverbed. The hurricane had all but subsided between 2.00 to 3.00 pm, those of us who were allowed to venture out did so, like the dove of Noah's time. The difference here was there was no dry land to search for. We knew what we were hoping to find. The adults thought we went out on the streets to ascertain what damage had been done: truthfully, our thinking was to find out how many fruit trees had fallen, and what feasts awaited us. And we were not disappointed: a wide and varied selection of fruits awaited us, ours just to pick up and take without the effort or danger of having to climb a tree. With our treasure in hand we returned to the 'shelter.'

When night fell we all stayed in the house, as the adults were uncertain if the hurricane would do an about-face and return to the island. This night passed very quickly. We didn't have any beds so when all the chairs were taken up I braced my back against the wall and made myself as comfortable as possible. It was only going to be for one night. Soon it was morning, but this morning though different. It was the morning after the first hurricane that many on the island had ever seen. Many didn't know what to expect. Everyone who had sought shelter in Pastor Hardy's house returned to their respective homes, or at least to where we knew we left our homes standing. Some people were fortunate to find their homes just as they'd left them; others were not so fortunate. Two houses opposite ours fell. Many people were homeless. Our house did not fall because of the propping we had done; but the force of the wind twisted the house somewhat.

When I stepped out that morning it was extremely windy. Outside was grey and there was a strange quietness. There were trees, utility poles and an assortment of debris strewn across the road. Everyone swung into action with whatever instruments they had to clear roads. There were remnants of houses everywhere. According to Rudolph (who was at that time a bus conductor) there was an attempt by the private bus operators to have a bus service going but the wooden bus that was being used at that time (with the tarpaulin rolled down at the side) was no match for the wind. The wind tore at the tarp and it became clear that the bus would never make it to its route destination, so at around 10.00 am the decision was made to take the bus out of service and forgo the attempt.

Immediately after the hurricane there was a call to mobilise all the available carpenters that could be found. Men who did not know a saw from a hammer cashed in; realising that money could be made, they bought themselves the necessary tools and became instant carpenters. The fact that they lacked carpentry skills didn't matter. A board needed to be nailed or a sheet of galvanised needed to be put back in place, a pailing (a fence) needed to be straightened or perhaps a pig or sheep pen needed to be tacked back together. The need/necessity for an instant fix gave these men work. Some of these men were subsequently referred to as 'stormy carpenters' and for many years after the hurricane, if a carpenter didn't do a good job they were referred to as a stormy carpenter.

Another set of people who 'cashed in' during the aftermath of Hurricane Janet were women called 'see-me-in-distress' (a play on the word 'seamstress'). A 'see-me-in-distress' was a woman that you went to when your usual seamstress had taken in too much work and at the last minute couldn't accommodate your garment. You then had to turn to the 'see-me-in-distress' who could cut, perhaps even stitch, but one thing for sure … everyone knew that it was 'she' and not the good seamstress who had made your garment.

The day after the hurricane the St Giles Scout troops were mobilised and sent to Carrington Village School. The Scout Master got all the senior Scouts together and told us that we would be manning the Carrington Village School Hurricane Shelter. We would be responsible for receiving emergency food and other supplies delivered by the Barbados Regiment (as it was then known) to the respective emergency hurricane shelters. The scouts then prepared and gave the rations to those persons in the shelter. We also provided, by the way of an open fire, hot water, first aid, etc.

I guess this operation lasted for about two to three weeks and we did an excellent job in administering the task given. Apart from the initial guidance given by the Scout Master, none of the boys exceeded 15 years of age. We, the St Giles Scouts, were highly applauded by all for a job well executed. Working closely with the Barbados Regiment after Hurricane Janet convinced me that I should join this military unit. That would not happen for another three years. I became Senior Scout and then Assistant Scout Master at St Giles after leaving school. I continued to serve St Giles and St Leonards thereafter as Scout Master.

In today's society there are many who would frown, if not laugh, at the idea of having a dollar added to their weekly wages. Most would think, "A dollar? What can a dollar more do, it can't make much difference?" In today's money a dollar means very little. But in 1956 a dollar more to your wages was monumental. A dollar more meant that Mammy could buy additional groceries and for me … well it meant that I would have more in my pocket. When the opportunity presented itself where I could now earn four dollars a week, I jumped at it. This new job took me to the Caribbean Confectionary Company where I would work weighing candy in what was called The Cold Room. It was my responsibility to give an account of the amount of candy that was made for the day. The expression, "child in a candy factory" certainly applied to me! I was surrounded by all my favourite candies: peanut candy crisp (a yellow candy shaped like a peanut with peanut butter on the inside), Paradise Plumb (a red, yellow and white candy) and mints. No mother or grandmother went to church without a clear or extra strong mint in her pocketbook/handbag.

Each day at the candy factory was an experience. I learned how all the treats from my earlier childhood got made. Sugar and water were blended together and put to boil. Steam was the method used to heat it to a boil. It was then poured onto an iron table where men with iron bars would stir, add colour and flavours, turn and kneed it until it was cool. Then it was placed into a machine that would roll, stretch, and mould it into shapes. These shapes were sent to the cold room for weighing. The candy was then wrapped by automated wrapping machines operated by women. The Engineer would remove the respective machine platter and set up for the next type to be wrapped.

For two years I was a diligent employee. I was always punctual and took great pride in my job. It was also while working here that I wore my first pair of long pants. These pants were dungarees (jeans); Mammy purchased the fabric and had our tailor make the pants, as there was no such thing as going to the store and purchasing a pair of readymade pants. These pants also gave Mammy additional 'ammunition': she would use the long pants, not so much as a bargaining chip, but as a means to keep me in line. If she thought you started to 'act like a man', when you were still under her roof and control, she would remind you that you weren't. For the most part I would hear, "Do you think 'cause you wearing long pants now you are a man? Well let me tell you that you are not. Those are my pants and I would take them off you and put you back in short one."

That was enough to reel back in whatever 'man-ish' behaviour had managed to surface. Once I'd started wearing long pants, I didn't want to go back to short. I did however wear short pants again for Scout duties and the Barbados Regiment .Scouting and the Barbados

Regiment taught me many life lessons, as did working at the candy factory. The 'life lesson' I learned there, came through the factory canteen where we were given lunch credit on a daily basis. One Friday, I went to collect my four-dollar weekly wages only to discover that, during the week, I had eaten up most of the $4.00 from the canteen account. That meant there was very little money to take home that week. As always, Mammy knew what to do. She made sure that I had some kind of packed lunch, but it was given to me with the warning, "See the factory canteen and don't see it." Needless to say, that never happened again.

My love for scouting remained, even as I worked full time. Scouting only required my obligations for about an hour a week after work and on Saturdays, so I was able to fulfil my obligations to my troop. As a matter of fact, even after I joined the Barbados Regiment, I remained involved in scouting, right up until the time I left Barbados. I rose through the ranks to become a Scout Master, both at St Giles and at St Leonard's.

As a Scout Master there were many duties and responsibilities, but there was also time for fun events and exercises. The scouts attended jamborees and went camping, where there were many opportunities for teaching and learning (tying the knots, learning survival skills: how to start a fire without matches, pitching a tent, etc.) There was one particular activity, an international scouting event that we all looked forward to. That event was Bob-A-Job. The Bob-A-Job meant that the scout would perform a job in the community (in homes or places of business) and the person for whom the task/job was performed would pay the scout a 'bob'/ a shilling (24 cents).

That meant that an industrious scout could make a bit of money as he went from job to job. Of course there were those persons in the community who saw this as way to exploit the scouts and get done those menial tasks that they didn't want to perform themselves or pay to get done. That notwithstanding, the person for whom the services were performed would sign a card stating the details relating to job and its remuneration. The money earned from this event was used for charitable causes.

I truly believe that scouting contributed greatly to the man I am today. There are times when I have to do a particular chore that involves ropes or twine and I will automatically resort to using one of the knots I was taught as a scout. Scouting taught me discipline and respect, the two core, fundamental tools that are mandatory in business, and my life in general. Lacking either shows in the way you conduct yourself and business; having both and employing them with due diligence reflects in your character. People do take notice of that; it matters to them that they are treated with respect. A disciplined individual has strength of character and can be depended on – that's a true scout.

"Once a scout, always a scout."

CHAPTER 13

Be careful what you wish for... you just might get it

"If you think education is expensive...try ignorance." AFRICAN PROVERB

When I was 17 years old, and very much against Mammy's advice, I joined the Barbados Regiment. I remember when I told her she was anything but pleased. She said to me, "I don't want any green berets in my house. You only setting yourself up to be soldier bait." I understood Mammy's fears and the way she was expressing them. After all, she had lived through two world wars and was concerned for her son in anyone's army. At the time I joined the Barbados Regiment, Mammy only had four sons at home. My brother Lemuel was now living in Guyana. The decision for him to live there was one borne out of necessity and a mother's desire to protect a child. So with Lemuel living in Guyana, Rudolph, my second oldest brother, became the one that Mammy turned to when she needed to discuss household matters. But at the time I knew none of this. I only became aware of this during the summer of 2011 while in Barbados gathering information and doing research for this book and conducting interviews. Rudolph was one of several persons interviewed; until the interview Rudolph had never spoken of the very important role he played in helping Mammy financially in supporting us and running the house.

I never knew that Rudolph had sacrificed his dream of becoming a teacher, and later a goldsmith, so that there would be more money available to help Mammy with us. How did this come about? Rudolph was afforded an opportunity to be trained to teach and also learn jewellery-making and watch repairing at one of the most reputable jewellery makers in Barbados – at the time, Holder Brothers – but he chose to take a job that would earn him more money. But, as I said, I was only made aware of this later, and so I worked hard to assimilate myself to life in the Regiment. I soon worked out that orders came from above and finished at the lowest rank; hence I sought to move up in rank as quickly as I could. It took me four years to move from Private to Sergeant. For some that might be a crawl but for me it was a monumental achievement. I'd left the lowest rung of the ladder.

I was enthusiastic about being a member of the Barbados Regiment and was able to divide my time between the Regiment and the Boys Scouts with comparable ease. In some ways the activities of both correlated – open air exercises, living under canvas tents and tracking, to mention a few. For me, the additional excitement in the Regiment was weapon training and drill exercise. As it was, the Barbados Regiment was a part-time militia. It was mobilised for two weeks every year and during those two weeks we were engaged in full-time training.

It was during the two weeks' deployment that we would sometimes be sent to one of the other islands. We went to St Vincent in 1961 and St Lucia in 1962. What I had not anticipated, dreamed or imagined, was that the day would come when I would stand on the deck of a battleship. That day came in August 1962 when I boarded the ship HMS Troubridge in the Bridgetown port and sailed for approximately eight hours to St Lucia. The HMS Troubridge was T-Class Destroyer of the British Royal Navy, so you can imagine the immense pride with which I stood on the deck. I can well remember the cardboard stiff feeling of standing there on this ship, occasionally walking around the deck and paying much attention to the various naval guns on board. I was wearing the very same green beret that Mammy was sure 'going to make me soldier bait' (also referred to as cannon fodder.) Neither Mammy nor I ever considered moment – her last boy standing on the deck of a British warship ploughing the Caribbean Sea heading to St Lucia.

HMS Troubridge (January 1969)

HMS Troubridge

As the HMS Troubridge pulled out of the Bridgetown Harbour I stood proudly on the deck watching the lights of the Barbados slowly pass from view, all the while anticipating what the lights of St Lucia would look like. Relatively soon they came into view. I was so excited on this exercise as I would also be meeting the people of this island for the first time, that I stayed on deck most of the time. The voyage on both the outward and inward journeys to St Lucia seemed effortless for this vessel, as it moved with ease on a rather tranquil Caribbean Sea. Unlike the previous year, 1961, the Regiment went to St Vincent on a locally-owned motor vessel owned by Captain George Ferguson and many of us became seasick!

CHAPTER 14

Joining the Regiment

"People know each other better on a journey"
AFRICAN PROVERB

On that day, as I stood on the deck of the HMS Troubridge, I was standing proudly as a Sergeant. I'd worked hard and had made this accomplishment in a much shorter period of time than other soldiers. However, I was under no illusion that someday, should I stay long enough in the Barbados Regiment, I would become a commissioned officer. I'd worked hard, done what was asked of me and more. I had given the Barbados Regiment that extra, yet nothing that I had accomplished so far – marksmanship, three stripes, drill instructor, etc. – would be taken into consideration to rightfully take me to the enviable rank of commissioned officer. I was more than eminently qualified for the position, but I would never see it because of one missing element.

Unlike the Ministry of Health (where I would later work) where I was able to prove that I was capable of performing as well as anyone, to be a commissioned officer I was missing one much-needed element: a secondary education. The Barbados Regiment could and would not be so easily swayed. There were rules, regulations and reasoning; though they made no sense (to me) they existed to keep me, and others like me, from the ranks of commissioned officer. I could out-shoot and out-perform the best of them, whether or not they had a secondary school education, but in the end none of that would matter.

I have to mention here that I DID have the opportunity to get the much desired (and much yearned for) secondary school education ... not once but twice. The first time was in 1952; about eight scholarships were offered by the Modern High School and, depending on how well I did in the exam, I stood the chance of being awarded a full scholarship. I took the exam but I didn't get a high enough score for a full scholarship; however, I'd done well enough to qualify for a half scholarship. I was ecstatic, holding my breath as this information was conveyed to Mammy. She didn't expend a lot of energy thinking about it. She simply said she couldn't afford it. I accepted and understood because I knew how hard Mammy was working to keep a roof over our heads and food on the table.

In as much as I understood, I also badly wanted that secondary school education. So, with the dream still alive in my heart, I set my mind on re-taking and passing the exam. I hoped that by the time the results came out things (or at least Mammy's feelings) might have changed. I re-took the exam the following year, but the results were the same. A half scholarship. Once again, the proposition was put to Mammy: would she be willing to pay the other half? This time around, Mammy's response was much different: she said, "None of the rest went to secondary school. So you won't be going. I can't make that difference between you all."

Mammy had spoken and, as always, her words were the law. I didn't go. To some it might sound harsh or unfeeling to so casually dismiss a child's dream but to Mammy her reasoning was sound. All her sons would be treated the same. All of my brothers had gone to St Giles and none had gone on to secondary school. There was no exception then and there would be no exception now. So, I let it go and I refocused my energies. I might not be going to secondary school but I wasn't going to let that determine who or what Collin Leroy Carter would become. I wasn't sure what I was going to do, but whatever it was I was going to be the best at it.

My discipline as a soldier was recognised by the one English officer who was there as Adjutant (Military Administrative Officer), a second from a British Regiment. He felt that I was a good candidate for Her Majesty's Army and, to prove his sincerity and belief in my ability, he said that he would provide me with a letter of recommendation outlining why I would be an excellent candidate for the British Army. I understood (without him telling me) that I would be able to rise higher in the ranks in England if it were based solely on my ability. But, just like the Barbados Regiment, even with his letter of recommendation I would not receive a commission in the British Army. He and I both understood that, in England, more than not having a secondary education stood in my way. Standing between me and that commission was the one thing that could not or would not be overlooked: my abilities and I were 'housed' in the skin colour that would limit (if not fully prevent) my rubbing shoulders with the privileged for whom commissions were an expected way of life.

It should be noted that when the call to arms came down to Barbados from Mother England in 1962, it was for over 500 Barbadian men to enlist in the British Army. These were men with varying levels of education. Scores of them answered that call. Of those who answered, two that I know of received commissions which allowed them to attend Sandhurst – the British officers' school for the privileged of the privileged; those expected to govern, achieve and otherwise attain the best that British society had to offer. But Mother England wasn't going to allow too many of us to rub elbows and dirty the sleeves of the privileged.

That notwithstanding, I must admit that the military helped to shape my life and, to some degree, prepare me for the difficult and demanding life I confronted as a Black person in England.

CHAPTER 15

The more some things change, the more things remain the same

"The hunter in pursuit of an elephant does not stop to throw stones at a bird" UGANDAN PROVERB

My membership of the Regiment also played a small part in procuring employment as an Aedes Aegypti mosquito Health Inspector. While working at the Caribbean Confectionary Company I applied to many Public Service Departments seeking employment of a clerical nature. Like other people I also had a list of things that I wanted, wished for, and was willing work very hard for. Some of these things I got and some I didn't. When I was 17 years old I wanted one such thing and was willing to work hard to attain it: that was a job in any government department. I guess in those days you felt that once you had a job in a government department, it was likely that you had a job for life until you retired and received a government pension. It was generally felt that a government pension was the golden nest egg for old age.

I was fortunate enough to obtain a government job, as a Health Inspector with the Department of Health. This was considered to be a good job and (to some people in Barbados at the time) it was a job that was well out of my league. The position as a Health Inspector brought with it a certain degree of legal authority, regardless of my age. Imagine, if you will, what it meant for me, a 17-year old young man from Carrington Village, to have acquired such a position without a secondary school education. The position was not the kind of job anyone imagined for a boy who attended St Giles, far less one that had left school at the tender age of fourteen.

However, the difference between me, and other people's expectations of what I should or should not be doing, was my determination and tenacity. I didn't see this position as something unattainable to me, but when I looked at it I simply said, "Why *not* me?" So, I went about doing what I could to get it.

The main function of this position was the eradication of the Aedes Aegypti mosquito; in those days it was better known as the Yellow Fever Mosquito. It was also the carrier of other tropical fevers. Training for this position was demanding. Those of us selected were given a series of lectures by the Board of Health and after these lectures we were tested on what we had retained. I scored very high and was short-listed for a position. I was Health Inspector, trained by the Board of Health. I was a confident and convincing Health Inspector and, to show that we were on a serious mission, I had proper picture identification. So my fellow Barbadians knew that they could trust me: I was a man with a 'position', dressed in a 'collar and tie'. Thanks to my training I can identify the eggs, larvae, pupae and adult Aedes Aegypti mosquitoes. I could also tell you, in great detail, about the habits of these mosquitoes; how they spread the dreaded diseases and how they could be eradicated.

Combating the Aedes Aegypti mosquito required the use of a flit (aerosol) can with DDT (dichlorodiphenyltrichloroethane), which I would spray into and on any receptacles containing stagnant water. Now, at the time, I was told DDT was harmless to humans, but would eradicate the Aedes Aegypti mosquito. This seemingly harmless white powder was mixed with tap water and sprayed around homes. Of course some people had their concerns about DDT, but with the confidence of my training and conviction of my so-called expertise in the substance, I confidently assuaged their fears and assured my fellow Barbadians of its safety by demonstration. How did I demonstrate that DDT was harmless? I tasted it. Yes, I would dip my finger in the white powder and ingest it. I didn't do this out of a sense of bravado or stupidity, but because I was assured by my 'superiors' that it was harmless.

In years to come I would discover that the assurance of DDT's safety was such a far cry from the truth that, even now, there are no words to adequately describe the personal anguish and torment I have subsequently experienced years later. I remember sometime in the 1980s (when DDT was banned) I listened in horrific silence to a radio programme as they discussed the enormity of the destruction that this chemical causes. I was immediately taken back to my days as a young man who not only ingested this substance but might have, unknowingly and unwittingly, exposed people, their property, livestock, gardens, fruits, and vegetables to this dangerous carcinogenic. DDT does not go away. The knowledge gained as an Aedes Aegypti Health Inspector was interesting but I found learning about the dangers of DDT to be (and please pardon the pun) 'absorbing'.

In retrospect, it is profoundly sad how we can go about our daily lives doing the mundane and ordinary things that make our lives fulfilling, yet we choose to be indiscriminately oblivious to dangers all around us, be they man-made, environmental, psychological and or physically. We sometimes have such a disconnect to our immediate surroundings that even if something appears to be out of sorts, or pose an immediate threat to life or limb, we see this thing yet make a mental note *not* to become involved. Sometimes, if pushed hard enough, we may even express our views … until we are challenged to provide supporting documentation or reasons to justify why we feel the way we do. Some will rise to the challenge. Many others will adopt the, "It's not my business" or, "I don't care" attitude. That mindset keeps us in blissful ignorance.

It's only when the light is turned on in our blissful dark cocoon (and oftentimes not of our choosing) and the danger is now glaring us in the face do we then respond. Often our response time is out of sync with the danger; we are too late and there we are, cocoon open and our unprepared asses exposed. Then it's glaringly obvious that we have nowhere to turn, run, hide or escape. Of course we can always fall back on a litany of regrets and woes but it will serve no significant purpose. It's too late.

Despite learning what I did about DDT I must look upon my job as an Aedes Egypti mosquito inspector in the full context of what this job afforded me at the time. In some measure the training and discipline greatly contributed to my self-control, strictness and general orderliness in life. In spite of my authority as a public health inspector to prosecute householders who became foul of the law, I only used this authority once. It was on an occasion when I visited the home of a constant offender. Her water barrel in the yard was teeming with mosquito larvae, as per usual. I attempted to show her the larvae and with a bombastic attitude, she invited me to show the findings to my mother. Of course that was the proverbial red rag to a bull, hence I prosecuted. She was summonsed to court and was fined fifteen shillings or fourteen days in prison. Her actions resulted in two other persons in the district being prosecuted; to this day I can still remember the names of the three defendants.

My dear reader, take note: every endeavour in my life has been an escalating learning curve.

CHAPTER 16

Stars in her crown

"Count not only my blessings but also count my worries and struggles as well" GHANAIAN PROVERB

While my mother was earning the stars for her royal crown which she would, at the appointed time (according to the book of Thessalonians 4:16 where it says the dead in Christ will rise and join him in heaven) she was also working her way up Golgotha's hill with the daily burdens of life. Mammy is being the perfect devotee to her church and equally devoted to us, her boys. We all understood how important that crown was to her and so we were doing our part to make sure we didn't do anything that would tarnish it or cause her to get one less diadem.

With her sons growing into young adulthood life (and women) brought circumstances into our lives that could not only have tarnished her crown but could have, most assuredly, not let her get one at all. If getting that much-desired crown depended on the rightness or wrongness of what her teenage sons were doing, then she would have found herself in the wrong 'crown distribution line. She would have been in the "Not Ever Getting One" line. Where Mammy was perhaps looking at her sons and feeling proud at the young men we were becoming, other people were looking at the fine young men we were, but for quite different reasons. These were the young (and sometimes not so young) women of our village, and even some of the surrounding villages. They were some who knew us (for lack of a better word), or were desirous of knowing us 'differently.'

Where Mammy saw young men on their way to becoming fine upstanding men and future husbands, women were seeing 'village rams'. To that end, we had one thing working in Mammy's favour, an expression I so often heard: "you are only held responsible for what you know". We might have been young and perhaps a bit reckless and foolish with some of the things we were doing, but we were never foolish enough to let Mammy find out what we were doing. At least, we convinced ourselves that she didn't know. We liked living so you can be assured that we worked hard to make sure that she never got near to finding out. Our hard work paid off; Mammy never found out so, by all counts, she couldn't be held responsible. Her crown was assured!

Once Mammy's crown was assured we went about the business of doing what we wanted and keeping it from her. However, on a visit to Barbados in 1969, Mammy validated my suspicions that she wasn't as oblivious to what we were doing as testosterone charged and driven young men. This came about one evening when she was on her way to church and I was talking to one of the young women who had come by to visit me. As Mammy headed out to church she said good night to us both and we said goodnight to her. She walked off a few paces and then stopped and called me to her. I went to her and she said, "Since you've come back all I can hear is Collin, Collin. Just remember that you have your wife and family in England. So if you feel that you are a jockey then know that my house is not the Garrison. If you want to ride go down to the Garrison; not in my house."

With that she walked on to church. Her observation took me a little by surprise and I smiled at how hard I was working to keep tarnish away from her crown.

BOOK IV

1960 – 1970
Her Majesty's Subject

Adinkra symbol, Fawohodie

Freedom / Independence
Fawohodie ene obre na enam
Independence comes with its responsibilities

Mishumaa Saba, The Seven Candles (Kwanzaa symbol)

**Symbols of the Nguza Saba — the seven principles
African people are urged to live by**

CHAPTER 17

My British Passport

"There are still those who do not know a lion when they see one." ASHANTI PEOPLE

In 1961 I was still a subject of Her Majesty the Queen and so I was issued a British passport. Independence was still a few years off for Barbados. The passport number was 72399 and my name was printed on it as 'C.L. Carter', not 'Mr Collin L. Carter' or 'Collin Leroy Carter' but 'C.L. Carter'. I was reduced to two initials followed by a surname. What my given name was bore no particular importance to the issuer of this document. I was issued one and that, regardless of the name imprinted therein, should have been enough for me. And it was. I was delighted nonetheless that the document was issued to me, one of Mother England's subjects. This passport was signed on behalf of the Governor of Barbados, who was Her Majesty Queen Elizabeth's representative at the time.

Armed with my British passport I was preparing to go and do whatever I could, whatever was required for me to show Mother England what a loyal subject I was. At that time in my life, the seasoning was complete. Like everyone else in Barbados, the English-speaking Caribbean or British colonies, I was willing to show allegiance to our beloved Queen. When I was at school, each morning I stood, along with the entire school body, faced the Union Jack and, in our most solemn and heart-felt voices, asked the Lord to bestow his benevolence on our beloved Queen. We thought nothing of standing with our hands on our hearts and singing 'God Save the Queen'.

"God save our gracious Queen; Long live our noble Queen; God save the Queen!
Send her victorious; Happy and glorious; Long to reign over us; God save the Queen!"

The days at school never got started unless our collective voices asked this one thing of the Lord. None of us standing there thought to silently add a blessing for our parents or, in my case, my mother, who was working her fingers to the bone to provide for my brothers and me. But there we were, imploring the Lord to bless and protect our beloved Queen, whose forebears so many years ago enslaved us and were responsible for the meagre existence that for so many of us was an accepted way of life. We all knew we didn't have a lot but, because most of us didn't know better, didn't fully understand how truly poor we were. In our minds and thinking, we just didn't have as much as the white people I saw in the St Michael districts, but we didn't think in terms of poor or rich. We'd been properly seasoned so we 'accepted' that the white people were rich and we, the Black people, were just where we were supposed to be: getting by, picking pea outta shit, catching our asses, or any of the other colloquial expression we used to express our state of impoverishment. The white man's seasoning of the Black man was intense…and effective.

However, years later, as my conscious awakening opened my eyes, I was able to look at that passport with an eye of scrutiny and see it for what it really was. On the face of this dark blue British passport number 72399 was a crest: that alone said a lot without really saying anything out of the ordinary to the casual observer. Back then it was an enviable object but, to the man I am today, every symbol on that crest and shield assails and insults my consciousness.

I look and think, "What unmitigated gall; a lion?" The Lion. King of the Beasts. King of the Jungle. But according to them, where is this jungle? Africa. So…why is this symbol of strength and the king of the greatest continent on earth representing a nation that was involved in the oppression of so many generations of my people? It was being used because of what it represented: it was the king; the head, the strongest; the one to be reckoned with.

It was only recently that I took another look at the unicorn and, to my great chagrin, the unicorn was chained! It doesn't matter that most pictures you see will depict this chain, nor does it matter that, more often than not, this chain is gold. This may not seem like such a bad thing, until one understands, as I now do, the reason for the chains. This is all part of myth or legend but bears a significant correlation to us as a people. Legend or myth has it that, "A free, unchained unicorn is a dangerous beast." This legend or belief had to be strongly and deeply believed because the unicorns in the Royal Coat of Arms of Scotland suffered the same fate.

I observed these mythological creatures and then the chains around their necks grabbed at me; the reasoning as to why these beautiful creatures were chained resonated within my awakened conscious mind. In the same way that a free unicorn is a considered a dangerous beast, is that why my free ancestors, once captured and enslaved, were then seen as dangerous beasts, to be captured and chained, subjected to the brutality they endured so as to break their spirits? So we can justly say that they knew that as Africans we would always seek our rightful freedom; hence we had to be restrained by the use of chains, cages and whatever means they could conceived? Today it saddens me that I still see so many of our people walking around proudly with the chains of our past still firmly attached to their brains.

CHAPTER 18

Going "over in away"

"Liberate the mind of men and ultimately you will liberate the bodies of men." MARCUS GARVEY

Two and a half months after I completed those war exercises in St Lucia I would be on another vessel, but this time the ocean would be way below me and it would be the clouds to be parted and not the ocean. My vessel would be a BOAC (British Overseas Airways Corporation) airplane. However, before I got to the point where I would be boarding this airplane there was the process of qualifying for this much enviable job: A bus conductor in England! There would at least be one part of the process that I won't have to think about … a passport. I already had one.

I had to apply for the job through the Barbados Employment Exchange (situated at Herbert House, Fontabelle in Bridgetown). After acceptance, I had to attend evening classes at St Leonard's School, where the class revised Maths and English. We were introduced to a London Transport 'waybill' and the work on the London buses. We were also given general information about England. After this, we underwent an X-ray and a medical.

The Barbados Government had advanced to each individual a loan to fund the passage (flight) and other expenses. Of course this loan had to be repaid and, to this end, a family member or friend who had land or a house, would act as a loan guarantor. Sadly, many of the travellers never repaid their respective loans and I do know some guarantors had moments of regret. I am happy to say that my guarantor did not.

Of course, there were goodbyes to be said: some obligatory, some heartfelt, some because Mammy said so. The hardest goodbyes would be ones to the life-long friends I was leaving behind. Before those most difficult goodbyes however were the ones to the elders of the village. Back then, the old people always said goodbye as if they didn't expect to see you again. The truth is, some never did. The tone was sombre. And, if they knew you from the time you were a child, they would reminisce.

You knew never to rush an elder if he or she were reminiscing. You listened patiently until the moments passed; they always did, although some took longer though than others. They would wish you well and all the best, admonish you to make the most of the opportunity, asked that you remember friends and family left behind and above all else, make something of yourself so that when you returned it would be clear that you didn't waste the precious opportunity afforded you.

I remember going from house to house in the gap, letting people know that I would be going away (or, as people said, "Over in away". "Over in away" was like that magical land in a fairytale when the author said, "In a faraway land..." I was going to this faraway land to live and work and (perhaps) play; the most important one was WORK.

Once the goodbyes were said it was time to head to the airport, but there was one more thing that had to be done. It was something that Mammy had done for my brothers Victor and Carl before they went "Over in away". Now she would be doing it do for me. This thing didn't have a particular 'name', but it seemed like it was some sort of finishing touch or seal she needed to give us: to satisfy her heart that she'd done all that she knew how. Mammy accepted you were leaving: now it was time for the 'private ritual' that she administered to all of her sons who had been fortunate to go "over in away". Other mother's might have given their children new clothes, money or even motherly advice. May Carter had one additional (and invaluable) item in her arsenal: Reindeer antler. Mammy called me to her and to my surprise she had a reindeer antler. Of course I wanted to ask her about it but the look on her face forbade any questions.

Without any fanfare or discussion Mammy prepared a drink for me. She had a glass on the table with a liquid in it. Into this she scraped some of the reindeer antler. When she'd scraped enough to satisfying herself, she stirred the mixture and presented it to me. "Drink that," she said. I took the glass and, without question, drank it. When I was finished she said, "Now you can go 'long wherever .'"

Ironically, it would be more than fifty years before I would hear anyone talk about reindeer antler, and it wasn't a member of my family. In February 2014, while in Barbados, I was listening to a programme and one of the sponsors (a health food store) mentioned reindeer antler and talked about the health benefits of reindeer velvet. That jolted me right back to the day I about to leave Barbados and that 'thing' that Mammy had done. As I was on the phone with Annette (my invaluable researcher) I asked her to Google and see what May Carter knew that none of us did.

According to: http://www.naturalelixir.com/antler.html, what we discovered was this:

VELVET ANTLERS OF WILD REINDEER
Caribou (*Rangifer tarandus*) from Siberia, Russia

HISTORY: The history of using velvet antlers for medical purposes counts more than 2000 years. The word "antler" itself derives from the Latin *Anteoculae* which can be translated as, "in front of the eyes". The first evidence of deer velvet use in medicine was documented on a silk scroll found in a tomb in Hunan China. The scroll dates back to 168 B. C. The use of antler dates back to the Han Dynasty 206 BC to 220 AD. Later in the 16th century several antler preparations including pills, tinctures, and ointments were listed in the medical text of Pen Ts'ao Kang Mu.

It should be admitted that the antlers use as a medicine was known not only to Chinese. Thus in Russia, the documented use of deer velvet dates to the late 1400s, when antlers were referred to as "horns of gold." Since then medicinal use of antler became so common that deer farming was introduced to Russia in the 1840s. But only since the 1930s have the first attempts to provide sound scientific research into antlers' therapeutic effectiveness been conducted by Russian scientists and pharmacists. As a result, more than 100 articles on the subject were published. Hundreds of articles have since been published in China, Korea, Japan, Russia, New Zealand and Canada. In the1970s Drs Takikawa

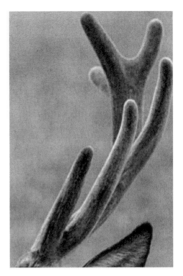

Wild reindeer antlers

and Kqjihara found that pantocrin sped up the healing process of damaged neural tissues. In 1988, perhaps one of the most important effects of velvet antler was discovered by Japanese scientists Wang and associates. They found that velvet antler has an anti-aging effect.

In 1999, the use of velvet antler was scientifically supported by clinical research in compliance with FDA regulations for its beneficial effects in treating arthritis. However, empirical evidence suggests several other therapeutically valuable actions including immune stimulation, anti-aging, protective and rejuvenating effects, and beneficial effects in blood and circulation.

In the North America this product has become known only in the last decade. Nowadays, the American antler market is expanding as more and more Americans turn to holistic medicine.

Thanks to modern technology, this information further confirmed that my mother was light years ahead in her knowledge and wisdom. I didn't know it then but perhaps that elixir my mother prepared has contributed to the longevity of my brothers and me as we've all, with God's grace, seen that promised 'three score and ten'. We now range in age from our mid-eighties to the mid-seventies. I am the youngest at almost seventy-seven years old. When I called Rudolph the day after

I heard the discussion on the radio, to my surprise not only did he know what I was talking about, but he too had gone through the same ritual. Not only that, but he was in possession of the very antler that we'd all 'sipped' from. That news made me very excited; I couldn't wait to see this piece of history that my mother so deftly used. I asked if he had any idea what the liquid was in the glass. Unlike me he knew. I listened in shock as he stated that it was, of all things, mercury.

Yes; mercury. The very substance that we are told today is highly carcinogenic. That word carcinogenic prompted a search on the internet. The excerpt below is from an article called: 'Mercury Toxicity' written by: David A. Olson, MD; Chief Editor: Tarakad S. Ramachandran, MBBS, FRCPI, FACP,FRCP. It contains a wealth of information, some of which states that there was a time that mercury was for medicinal purposes. I found this to be very eye opening and have included it to further show that, although my mother had no formal or medical training, she was able to administer this elixir to 'protect' her sons and (as far as we know) not cause harm to any of us.

BACKGROUND

Mercury in any form is poisonous, with mercury toxicity most commonly affecting the neurologic, gastrointestinal (GI) and renal organ systems. Poisoning can result from mercury vapor inhalation, mercury ingestion, mercury injection, and absorption of mercury through the skin. (See Etiology and Prognosis.)

Mercury has 3 forms: (1) elemental mercury, (2) inorganic salts, and (3) organic compounds. Perhaps the most deadly form of mercury is methylmercury. Only 2–10% of the ingested mercury is absorbed from the gut, and ingested elemental mercury is not absorbed at all; however, 90% of any methylmercury ingested is absorbed into the bloodstream from the GI tract.

Organic mercury compounds, specifically methylmercury, are concentrated in the food chain. Fish from contaminated waters are the most common culprits. Industrial mercury pollution is often in the inorganic form, but aquatic organisms and vegetation in waterways such as rivers, lakes, and bays convert it to deadly methylmercury. Fish eat contaminated vegetation, and the mercury becomes biomagnified in the fish. Fish protein binds more than 90% of the consumed methylmercury so tightly that even the most vigorous cooking methods (e.g., deep-frying, boiling, baking, pan-frying) cannot remove it. (See Etiology.)

For centuries, mercury was an essential part of many different medicines, such as diuretics, antibacterial agents, antiseptics, and laxatives. In the late 18th century, antisyphilitic agents contained mercury. It was during the 1800s that the phrase "mad as a hatter" was coined, owing to the effects of chronic mercury exposure in the hat-making industry, where the metal was used in the manufacturing process.

In 1889, Charcot, in his Clinical Lectures on Diseases of the Nervous System, attributed some rapid oscillatory tremors to mercury exposure.

In Wilson's classic textbook of neurology, published in 1940, Wilson concurred with Charcot's attribution of tremors to mercury poisoning, but also described mercury-induced cognitive impairments, such as inattention, excitement, and hallucinosis.

The business of my going over in away proceeded like all others. A car hired, or a family friend would come to take you to the airport. Back then, going to the airport was a *major* event; not just a family affair but also a neighbourhood/village affair. People put on their best clothes to come and see you off. They milled around; some cracked jokes. Some reminded you that they knew you 'back when'. Some didn't know what to say or do…or even why they were there. But they felt they had to be – after all, you were going away. And of course they would be tears – enough to float the plane if it were a boat.

Now that I'm in the funeral business, to me, coming to the airport to see a person off was and is akin to attending a wake. The actions were the same: people come to a wake to say goodbye to the person leaving.

Just like being dressed to see you off on your final farewell, people came to the airport decked out in their Sunday best. Men wore suits, ties, shirts that were properly stiffed, starched and ironed, dress shoes, socks, and hats. The ladies wore coat suits, dresses, skirts and jackets, hats, gloves, stockings, and shoes with heels. No one would dare to leave home for the airport without being properly attired.

I was May Carter's last boy so I had to look the part. In my case, Mammy got me a Wilson felt hat. I'd never worn, far less owned, a felt hat before but all men who were going 'over-in-away' wore one. Mammy wouldn't have me looking less than any other man. I remember leaving home with my brand new felt hat. I may even remember boarding the plane with it but after that I have no recollection of it. I'm not sure whatever happened to it, but I think I might have left it right there on BOAC plane (or on the bus or on some counter or ledge along the way). Bottom-line is that I wore that hat for the first and last time. I don't know if I ever told Manny I'd lost her precious hat. I don't think I did!

I may not have had any secondary school education, but the expectations of my family, friends and peers were the same for me as they were for those that did: "make much of this opportunity because we are waiting with high expectations to see what you are going amount to." You were expected to achieve. There was no such thing as going "over-in-away" and engaging in slothfulness, laziness, or any social behaviour that would bring shame or disgrace, or make someone think that a rare and prime opportunity was wasted on you.

After the send-off at the airport there would be sense of loss for those left behind. Without phones to call home, you had to write. Even with these extreme conditions, if people didn't hear from you 'out of sight' never meant 'out of mind'. People would ask about you or talk about you. When they did it might be, "Yes. Collin, May Carter last boy, he's over in 'Away'." A son could end up in the 'duck's guts' if he went over-in-away and didn't send home anything for his mother. Getting a barrel from the child, husband, wife or family member from away was a status symbol. All of these things would be on your mind creating psychological pressure for you. Failure wasn't an option and there was no fall back excuse. You couldn't say I didn't have a secondary school education; not then. People knew that in over-in-away you could go to school older, and for longer, than in Barbados. Even the old people would tell you, "Learning better than silver or gold."

So there I was – I had said my goodbyes and was on my way to this illusive place, where much was expected from anyone who went there. Much was expected of me and I knew it. Once on board the plane I sat and thought. There was much to think about. How would I do all that was expected of me when I wasn't even sure what, if anything, was waiting for me?

Aboard this aircraft were over one hundred and fifty Barbadian men and women, heading to England to work for British Transport Services, the National Health Service, or J. Lyons Teashop. My days of being readied to defend my homeland were quickly receding as the 12-hour plane journey drew closer to England. Back in 1962, it was impossible for a passenger plane to fly non-stop from Barbados to London, and our plane made a refuelling stop in Santa Maria, one of the Portuguese islands in the Azores archipelago. Once the plane had touched down in England, I knew that my life was going to change; but it wasn't going to take months, weeks or even days. Change would come within a matter of hours!

CHAPTER 19

Arrival in London

"Wisdom does not come overnight"
SOMALIAN PROVERB

My arrival on that night, Friday the 2nd of November 1962 was about to dispel any 'myths'. I was here, at Mother England's doorstep, having been requested by her to come and once again sacrifice. I had only a few hours ago turned twenty-two and here I was; along with another one hundred and fifty young Barbadian souls, stepping off a BOAC plane to do our bit for 'Queen and Country'. We were just the latest in a long line who had repeated history: During World War II, between 1939 and 1945, thousands of Caribbean young men and women had left their shores to sacrifice for Mother England. At the time I was a mere stripling, but now, here I was, for all intents and purposes, a man, making my own contribution.

Unlike the previous exodus of young Barbadian men who came before us, none of us really knew what we were headed to. Those young men went because of the war; they were going to fight for and protect Mother England. In our case there was no war, we were essentially coming to England to do jobs that its white, working class citizens felt were 'beneath' them. Unlike other West Indian islands, England had a contractual agreement to allow Barbadian nationals to go to England for employment: major employers included the British Army, London Transport Board, the Ministry of Health and the National Health Service, British Rail, Lyon's Tea Shops, the hotel industry and automotive factories. We were told these jobs held promises of a better future, a life much different to the ones we were living in Barbados and the English speaking Caribbean. What we were *not* told was that we would be facing abject racism and be thrust into a racial and social war, the likes of which most of us had never heard of, far less experienced.

In fact, at this time I was more than willing to make a sacrifice 'for Queen and country'. The notion of joining the British Army first entered my mind as a member of the Barbados Regiment, when in 1962, 500 young Barbadians were invited to join the British Armed Forces. Thanks to the Barbados Regiment conducting military exercises, I had been able to travel to St Vincent in 1961. They had planned further military exercises in St Lucia in mid-1962 and I was keen to go, but as a result of attending these manoeuvres, I had missed the opportunity to leave Barbados and join the British Army. So it was when I returned to Barbados from St Lucia that I'd made plans to go to England to work for London Transport.

I was still very much a part of the Barbados Regiment, and in October 1962 I had been asked by the Adjutant, Major Brown and the RSMI (Regimental Sergeant Major Instructor) Bluck if I would volunteer to be a sentry at the Cenotaph for Remembrance Day at the beginning of November. I had told them that I would not be in Barbados, as I had sought employment with London Transport and would be leaving in the first week in November.

They had asked me to re-consider my job with London Transport and to consider joining the Army. They were very persuasive and, as I thoroughly enjoyed being a part of the Barbados Regiment, I agreed. Paperwork was prepared and arrangements were made for me to join the Royal Leicestershire Regiment on arriving in England. So, when I left Barbados, I had the option of either joining the British Army or working for London Transport.

We arrived at Gatwick Airport on that Friday night at 8.30 pm. After leaving Immigration and Customs we were met by Barbadian Liaison Officers who provided us with envelopes containing money and calculations as to how this money was dispensed. There was an outline on the envelope indicating how much was paid in advance for rent, the bus conductor's license, and enough to tide us over until we received our first pay packs. The amount in the envelope was equal to approximately two week's earnings.

We then boarded one of the waiting London Transport buses. This boarding was a precise and orderly roll call. Liaison Officers had been assigned to us; each one had a list and when they called out the name of each new arrival, that person would then board their respective bus. Each bus had a specific set of lodgings addresses. Not all of the landlords were West Indians; some of them were white. The few white homeowners didn't take West Indians as tenants because they had no affinity, nor liking, for coloured people (that's what we were called in the 1960s). However, they were paid good hard cash, and this weighed much heavier on them than their prejudices.

As I boarded my assigned bus, my mind drifted over parts of the process that had gotten me to where I was; in England, facing a future that, although quite uncertain, held many assurances. Apart from those who had arranged to stay with relatives and friends the rest of us boarded London Transport buses and headed off. On the journey from the airport there was a degree of excitement and our eyes were peeled. We were in England! Every coloured person we saw walking on the street drew our attention. Someone would exclaim, "Look, a darkie! Look, anotha wun!"

However, the excitement soon turned to concern as we started to wonder whether or not the bus driver really knew where he was going. We saw repeats of what we thought were the same streets, shops, pubs and banks. On this, our very first night in England, we thought we were lost. At some point someone asked (in a muffled voice): "Man, yah tink dis driver know wuh de ass he gine? This is pure shite!" This brought about peals of hysterical laughter and somewhat lightened the mood. But we were still concerned, having only journeyed between Seawell Airport to St Lucy where sugar canes, breadfruit, mango and mahogany trees, cus cus grass hedgerows, one or two familiar churches, and rum shops were our landmarks. This endless string of buildings, a few 'darkies' and stores all looking alike, were all the more mind-boggling. This trip from Gatwick to London seemed never-ending.

These thoughts started to dissipate when we realised we were not lost. To our relief the bus started making stops to drop off its passengers. At each respective address the Liaison Officer called the names of the 'tenants' who would them disembark. Eventually, the bus stopped at my new 'home': 19 Heathlands Road in Stoke Newington, North London. My name was called, along with Michael Archer and Anthony Barker.

We got our suitcases and got off the bus. Although, by this time, it was well after midnight, the landlord, a Trinidadian by the name of Mr Lynch, was obviously expecting us. Despite the fact that Michael, Anthony and I were 'strangers', we soon discovered that we were expected to share ONE ROOM, and not just for this one night! This was our accommodation; our new home. As was (and still is) my nature, I questioned this singular accommodation. No answer came that night. The landlord simply said to me: "I'm not going to discuss it or argue with you tonight. You all guys had a long flight. You have a good sleep and tomorrow morning it will all start to manifest itself. I'll wake you about 9.30 am." Before retiring, Mr Lynch showed us the bathroom. I would later discover that it wasn't 'our' bathroom – it was to serve seven tenants.

Mr Lynch then told us to be ready in the morning by 9.30 am so that he could take us to the High Street to purchase a few requisite items. He then left us alone. In the room were two beds, a single and a double, a small dining table, three chairs, a wardrobe and a paraffin heater burning in the centre of the room. We decided that Michael and I would share the double bed and Anthony would have the single. I use the words 'double bed' generously, as it was barely big enough to hold the two of us.

CHAPTER 20

First morning in England

"If you find no fish, you have to eat bread."
GHANAIAN PROVERB

Morning came too soon and we heard a knocking on the door. It was Mr Lynch, the landlord who, as promised, was going to take us to the High Street so we could purchase some pots, pans, etc. We pooled our resources together to buy a teacup and saucer each, one knife, fork and spoon each, one third of two saucepans, one third of a frying pan, one third of two pots and some food items – just enough to give us a start.

Before leaving the house Mr Lynch asked his wife to prepare us a quick breakfast which we ate. Before we left, there was something that Mr Lynch needed to show us. He took us to the kitchen assigned to the tenants and pointed to the cooker (stove) which had four burners. He informed us that *only one* of the burners was allotted to us. The other burners had been assigned to the other tenants. He said that if at any time we wanted to use any of the other burners, we should first check with the relevant tenant so as to avoid unnecessary arguments.

He showed us the bathroom again which, like the kitchen, was communal. The entire house was clean, very well laid out and organised. We were allowed a bath on Saturdays or Sundays. The bath required gas to heat the water and had a coin operated metre attached.

Mr Lynch said he would put the money in the gas metre on the weekend. If we wanted a bath during the week we should first check with him or his wife. I found the idea of surviving on one bath a week rather strange, but we quickly adjusted to this weekly ritual, especially as I realised how fortunate we were to have the luxury of a bath in the house.

I say 'fortunate' because I discovered at that time at least 90 per cent of the houses in England didn't have indoor bathrooms, which meant that most people had to utilise public baths. It took many years, grants and gentle persuasions from local authorities/councils for white homeowners to install baths. Many of the homes were over 80 years old; to the homeowners, installing an indoor bathroom often meant sacrificing a room in the house and they were accustomed to the houses just as they were. The same situation was often true of the toilet, which was usually located in the back yard. Some of them might not have been as far away as from the house as our pit toilets were in Barbados, but outside *was* outside. At least in Barbados it was warm. In England, people had to relieve themselves in all weathers!

When I arrived in London it was winter. England was dark, wet and cold and my first winter was going to be the worse. In those days houses had no carpets or central heating. Pipes froze and burst, chimneys on houses and factories spewed endless smoke, soot and coal particles transforming the sky into an endless frigid blanket of grey, thus significantly reducing any 'daylight'. None of us had ever experienced a winter and were totally unprepared. We were not told by those who had recruited us what the winter and smog was like or what to really expect. We didn't have the appropriate clothing…but how could we? We could hardly purchase a winter coat in tropical Barbados.

Upon leaving the house that first morning, the first person we encountered on the street was a man; he was a stranger to us but, as is customary in Barbados we 'spoke' and said, "Good morning." His abrupt reply was, "What's so bloody good about it mate?" We were shocked and surprised, as we didn't expect to be greeted with such open hostility. Mr Lynch immediately pointed out that in England unless you knew the person you didn't say good morning, good evening or good night. You simply didn't 'speak' to them. He made it clear to us that whilst 'speaking' was correct and polite behaviour in Barbados (strangers included), it wasn't done in England as we could offend the individual. It was a lesson we learned quickly…and well.

We walked along Heathland Road, crossed over Manor Road and continued along Bouviere Road, eventually taking a left turn onto Stoke Newington Church Street. About thirty yards ahead was Abney Park Cemetery. The first thing Mr Lynch pointed out to us was graffiti on the cemetery wall which read: "Niggers out! Niggers go home!" Mr Lynch told us that England was as racist as anywhere else in the world: this graffiti didn't mean that niggers were to keep out of the cemetery. It meant that niggers should get out of Britain.

Mr Lynch took us to the newsagent; a small shop which primarily sold newspapers, cigarettes and confectionary. He said: "If I had a room to rent I would ask the newsagent (the person who owns and runs this paper shop), to put a card in the window to advertise it." In those days this was common practice for anyone with rooms to rent or items to sell. The advertisements would typically be written on pieces of card (about 4 inches by 3 inches) and placed in the shop window. The newsagent would be paid some small sum for this service.

In the case of "rooms to rent" they often came with restrictions, which today would be illegal and considered downright offensive. Many of the cards would read: "No Children, No Dogs", but what was most shocking to us was that most of them blatantly stated: "No Coloureds, No West Indians". Some even had stronger language, such as "No niggers need apply". Many adverts said: "No Irish, No Niggers, No Dogs" and some among us (perhaps as a way to try and mast the insult) 'joked' that at least we were placed above the dogs. Mr Lynch said: "This is the reason why rooms are not readily available to West Indians." That immediately helped us understand why three of us had to share a room.

The information gained during the trip to the High Street showed my questioning of Mr Lynch on the night of our arrival (why the three of us had to share one room) to be both premature and naïve. I had asked my question only based on what I'd perceived: he lived in what we Barbadians call 'a big upstairs wall house' and, to the average Barbadian, this implied that anyone who lived in such a house was 'well off'.

After our 'rude awakening' tour, Mr Lynch took us to the Woolworths store where we bought the necessary items and food stuffs for cooking. We returned home, our roommate Barker asked if he were to leave first, would he be refunded his share of the money used to buy the kitchen utensils. I told him that if I were to leave first I would not ask for a refund. That was the end of that discussion.

I went back to that room, conscious that I was sharing a room with two guys who were not my friends and whom I'd only met on the flight to London. I had to share, not because they weren't rooms to let in London, but because the accommodations I saw advertised were not for Black people. The thoughts just started flooding my mind. If I were a white Barbadian I would at least have been given an audience. Why did I have to stay in that room from November until April the following year? Was it simply because of my colour? My Blackness was not only a colour, but it confined me to a condition – living in racist Britain. That was my most profound experience in Britain. Now I questioned myself: "Why is it that I was born Black, should die Black and, between those two events, why is it that I should be treated in this way just because I'm Black and I didn't make myself Black."

In other words, if I knocked on any white person's door looking for a room to rent, all they would see was a Black man and they would experience all their negative connotations relating to my race. They would probably have politely said: "Sorry, no rooms to rent here!" Whether or not this was the truth, they would have said the room was gone.

Did I mention that it was winter and I didn't have a winter coat? Not having a winter coat made me discover just how cold it was, especially since I had just left that lovely, warm, beautiful island of Barbados. However, one of my roommates had previously travelled to America and had a winter coat. He was not selfish with his coat, and for that I will be eternally grateful. Until we could afford to buy winter coats, the three of us shared his. When we ventured out to explore our new surroundings the owner of the coat (naturally) wore his coat, so the two of us padded ourselves as best as we could to brave the elements. If it meant wearing all the clothes we had (including pyjamas) then we did. Being warm, staying warm was optimum. Thankfully, about a week after I arrived I was able to purchase my own coat.

Another discovery I made was that neither of my two roommates could cook, so most of the cooking duties fell to me. If I had to go out whilst they remained at home, they asked me to cook. I charged them about a shilling each for cooking. Mable Carter knew how to 'turn a dollar' and, thanks to her, I could not only wash and clean but cook too (and earn some money in the process). All thanks and praise to Mable Carter; she had the vision and foresight to teach her boy children to do these 'domestic chores'. She well knew that one day these skills would come in handy.

CHAPTER 21

My first few days – Finding my way

"In new surroundings a hen walks cautiously"
CAPE VERDEAN PROVERB

Most of the Saturday, 3rd November 1962 was spent in the house. It was very cold and foggy outside. I was missing Barbados: my mother, friends and activities, the Barbados Regiment, the Boy Scouts and even my work as a Health Inspector. England was not only cold, dark grey, damp, unfriendly, smelly, and dirty but most of all it was old, with seemingly endless rows of joined together unpainted, grey, sooty-looking houses. The streets were no different. The people were strange looking, draped in their drabbed black, grey and brown clothes with their curious yet dismissive stares. Heathland Road and its environs were then and still are a Hasidic Jewish area.

No starry skies at nights, trees without leaves, no blue skies, no night choruses from frogs and crickets. Most importantly, I was a young coloured man – a darkie – in a white man's country. Questions came rushing to my mind: "Are you going to stay until you achieve your objectives? Will you work hard, save up your passage and return to Barbados as soon as possible? Will I be able to withstand the anticipated racism that I felt was in store for me? What would the work be like as a Bus Conductor on a London bus? With my training as a soldier and recommendation from the Barbados Regiment should I join the British Army?" The question I knew that I could answer was,

"What will my mother and peer group say if I returned to Barbados within a few months?" Answer: "Boy you are a failure." "You had a good chance!" "Man you blow it!" or "You rob somebody else out of a chance." It was the answer to this question that helped me to conclude, "Collin Carter, you are going to stay and make good. You are going to work hard, pay back the Barbados Government, save some money and, above all, you are going to find yourself in school at night and build on the basic education you got."

By Sunday morning, having discussed my thoughts with my two roommates, we jointly agreed that we would be staying for the long haul. We would give England our very best shot. We were now ready to get on that London Transport bus that we were told was coming to get us on Monday morning at 6.30 am, 5 November 1962. That evening, the landlord (Mr Lynch) invited us to watch TV in his flat; we were anxious to see this thing called television. There weren't any in Barbados when we left. What we did have were eight cinemas, a mobile cinema (a movie cinema on wheels) and the occasional projector slide show which was called Magic Lantern; but no TV as yet. Mr Lynch encouraged us to at least watch the nightly news when we could.

Just being in England less than two days and my brief encounters were having an impact and stimulating my thoughts in ways that had never done before. I was confronting the problems of race, thinking positively about my colour and getting used to the new culture, food, climate and general surroundings. As I prepared myself to assimilate to my new home, I'll confess my ignorance of the knowledge that Black people had lived in England in reasonable numbers from the 16th century. At that time, most of them were enslaved. Between 1794 and 1819, Black people fought for rights and freedoms, not only for themselves but also for the white working classes. Men like William Cuffay, David Duffy, Benjamin Prophit, Robert Wedderburn and William Davidson (who was hung on 1st May 1820). Women were also involved. In 1870, Charlotte Gardner, an African woman, was hung at Tower Hill along with four whites for taking part in the Gordon Riots of June. If, by some miracle, she had managed to live until our arrival, she would have told us and white England of the sacrifices she made as she fought for her rights and theirs.

Two days after I arrived in England – 5 November – the English celebrated Guy Fawkes Night[2] when children made effigies of Guy Fawkes and carried them around, begging people for money. I had never spoken with, heard, or come face to face with anyone from the British working class, let alone a 'Cockney'[1]. So I didn't know what to make of these dirty little white children, the likes of which I'd never seen, presenting you with this effigy and begging you: "A penny for the guy!" Within the vicinity of my lodgings were very small pre-fab houses, side-by-side, looking like twenty-foot containers. They really were no better than our modest chattel houses in Barbados. Was this really England? Where was the green and pleasant land I was taught about, and read about? Smoke belched from every chimney. There was a strong residual smell of burning cinders. The milkman delivered milk and unwrapped bread to customers' doorsteps. The paraffin[3] (kerosene) man ringing a bell, letting you know he was selling his heating fuel, the Rag and Bone man (scavengers of meal and junk) coming along on a horse-drawn cart to collect anything that wasn't screwed down, and the many second-hand shops selling second hand clothes: all of this I observed during my fist few days. It was all a bit of a shock, as no one had ever spoken to me about these conditions, nor had I read about it or seen it on our beloved mobile cinema in Barbados.

By Sunday, 4 November 1962, I was ready to hit the London streets on my own. At that time, two of my brothers, Victor and Carl, were living in north London, but they didn't know that their little brother was in England. Victor had left Barbados for England in 1958, after which he made very little contact with the family remaining in Barbados. Carl had followed in 1961. They were both living together but I always wanted to be on my own, even if that meant sharing a room with two strangers. Truth be told, after three days, my roommates were feeling less and less like strangers. Michael and I were quickly becoming like brothers and the Jamaican tenants in the house were like family members.

Victor was employed with British Rail as a train guard, and Carl was working as a bus conductor for London Transport. It was coincidental that my first address was only about 9 bus stops away from them in Finsbury Park, north London. I asked Mr Lynch for directions to Finsbury Park. He introduced me to my first London road map – the famous "A-Z" which was easy for me to read as I had learned map reading in the Boy Scouts.

My first mission was to 'surprise' my brothers. As instructed by Mr Lynch I caught the 106 bus and asked the bus conductor to put me off at Rock Street, Finsbury Park. He did and I made my way to the address where my two brothers were living. My brother Victor did not readily recognise me when I showed up. He thought that if I was coming to England I would have told him or my other brother so for him it was a great surprise. He asked me when I arrived and where I was staying. I told him. My brother Carl was at work but Victor was glad to see me and invited me up the stairs to his two-room apartment. As we reached the top of the stairs I noticed that his cooker was installed on the landing area with a ceramic kitchen sink next to it. Also on the landing was a coffin-shaped galvanised bathtub standing on its end. I asked him what it was used for and was astonished when he told me it was his bathtub! We too had a bath tub in Barbados which we used for the same purpose (and also for washing clothes) but hey Man! We were now in London, for heaven's sake! I begged him to please explain this me? "Well you see Collin there are very few houses in England with baths or bathrooms."

So I asked: "Does everyone have one of these galvanise tubs?"

"No." said Victor. I asked: "So how do people in this place bathe with tubs and no bathrooms?"·

"They go to the public baths and pay; maybe 3 or 6 pence for a bath." said Victor

"Oh! I exclaimed. "Just like the public baths back home in Carrington Village,

"Yes, but in this country they use cast iron bath tubs not showers like back home."

"What are you doing about a bath?" He asked me. I told him I'd had a bath that morning. His next question was "How?"

I said, "The house where I'm living."

"De house where you are got a bath?"

"Yes, Vic."

"Boy; you real lucky!"

Victor, his wife Geraldine and I talked and he expected me to fill-in all the pieces about home since he had left. His two-room apartment was very well furnished and it was all his own furniture. The floor was carpeted and really nice. We talked about everyone and what we knew. He told me about the 'dos and the don'ts' of England and general banter ensued. I did mention that I was on my way to see my old friend Wilbert Connell who was someone he also knew. Mammy had given me a package for my brothers: her special heavy sweet breads, a winter cap for Carl and other bits. Package delivered and chatting exhausted for the evening, I took my leave and Victor said that he and Carl would visit me the following night.

As I told Victor, Wilbert Connell was my next stop. We had kept in touch after he'd left Barbados in 1960. We were both keen photographers. As strange as it may sound now Wilbert's mother had given me about six green avocado pears to take for him and I was anxious to deliver them. Wilbert was now living in Westbourne Park in west London; as it was winter, by the time I got to there it was dark. I knocked the front door: as was the custom in those days, the number of knocks corresponded to the floor of the house (two knocks for the second floor, etc). Wilbert opened the door and I could see from the expression on his face that he was both surprised and extremely pleased to see me standing there. We greeted each other like long lost brothers do: a big bear hug that turned into a sway, pats on each other's back and BIG SMILES!

I stepped into the passage and stairway was in darkness. Wilbert explained to me that the lights weren't working and, as I begun to ascend the stairs to his room, he begun to instruct me in a cautious voice. He said: "Walk carefully and slowly coming up the stairs." Before his words could register properly my foot found a hole in the staircase. With my foot in the hole I asked: "Man what kinda rat hole you live in?"

Wilbert replied, "Man ah trying to get somewhere else."

Having been forewarned I removed my foot from the hole and exercised greater caution as to where to place my next step. I continued up the stairs and entered Wilbert's room. Sadly, of all the rooms I had seen in England (even years later) this was by far the dingiest. The house had fallen into great disrepair: the wall paper was peeling, the linoleum (lino) was worn and needed to be replaced and he didn't have a bathroom. Knowing Wilbert as I did, there was no way he would have lived under the same conditions in Barbados. The proud Bajan man that I knew him to be wanted to get out.

Wilbert and I had a long discussion and, as was customary, he wanted the 'ball-by-ball' commentary (i.e. the latest news) that the last known "arrivee" would bring. Not too long after that I would be asking others the same questions. We discussed our common interest (photography) and he took happy delivery of his avocado pears. By the time I returned home to 19 Heathland Road it was about 10.00 pm and I had to ready myself for the next morning and the 6.30 am London Transport bus. Ironically, the same bus that had picked us up from the airport would take us to begin our training at the London Transport Training Centre at Chiswick Park.

It was during these first few days in England that I ran into an old school friend, Orville, who had been one of my contemporaries at St Giles. He had also come to England to work for London Transport and asked me what garage I was going to. You will remember that I mentioned earlier in this chapter that I had the option to join the Royal Leicestershire Regiment, and I was still determined that this would be my course of action. I told Orville that, instead of working on the buses, I would be joining the Army. He strongly advised me against such action: I was unaware that at that time, many of the young men from Barbados who had left the island in 1962 to join the British Army had been sent to Yemen to assist British troops in the North Yemen Civil War. That conflict lasted from 1962 to 1970 but it's ironic that, today, war continues to rage in that area in 2017.

He suggested that I work for London Transport for three months; then, if I didn't like the work and felt that I should still join the Army,

I could take up my position with the Royal Leicestershire Regiment. He did however point out that, whichever option I took, I would need to be prepared for the rampant racism that existed not only on the buses and in the Army, but in England as a whole. He felt that this racism would be one of the deciding factors in my final decision.

I have to 'jump forward' a bit and tell you that I took Orville's advice, delaying my entry into the Royal Leicestershire Regiment to work for London Transport. He was right; the racism to which I was subjected was rampant. In spite of this, at the end of the three months I decided to stay with London Transport. I decided I was not prepared to join the British Army and risk being injured, maimed or even killed fighting in a war that had nothing to do with Black people.

MONDAY, 5 NOVEMBER 1962

The bus arrived at 6.25 am. No longer did 6.30 am mean 7.45 am, like keeping Bajan (or so-called West Indian) time! Along the way, the bus stopped to collect other trainee conductors and we arrived at Chiswick Park by 8.00 am.

We were introduced to our tutors and the classroom. We had been taught some of the processes before leaving Barbados; what was now necessary was the practical/hands-on training on the buses.

On completion of the first day we had to find our way back to our lodgings, which was approximately ten miles away from the training centre. We used the Underground and bus services to make the journey home.

TUESDAY, 6 NOVEMBER 1962

We had to find our own way to London Transport Training Centre. We arrived about 15 minutes late and were severely reprimanded for not being punctual. We were given a stern warning that "under no circumstance must we ever be late again" otherwise we could not be considered for the job because "London Transport passengers came first". What a learning curve! In Barbados, if it looked like it was going to rain (or if it did!) that was good enough reason to be late for any job and you expected your boss/ employer to understand that. Now this was a whole new ball game; we were in England. You were not expected to 'shelter' from rain or snow: whatever the weather, no matter how atrocious, you got to work on time. "Our passengers come first." That statement was repeated to me some three years later: I'd requested all early duties so that I could attend college in the evenings, but my request was refused. It was then that I immediately concluded there was no real future on the buses for me. I would never put London's faceless commuters before myself.

After the second day at the Training Centre we were issued with uniforms and instructed to report to our respective bus garages, in uniform, for practical training the next day, Wednesday, 7 November, then return to the Training Centre the following week. On that Wednesday morning, we caught a route 106 bus from Heathland Road to Clapton Bus Garage where we reported for Practical Training. We boarded the bus and to our surprise the conductor was an attractive female who greeted us with a 'real Caribbean smile.' We asked her if she would tell us when we arrived at Clapton Bus Garage and with another beautiful smile she said: "Certainly!"

Michael, Anthony and myself sat on the bus looking all new-brand in our snow-white plastic cap, heavy white shirt and tie, black silver buttoned double breasted jacket and trousers with light blue stripe on the seam. The 'Caribbean smile' Conductress told us when we got to Clapton Bus Garage. We got off and reported to the garage manager, who allocated us to our respective conductor instructor.

FOOTNOTES

1. The term 'cockney' has had several distinct geographical, social, and linguistic associations. Originally a pejorative term applied to all city-dwellers, it was eventually restricted to Londoners and particularly to 'Bow Bell Cockneys': those born within earshot of the Bow Bells, the bells of St Mary-le-Bow in the Cheapside district of the City of London. It eventually came to be used to refer to those in London's East End, or to all working-class Londoners generally.

2. Guy Fawkes Night, also known as Bonfire Night and Firework Night, is an annual commemoration observed on 5 November, primarily in Great Britain. Its history begins with the events of 5 November 1605, when Guy Fawkes, a member of the Gunpowder Plot, was arrested while guarding explosives the plotters had placed beneath the House of Lords. Towards the end of the 18th century reports appeared of children begging for money with effigies of Guy Fawkes, and this custom remains to the present day. The present-day Guy Fawkes Night is usually celebrated at large organised events, centred on a bonfire and extravagant firework displays

3. Before the advent of central heating, paraffin (sometimes called kerosene was widely used to heat homes.

CHAPTER 22

Even in England, you can find an old friend

"Do not vacillate or you will be left between doing something, having something and being nothing."
ETHIOPIAN PROVERB

I never gave much thought to getting about on my second day. Nor did I fear any danger. After all, I was twenty-two years old and had left Barbados to come to England: there was a sense of adventure. It also helped that, although I'd had a brief 'introduction' to racism, I was unaware of the racial dangers lurking. I was 'introduced' to one of the dangers about a year and half year later; it came in the form of a racist attack from groups of young white men. These attacks would be especially prevalent if you were on your own.

ON BEING A "TENDERFOOT": FIRST DAY AT WORK

We were allocated to our respective buses and conductor instructors, and off we went on a double-decker bus as a trainee bus conductor. It would be fair to say that my first reaction was a measure of excitement: being dressed in this brand new naval-looking uniform, and having a bus instructor who was first real 'Cockney-speaking' Englishman I encountered. I never expected to hear that tone of voice and that kind of accent coming from an Englishman. I suppose it was a learning experience and compromise for us both: I had to get used to his speech pattern and he had to get used to me with my hard Bajan accent! I had to reduce the pace of my speech by about fifty per cent whilst simultaneously increasing my listening 100 per cent to understand what he was saying.

In addition to my instructor's accent, I also had to get use to the various nationalities, accents, tones of voice, and the British class system. In those days, the 'Dockers'[1] would be wearing what we called a black donkey jacket and probably some blue dungarees. In the city there would be the 'City gents' who would be wearing the Parson Gray suits, bowler hats, shirts and ties and most likely carrying an umbrella and a briefcase. The 'office cleaners' (also called charwomen) would be wearing aprons under their winter coats. Some of them had their heads tied with a scarf, reminiscent of the character 'Flo' in the Andy Cap cartoon strip. This was the first time I was exposed to the British working class and it was somewhat of a 'culture shock'. Up until then, all the Englishmen I'd ever met had primarily been those who had been seconded to the Barbados Regiment and who had portrayed a 'middle-class' upbringing. So, as you can imagine, initially it was difficult for me to believe or accept there were white working class poor that I encountered along my work route.

Up to that time everything that had been portrayed to me about England was exciting, glamorous, intriguing and even captivating. But this England: the docks, bombed out areas such as Bethnal Green in East London, the docklands slums, the living conditions of the working-class poor and the overall 'grey-ness' of it all: these were never shown to us, they never told us anything about that. And years later, on my visits to West Africa, I was reminded that here, too, were images that I had never been shown, or told about: modern capital cities and motorways, skyscraper buildings, good infrastructures. The pictures they always showed us of Africa were always the worst: poverty, famine, war and corruption.

The '277' bus route that I worked passed through the West India docks; the first time I saw the social conditions and housing in the area I realised I was seeing the British working class as it truly was. This made me feel I was in the equivalent of Chapman Lane,

Barbados, or any of those very urban ghettoes in Bridgetown: Nelson Street, New Orleans ("The Orleans") Vine Street, Spruce Street or Cypress Street. Seeing 'this' England made me realise that, socially and economically, these people who we were taught that we should 'worship', were no better than us. In fact, in some cases, they were far worse off that we were.

I was of course aware that racism existed in Barbados, but I had never experienced it in the hostile and almost-violent way that I was experiencing it now. To me, these poverty-stricken white people were very much like the 'red legs' of St John, Barbados[2] yet, because of my skin colour, they felt and behaved as if they were superior to me and my people. These poor-whites were venting their pent-up racism on us, because of our high visibility: our Blackness. These are the same kind of people who, if we'd met in Barbados and they'd had a good wash, we would probably look up to. But here in London, their standard of living was no better than that of the poor people of Carrington Village. In fact, it was worse: dirty little snotty-nosed children running around; the houses untidy and dirty; rude and smelly people getting onto the buses; people walking the streets eating fish and chips out of a newspaper; unwrapped bread left on the doorsteps next to milk.

I needed time to come to terms with this side of England. I kept asking myself: "Am I really in England? Is this really England?" There was a certain amount of emotional and mental conflict within me: like thousands of other Caribbean people, I had been 'conditioned' to believe that white people were better than us, without exception. But I now had to have a different view of people I once believed to be socially, economically, financially and intellectually my superiors. It changed my whole concept of what England really was, compared to the picture that had been painted for us in the Caribbean. Upon reflection, it's hard to imagine that I would have still come to England had this aspect of the country been laid bare before me. Then again, if I had been told about it prior to leaving Barbados, I probably won't have believed it. As I had done since the age of about five years old, I would have continued to believe that England was the green and pleasant land, the Jerusalem that I sung about as a child in school.

I may have had to revise my opinion of white people but, regardless of their economic standing, their belief in their superiority remained resolute. What I sometimes found particularly vexing that when these same dirty, unkempt, smelly people boarded the bus they offered their fare to the white instructor, who invariably said to me: "Take the money." Even though it was obvious I was the Conductor (as I had the ticket machine around my neck and the money bag), none of that made a difference in their prejudiced, racist eyes. The Instructor was there: he white and so they would hand him the money and ignore me.

He often had to direct these passengers to pay me and many of them made it obvious that they would prefer not to. Not all the passengers did this, but there was a significant minority that tried to make you feel less than human. These subtle slights were their way of letting you know they didn't want to deal with you. There were times when I was giving back change and some of them would make sure that their hands didn't touch mine.

This behaviour didn't really change until years later; to give a day-by-day account would be repetitious. Like May Carter, I knew I had a short fuse and at any time anyone of them could be the match to set it off. So I kept my 'short-fused self' out of their way as much as possible.

As time went on I became more adept at doing my job and adjusting to life in England. After six months of living with my two roommates, my brother Victor helped me to find a room, my first place on my own. The difference here however was that I wasn't sharing a room or a kitchen. It was a modestly-sized room with a cooker, bug ridden bed, small wardrobe, a small dining table with two dining chairs, linoleum covering the floor boards, and a communal bathroom with a bathtub. I caught water from the bathtub tap in a bucket and used the same for cooking. My new home was in an area called Finsbury Park, no more than eight bus stops away Stoke Newington. This room (despite the bug-ridden bed) gave me a lot more things:

room to breathe, to entertain and most importantly something that was paramount to a young man like me – privacy. I was now truly my own man with my own key, but I wasn't truly alone; brother Victor lived on the same road, almost opposite to me, so I was able to visit whenever I felt wanted.

FOOTNOTES

1. In 1960s Britain, a 'docker' referred to any man who worked as a manual labourer on the waterfront, loading and unloading ships.
2. 'Red Leg' is a term used to refer to poor whites that live in Barbados, St Vincent, Grenada and a few other Caribbean islands. Their forebears came from Ireland, Scotland and the West of England. According to folk etymology, the name is derived from the effects of the tropical sun on their fair-skinned legs. In addition to "Red Legs", the term underwent extensive progression in Barbados and some of the following terms were also used: "Poor whites", "Backra Johnny" and "Ecky-Becky". Historically, everything besides "poor whites" was used as derogatory insults.

CHAPTER 23

No longer England's bastard child

"Once you wake up the mind of a man you can't put it to sleep" ZORA NEAL HURSTON

Prior to setting foot in England I had associated the country, its power, authority and stark whiteness to the only other 'supreme' authority I knew – God. As a child I was 'introduced' to God who was also white, all knowing, superior and omnipotent. I'd transferred all these qualities and expectations to England thereby giving it a presumed superiority. Mr first landlord, Mr Lynch encouraged me to watch the evening news and the information I gained opened my eyes. On the news I saw conscious brothers and sisters in the United States: Stokely Carmichael, Malcolm X, Elridge Cleaver, George Jackson, Angela Davis, Martin Luther King Jr, Huey Newton, Bobby Seale, Elijah Mohammed and many others who were making their voices heard. Black people were making history. They were reclaiming themselves and were saying: "We don't want to be known as coloured, we don't want to be known as darkies. We are Black. We will no longer accept your second or third class citizenship; we demand human and equal rights and prepared to fight for them. We've been controlled by white power for over 300 years and what we are demanding now is Black power."

While I lived in Barbados, I was oblivious to all of this because there was no television. That 166 square miles called Barbados was my world. I didn't hear anybody in Barbados talk about these things. The history I was taught never showed any Black person contributing to the shaping of the world. None of those responsible for 'educating' me told that we were the descendents of a people who had made a monumental contribution to human development. On reflection, the 'holy rollers' and my Sunday school teachers were also remiss, because they never once taught me, or even suggested, that Black people existed in the Bible. They neglected to tell me that there had been slave revolts and revolutions in the Caribbean. No one mentioned Bussa, an African slave who in 1816 had led a revolt on a plantation called Bayley's in St Philip, Barbados. Nor did they mention Nanny Grigg, a domestic slave from an estate called Simmon's, or the role she played in helping plan Bussa's revolt. I'm sure that, had someone told me about Samuel Sharp or Washington Franklin (both Jamaicans who led two separate revolts) or the Haitian Revolution, or even the Nile Valley Civilisation, I would certainly have had a stronger sense of who I was. I would certainly never have been found flailing upon England's doorstep.

My education should have taught me about the Baptist War in Jamaica where up to 60,000 slaves were willing to die for their freedom. I would have known about "Tacky's Rebellion" which took place in Jamaica in 1760. The leader of this rebellion was an African Chief who had been made an overseer at Frontier Plantation. Sadly these brave men were betrayed by one in their midst, a slave from another plantation who saw their bid for freedom as an affront to the way of life to which he'd been 'seasoned'. This betrayal led to Tacky being killed and the remaining rebels committing suicide rather than be enslaved again.

But my teaching was white-washed and so Haiti's dominance over the French was never taught. The word 'reparations' would not have been foreign to me. They would have taught me about Toussaint L'Ouverture, who led the Haitian Revolution (1791-1804): a slave revolt in the French colony of Saint-Domingue (modern-day Haiti), which culminated in the elimination of slavery there and established the Republic of Haiti. It was the only slave revolt which led to the founding of a state and is generally considered the most successful slave rebellion ever to have occurred in the Americas. I would have learned that after the Revolution, France demanded that Haiti pay them 150 million gold francs, as both recognition of the country as a sovereign republic and as 'compensation' for the loss of slaves and its slave colony. Even for decades after I was born, Haiti continued to struggle to repay this debt, a financial hardship from which, to this day, the country has never economically recovered.

Hearing what my Black brothers and sisters were saying and doing in America would not have been a revelation, because I would have known that they were continuing the revolution our ancestors had started. Closer to my Caribbean home, I would have known the story of Clement Osbourne Payne, a Trinidadian born of Barbadian parents. I would have known of his trip to Barbados in 1937 when he came to let Barbadians know of the struggle that the people were experiencing in Trinidad; and that they too had a right to demand better working conditions and wages.

Clement Payne was a Trade Unionist who was viewed by the authorities as a dangerous revolutionary. He had only been in Barbados a few days when he held a meeting in Golden Square. As always, they were those who became disturbed by what he was saying and wanted him out of Barbados before he opened any more eyes. They had no legal grounds to deport him, so they used a very minor mistake on his entry document as proof that he intended to defraud the government. Baba Clement Payne believed he had been born in Barbados and wrote this on his immigration entry form. But it was proven that he had in fact been born in Trinidad: according to immigration law at that time, Trinidad was still a British colony. None of this should have mattered, but for this minor detail they charged him with intent to defraud the government.

The charge, though frivolous, had to be addressed. Intending to have a 'word' with the governor regarding his arrest, Payne and 300 of his followers marched to Government House. They were singing and dancing along the way and were asked to 'cease and desist'. They didn't and, as a result, Clement and some of his followers were arrested. He was the only one who was denied the right to raise bail and was remanded to custody. Facing expulsion from Barbados he intended to fight the case but his young lawyer, Grantley Adams, encouraged him not to as it could get ugly for him. On the night of 14 July 1937 Clement was expelled from Barbados. When his followers found out what had happened there was a massive four-day uprising. When the smoke cleared from the police guns, 14 people were dead (even until today these numbers are disputed), 47 were wounded and 500 were arrested.

Marcus Mosiah Garvey visited Barbados in October of that same year; 1937. This was more 'knowledge' that I should have been taught at school, but I was now in my early twenties and only just 'learning'. I would have wanted one of my teachers to tell me that, in the midst of the crowd on that October night, was a 17-year-old young man by the name of Errol Walton Barrow. Today, Errol Walton Barrow is revered in Barbados as the 'Father of Independence'. But back on that October night he was just an impressionable young man who, after hearing the words of Marcus Garvey, would walk away from that meeting with a new fire burning in him. I would someday have the privilege of meeting Errol Barrow, and hearing him tell me of that meeting made me envious that I had not experienced the moment, or at least have had someone tell me of it in my formative years. Errol Barrow told me of the impact Marcus Garvey's visit and speech had on him that night at the Queen's Park Steel Shed in Bridgetown, Barbados. It would be a speech that our future first Prime Minister and Father of Independence would personally describe as, "One of my most informative and political experiences."

The latter half of the twentieth century was a very interesting time; here I was in England going through a process of de-education and re-education. Apart from the civil rights movement and other conscious groups in the United States all making demands on the system, there were the 'hippies' or 'flower power people' campaigning for a new order of things, John Kennedy was assassinated in 1963 followed by the assassination of Malcolm X and Martin Luther King Jr., social unrest in the Caribbean especially in Trinidad, students unrest in Canada, the Baader-Meinhof group and Rudi the Red in Germany. Not neglecting to mention that our young men from Barbados were off fighting a war in Yemen in 1962 that up to this day mesmerizes me and up to the present, June 2017 this war is still raging. The past is not dead and buried, but very much alive and always with us.

CHAPTER 24

The Phantom, Mandrake the Magician, Lothar and religion

"Let stern lessons of yesteryear be your food, your drink, your rest" JOSEPH SEAMON COTTER

Here I was with eyes and ears wide open, absorbing every bit of knowledge that was coming my way. I wondered how it was possible that those responsible for educating me didn't tell me about my ancestors and the positive contributions made by our people? Why didn't (or hadn't) anyone write the kind of books that would make me proud of my people and replace all the negative images of my Ancestors that had been implanted in my young brain?

Somehow, along the way, I was introduced to comics that had heroes I idolised. These heroes were Mandrake the Magician with his sidekick Lothar and The Phantom who was also called "The Ghost Who Walked". He was shown to be the most knowledgeable man in the so-called 'jungle' (which of course was Africa); even more knowledgeable than those who were native and indigenous to the region. The Phantom lived in a region called Bangalla and there he dwelled in a Skull Cave. He had a white horse called Hero, a black wolf called Devil and he also had a sidekick: an African-a pygmy named Curan.

Here I want you to take notice: because it was white, the horse was named Hero. His wolf (equally important to him but because of its black colour) was called Devil. Need I say more? There was also

**The Phantom, Mandrake the Magician and Lothar (top right)
and Guran and Wolf**

a noticeable difference about The Phantom: as a child I thought nothing of it but, as I grew into my Black consciousness, I would be able to make a correlation. Traditionally (and whether in fact or fiction), many slave masters on plantations throughout the Americas and the Caribbean had white wives but never seemed 'satisfied' with them. No, they lusted after (and often got) every Black girl and woman on the plantation. However, in this regard the Phantom stood in stark contrast. He didn't desire any of the African women or girls that he encountered.

Even though he was surrounded by as many richly-hued women as those plantation owners, he did not find one that was fitting or desirous enough for his bed. He needed, found and kept just for himself a white woman named Diana. The 'correlation' of this is that many of today's Black men are behaving just like the Phantom: with the millions of richly-hued Black women out there, there are those Black men who are unable (or unwilling?) to find one that's 'good enough' in this sea of beauties. They are following in the Phantom's footsteps … only a white woman, a 'Diana', will do.

Tarzan was also a firm film and comic-book favourite, yet he too was part of the racist stereotype: here was a white man 'crowned' "King of the Jungle", a 'benefactor' to the 'natives' (Africans)…and his white 'wife' Jane.

Thanks to my work on the buses, I was meeting *real* African people. I was beyond excited and hoped that my feelings of surprise weren't showing. I say 'surprise' because none of the African people that were getting on the bus looked anything like the Africans I'd seen in my favourite childhood comic books. Other than a variation in skin colour, there was nothing different between them and me. They looked every bit like my brothers and sisters. But I should not have been surprised; I was getting my history lessons from comic books written by white people who probably had never set foot in Africa! But I must admit Mandrake and Phantom were two of my favourite comics and I eagerly looked forward to each new strip in the daily paper. To supplement my yearnings we exchanged comic books within our peer group. Overall though, I'm not sure which of these was the worse example of showing African people to be ignorant or dependant on being 'saved' by a white man.

These comic book characters wielded enormous power and influence over their friends. With a few 'magic tricks' Mandrake was able to impress Lothar enough to walk away from his seven nations where he was Prince. He also walked away from his responsibilities of being ruler when his father died. As was custom, Lothar was set to 'inherit' the twenty wives of his father. A part of me could understand him not wanting his father's wives, but what I now understand is that his actions are very much reflective of the actions of many Black men today. If a responsibility seems to be too arduous, then just walk away from it. Leave it for someone else. Lothar walked away from his responsibilities to follow a white man all over the world.

As a child I was envious of Lothar and Guran. They were, after all, my heroes. No one was telling me that I had nothing to be jealous of. No one was telling me that their depiction of my African brothers and sisters was wrong and based on unadulterated racism. No one was saying that their implied cannibalism (the bones in the nose which were supposed to be the skeletal remains of their devoured victims) was again a figment of the writer's imagination.

As I stood there looking at my brothers and sisters without bones in their noses I felt sorry for the child that, because he wasn't taught any better, didn't know any better. I couldn't help but remember the same little boy who cheered when the cowboys shot and killed the Indians. As that boy became a man, I learned that they weren't 'Indians'. They were indigenous people who, just like the Africans, had been abused and displaced so that white people could acquire the riches of their lands.

CHAPTER 25

Surging forward

"Hold fast to dreams, for if dreams die, life
is a broken winged bird that cannot fly."
LANGSTON HUGHES

I didn't have time to look back. In terms of my knowledge I was surging forward and night after night, as I sat there watching the news, I felt a stirring. At the time I wasn't sure what the stirring was, but with hindsight I now know. It was the awakening of my previously-comatose Black consciousness, which was quickened by the words and actions of my Brothers and Sisters in America. They were making demands, which I found both foreign and almost unimaginable. My seasoned, shackled mind had been deeply steeped in muck and mire of colonisation and couldn't fully grasp the concept of what they were doing. It would take a process of mental liberation before I would be able to. After all, I had been 'seasoned' to see England as the 'Mother Country' and I was one of her so-called 'sons'. So how could all that she and her descendants had done to me and my ancestors *not* be right?

Not for one minute did I question what Africa's children in America were doing; in fact, I was intrigued. To my ears, what they were shouting was a rallying cry. They were asserting themselves; saying they'd had enough of the injustices, mistreatment and abuse being dumped upon them by Uncle Sam and weren't going to take it anymore. I looked at these Black brothers and sisters that looked like me; I then took a closer look at my white 'surrogate mother' and in a moment of celebration realised that although I (like the rest of the Caribbean and its colonised children) considered her to be 'mother', I didn't look anything like her. I was actually her adopted bastard child and I didn't belong. That is why her white children were treating me (and my Brothers and Sisters) the way they were. But we had been so 'well-programmed', so 'seasoned', that when "mother" said she needed our services for war, bus drivers, nurses, we answered the call without hesitation.

After all, it was once such call that now had me in her backyard experiencing a full frontal assault of racism, prejudice and a hatred of me simply based on the high visibility factor I presented. My being Black wasn't just colour. To the children of the 'motherland' it was a representation of all things evil, negative and demeaning. That is why they felt a God-given, white-given right to hurl their most vile expressions of hatred my way. To my now-awakened mind that I had no rights, claims or privileges. I was an object to be vilified.

But I had heard the cries of my real brothers and sisters and was no longer a bastard or an unwanted child. I belong to them, their struggles. This colonised man who had left Barbados ("Little England") to go and serve the motherland was throwing off the mental shackles of colonisation. Like my ancestors, I too was now willing to demand, fight and if necessary, die for my rights. I was no longer Mother England's 'bastard child': I was Africa's legitimate child and felt a sense of pride that until now was unbeknownst to me. I began to learn who this history of my ancestral mother was and why her enslaved children had been kidnapped and dispersed to almost every corner of the world, exploited and abused, just to satisfy the greed of Europeans.

The pride of Son-ship I was now feeling could not be quenched. Africa's child wanted all that was due him and he was going to start working for it, both physically and mentally. How hard, how long, how indefatigably was unknown by this genie who was now out of the mythical bottle of mental enslavement. No one was going to get him back in that bottle of conscious-darkness. The burning desire for liberation could not be quenched. I wanted to hear, see and learn much, much more. Little did I know how integral a part working on the bus would play. I certainly never imagined that it would afford me the opportunity to meet a man that would be instrumental in my conscious learning and growth.

The bus was an ideal place to meet people and I met people from all over the world. I was particularly excited about meeting people from Africa. These people didn't exhibit any of the characteristics of those Africans that were depicted in Tarzan films, or even in my unconscious mind. They certainly didn't have bones through their noses. As I was the Bus Conductor all kinds of Black and Caribbean people would talk to me, especially the Caribbean ones. We gravitated towards each other like magnets. The conversation usually started by asking which island you came from or how long you'd been in the country. It could then gravitate to whether you knew about any rooms to let. It was during one of these conversations that I was introduced to an interesting group. I met a fellow West Indian, an Antiguan by the name of Brother Chambers who, during the course of our conversations, told me about the Notting Hill Riots[1] that had taken place in West London four years prior to my arrival. He also told me about the racially-motivated killing of an Antiguan carpenter named Kelso Cochrane[2].

Brother Chambers was keeping abreast of what conscious Blacks in America were doing and this helped to fuel my passion. They were doing their research, questioning white people's story about themselves and about us. They saw the need to identify with Africa. My mind, which had been shackled while I lived in Barbados, wanted to know more. I wanted to see the conscious brothers and sisters in America take pride in their Blackness.

Thanks to this agitated sense of pride, I was now seriously thinking about race. Brother Chambers invited me to a meeting, where similarly-conscious Brothers and Sisters discussed issues of the day that affected Black people. As I was unmarried at the time, I was happy to attend. We gathered in the two-room flat of a brother from Trinidad named George Joseph.

The group size varied; sometimes they were as many as two-dozen individuals, other times there were as few as eight or nine people. The group was made up mostly of men, but there were also a few female members (sisters).

FOOTNOTES

1. The Notting Hill riot is popularly believed to have been triggered by an assault against Majbritt Morrison, a white Swedish woman, on 29 August 1958. She had been arguing with her Jamaican husband Raymond Morrison at the Latimer Road tube station. A group of various white people attempted to intervene in the argument and a fight broke out between them and some of Raymond Morrison's friends. The following day, Majbritt Morrison was verbally and physically assaulted by a gang of white youths that had recalled seeing her the night before; the youths allegedly threw milk bottles at Morrison and called her a "Black man's trollop". Later that night a mob of 300 to 400 white people, many of them Teddy Boys, were seen on Bramley Road attacking the houses of West Indian residents. The disturbances, rioting and attacks continued every night until 5 September. The riots caused tension between the Metropolitan Police and the British African-Caribbean community, which claimed that the police had not taken their reports of racial attacks seriously. In 2002, files were released that revealed that senior police officers at the time had assured the Home Secretary, Rab Butler, that there was little or no racial motivation behind the disturbance, despite testimony from individual police officers to the contrary.

2. Kelso Cochrane was born in Antigua and moved to London in 1954, where he settled in Notting Hill and worked as a carpenter. After fracturing his thumb in a work accident, he attended Paddington General Hospital. While walking home shortly after midnight on 17 May 1959 the 32-year-old Cochrane was set upon by a group of white youths, who stabbed him with a stiletto knife. Three other men arrived on the scene, and the youths ran off. The three men took Cochrane to hospital, where he died an hour later. His funeral procession, on 6 June 1959, was attended by more than 1,200 people.

CHAPTER 26

The second floor flat

"Struggle is strengthening. Battling evil gives us the power to battle evil even more." OSSIE DAVIS

Brother George's flat was in Stoke Newington, on the second-floor flat of a shop on Brighton Road. There was sub-post office on the ground floor and on the first floor was Gillie's Barber shop; Gillie was also from Trinidad. At George's flat we discussed all aspects of international revolutionary struggle, the problems that confronted us as a people, how to deal with them and how best to show solidarity as a united group. We planned what action(s) we would take and made banners and placards. We picketed embassies: the South African, American and what was then the Rhodesian[1] embassy. We picketed police stations where Brothers had been arrested, incarcerated or even died. At every instance of what the authorities would term our 'civil disobedience' we displayed placards with our particular grievance(s), and on every one we drew a pig's head wearing a police helmet. The police were the vanguard of institutional racism and our protests reflected this. You could say that it was a virtual '*hot house*' of activities. We met every Sunday but depending on what was going on or needed to be done, we met during the week.

The Haitian, Cuban, Chinese, Russian, American and French Revolutions were an integral part of our discussions, giving us a clearer understanding of the reasons why people rose up and revolted, especially when oppressive governments ride roughshod over their people. We all had Chairman Mao's *Little Red Book* which became our new temporary bible. We endorsed the following quotations:

"Political power grows out of the barrel of a gun."
"Learn from the masses and then teach them."
"The power of the people is greater than the man's technology."
"Dare to struggle and dare to win."

Let me be clear here. I think we were intelligent enough to realise that we couldn't stage a revolution in the true sense of the word within African or Caribbean countries; simply because our people were still so 'seasoned'. Instead, we felt that political leverage, raising the consciousness of the people, being advocates for the people, agitating the people, all of these would be the best forms of 'revolution'. We understood that we were in no position to undertake an armed uprising because we had no arms. We still don't. I'm not talking about street gangs with sawn-off shotguns: how many African and Caribbean countries have a nuclear capability? NONE. Because of this, the Black man is in no position to wage that kind of warfare. Instead, as I've mentioned previously, our emphasis needs to be on growing food rather than on manufacturing arms. Fundamental education of our people is necessary. To eliminate the centuries of 'seasoning', it is the post-traumatic slave syndrome experience that we must work assiduously to de-educate, then re-educate our people. Our revolution has to be based on the consciousness of the people and using what materials and energies we have to formulate plans that would benefit us, both as individuals and collectively.

But let's go back to our meetings. In time we understood the nature of the struggles and felt empowered by these new thoughts. I was fundamentally moved by the ideology espoused in this little book. It was clear to me that, for there to be growth, sometimes the actions that must be taken can be viewed as gruesome. The teachings about the revolutionary movement showed me how a man with vision and determination can influence a group of people to bring about mass changes. When we looked at Cuba and saw how the Cuban people, with far less resources, resisted the might of the United States and did so for over five decades, then this would give us some indication as to the kind of war we had to wage.

We were heavily influenced by the Black Panthers and the Black Power Movement and aligned ourselves with their struggle. We felt that their situation and ours was very similar and so kept a keen eye and interest in what was happening with them in the United States. As I was embracing the teachings of the *Little Red Book*, I was introduced to another book, *The Philosophy and Opinions of Marcus Garvey*. By the time I had finished reading this book I was convinced that it gave us the 'blue print' of what we, as a people, have to do to liberate ourselves. The book was my inspiration and gave me a broader picture of what I had to do to move myself from a place of dependence to independence. Now, decades later, I can say that these teachings laid the foundations that drove me to becoming the man I am today, a man with a profound sense of Black consciousness and a totally committed Pan Africanist.[2]

Black consciousness incorporates questioning how and why we are at the bottom of the human ladder. How did it happen? Where and why did this decline start? As a Pan Africanist who has a solid foundation of Black consciousness I have to do what I can to offer my Brothers and Sisters a hand. Not just by giving him/her a few dollars but to see how I can help to uplift him/her so that he/ she can do for self.

I've been asked if I think my life would have turned out differently had I not been introduced to the *Little Red Book*, or Marcus Garvey's *Philosophy and Opinions*. My answer is: "I don't know". One never knows how one's life would have turned out if certain things did or didn't happen, but suffice to say these two things occurred at a time of my life when I was in a place of growth; I could accept and see the good in both of them. For me, it's the same as asking what I think my life would have been like had I never left Barbados. Again, I don't know; I can only work with what is known. What is known is that I left and, as a result, was introduced to a group of very forward thinking

Black Brothers and Sisters. That meeting left an indelible mark on my life.

As a student at St Giles School my voracious appetite for learning never left me. As I grew in to my Black consciousness, my appetite grew even more. I wanted to know and it wasn't enough for someone to tell me: Collin Carter likes to know for myself and the only way that could happen was to seek out this learning. I made it my business to get my hands on anything that would advance my knowledge. This is one of the fundamental principles that have pushed me into any and all directions to not only acquire knowledge, but share it. I use every method at my disposal to acquire knowledge: reading, internet searches, lectures and extensive travel. And I don't just spoon-feed people with information: I tell them how and where I obtained it. If you are interested, you too can obtain it.

FOOTNOTES

1. Rhodesia is now modern-day Zimbabwe.
2. Pan-Africanism is the idea that peoples of African descent have common interests and should be unified. Historically, Pan-Africanism has often taken the shape of a political or cultural movement. There are many varieties of Pan-Africanism: in its narrowest political manifestation, Pan-Africanists envision a unified African nation where all people of the African diaspora can live. (African diaspora refers to the long-term historical process by which people of African descent have been scattered from their ancestral homelands to other parts of the world.) In more-general terms, Pan-Africanism is the sentiment that people of African descent have a great deal in common, a fact that deserves notice and even celebration

CHAPTER 27

Black: Not just a colour, but a condition

Leaving Barbados was a good thing. In fact, it's the best thing that I've probably ever done in my life. Had I not done so, I would probably still be ignorant with my body free from chains, but my mind still in shackles. Like many so-called Black Barbadians I thought that white people, our enslavers, were wonderful and, being fortunate enough to be made in the enviable image of a blond, blue-eyed God and his only begotten son only added to this aggrandisement. This was (and is) a manifestation of the mental enslavement that formed the social engineering used to break the African. It should *never* be forgotten that Barbados was the headquarters of 'seasoning'; that horrendous process where, over a two to three year period, the enslaved African was 'seasoned' into the 'perfect' nigger. While most of these 'seasoned' slaves were kept in Barbados, many were shipped to America. These seasoned slaves weren't kept out of a sense of 'affinity'; it was (and remains) about trade and money. Slaves were trade and our enslavers always needed something to sell.

As I've mentioned previously, the England I encountered on my arrival fifty years ago was not the England of my expectations or imagination. My imagination had been deeply seeped in the stories told, read and shared by those whose duty it was to keep the African mentally enslaved. My imagination was also stimulated by the school books and films shared by the British Council (which was then situated in White Park Road, St Michael). On some Saturday mornings, we young boys would go and watch these films; where we would be awed by the greatness of Mother England and her privileged white children, who lived lives seemingly much easier and better than ours.

We remained ignorant but if I were to cut us any slack I would have to say not all of our ignorance was our fault. English historians pretended to be unaware of a Black presence in Britain for more than two millennia. There is evidence of Black involvement as far back as the Roman Empire, when Black soldiers (mainly from Nubia[1]) were sent to fight in ancient Britannia.

As with any group of people that ventured to another land; some of these Blacks remained in Britain. What had happened to us was a result of the systematic white-washing of Mother England's and the world's history. The intent was to remove any aspect of colour from British history. Our contributions to human development go back as far as 6000 BC. Mother England felt it necessary to eliminate this fact from her white children's mind, so as maintain a comfortable delusion: Mother Africa's kidnapped, stolen and enslaved children had done nothing positive or good to make their life easier and better, and were certainly not capable of great things. Therefore, they deserved to be slaves, to be scattered throughout the Diaspora, raped, abused, worked to death and murdered.

It was to this England that on 22nd June 1948 a few ex-soldiers who'd fought in World War II, plus others who had managed to get the requisite £28 to pay for the voyage, journeyed to England on the HMT Empire Windrush. For the soldiers it had been a long awaited return from a military leave; for the others who descended the gangway, this 'green and pleasant land' was about to be their new home. They had made it to Mother England. These Caribbean folks were hopeful of a future brighter than the one they had left behind. Now that the war was over, the process of rebuilding (albeit with a greatly reduced work force) had begun.

We all believed they were coming home to the 'Motherland'. We had expectations that this country would embrace or make room for us. We did not know that at no time in its existence had England ever wholeheartedly been accommodating to Africans. At best, the English were tolerant to some degree; at worst they hoped we would leave and go back from whence we came.

Despite initially welcoming Commonwealth immigrants, Enoch Powell, then Minister of Health under the Conservative government, suggested the idea of 'reparations' (funding people, mainly those of African and Indian descent, to leave Britain). He felt his endorsement of a ticket of fear, an anti-Black campaign would serve him and his kind best. On 20 April 1968, he made a controversial speech in Birmingham in which he warned his audience of what he called, "... the consequences of continued unchecked mass immigration from the Commonwealth to Britain."

As I look ahead, I am filled with foreboding. Like the Roman, I seem to see 'the River Tiber foaming with much blood'. That tragic and intractable phenomenon which we watch with horror on the other side of the Atlantic but which there is interwoven with the history and existence of the States itself, is coming upon us here by our own volition and our own neglect. Indeed, it has all but come. In numerical terms, it will be of American proportions long before the end of the 20th century. Only resolute and urgent action will avert it even now.

Even though it needed our labour desperately at the time, the Mother Country didn't want us anymore than she wanted the plague. The white people of Britain reacted to us as if Black people were new to Britain. But in those days we weren't called 'Black', we were called "Coloured. To add insult to injury, before our awakening many of us referred to ourselves by even more derogatory terms, We called each other what whites called us and saw nothing wrong with it: 'nigger', 'darkie' and 'wog' (short for 'golliwog'). My mother would called me 'nigger man' when she was angry with me and I would answer with no feeling of insult. For such a long time, as a broken people we accepted whatever derogatory name white people elected to call us.

The word 'Black' didn't come into 'vogue' as a positive description for people of colour until around the mid-1960s), when revolutionary-thinking brothers and sisters in America made the word an acceptable one. The fight to free our minds was a long, hard one, but their hardest fight wasn't with white people, it was with us and continues to be. For so long, the word 'black' had been deemed as such an offensive word that we didn't want it. 'Coloured' was bad; 'nigger' was worse; but 'black'? Nobody wanted to be referred to as 'black'. 'Black' meant African. African meant slave. In our minds we were free and freedom meant getting some distance away from being Black.

The brothers and sisters in America didn't give up on us. They liquefied 'Black' and gently drip-fed it to us. When we got used to the taste, they solidified it until we, the descendants of enslaved Africans, could finally shake off that link from our mental chain and feel comfortable. Not just proud to call ourselves 'Black' but to demand that other races also call us 'Black'. Once we had understood and accepted the beauty in the word, 'Black', we could each state proudly that, "I am Black, with an upper case 'B', and proud of it." We finally had a name that we had chosen ... it was ours. The activities in the US had an effect on other conscious young men in the UK and thus other organisations were formed, such as the Nation of Islam, the UK Black Panther Party, British Black People's Association, Hackney Black People's Association and North London African Association. These organisations worked tirelessly to combat and address the many institutionally racist conditions under which Black people had to live.

Never fail to remember that this achievement did not come easily. It was hard fought and very often it was our own people with whom we had verbal and psychological wars. Once we started to call ourselves 'Black', white people had to sit up and listen; they could no longer use the word 'black' as an offensive insult nor in any other derogatory sense.

In those early days of *our* struggle for racial identity, the Indians were also being subjected to the same kind of racial hell as we West Indians. They were being abused, harassed, assaulted and racially discriminated against by white people and white institutions. They, in turn, referred to themselves as 'coloured'.

However, once we had found our own identity and began calling ourselves 'Black', and insisted that others do the same, the Indians could not accept the term. The Indians did not want to be associated with the word 'black'. They sought to find another socially-acceptable 'label' and came up with 'Asian'. Being traditionally class- and caste-conscious, they preferred to not identify themselves with Black people.

FOOTNOTE

1. Nubia is a region along the Nile River located in what is today northern Sudan and southern Egypt. It was the seat of one of the earliest civilisations of ancient Africa and was home to one of the African empires. Nubian history can be traced from at least 2000 B.C. onward.

CHAPTER 28

Setting things right

"When spider webs unite they can tie up a lion."
AFRICAN PROVERB

I've always had a strong sense of what I consider to be right/wrong, fair/unfair, proper and/or humane treatment of Black people. As the 1960s unfolded, it brought with it a deeper sense of consciousness in African people. We were no longer willing to sit idly by and let another people dictate what they felt was right for us. The revolutionary Brothers and Sisters had decided it was time for us to be heard and we were willing to risk whatever repercussions or consequences to garner African liberation.

As I grew in consciousness, so too did my sense of doing whatever I could to assist in this advancement. The liberation of all African people was (and remains) our unified goal. I listened as my conscious brothers and sisters all over the world fought against capitalism, oppression, exploitation, racism and the myriad of other ills that are adversely affecting us. In Africa, the Caribbean, Britain, Latin America, France, Canada, China, America and Europe, wherever people were oppressed, the goal was the same: to bring down the tyrants of oppression. We were united in our efforts to improve the conditions of Black and oppressed people the world over. Students, workers and revolutionary brothers and sisters were protesting.

Some of these fights spilled from one area of the world to another. Such was the case of the student protest in Canada at George Williams University in what later became known as 'The Sir George Williams Affair'. In May 1968, six West Indian students accused biology professor Perry Anderson of discrimination due to unfair grading practices. The administrators did not appear to take the matter seriously and students initially organised meetings, sit-ins and peaceful protests. But they became disgruntled when the administration continued to take action and on 29 January 1969 over 400 Black and white students left a meeting and occupied the university's computer lab. It was a peaceful protest until 11 February, when negotiations broke down and the riot police were called in. As a result, the computer lab was destroyed, resulting in over $2 million in damage. Ninety-seven students were arrested, but the charges against most of them were eventually dismissed. Several of the occupiers had privileged backgrounds, coming from wealthy West Indian families. Among those arrested were Roosevelt Douglas (who was the son of one of the richest men in Dominica who later became the country's Prime Minister). Also deeply involved in the protest was Cheddi 'Joey' Jagan Jr, the son of Guyana's Prime Minister, Cheddi Jagan.

This student protest gained headlines in Europe and the Caribbean, far beyond the campus borders of Sir George Williams University. Like all good fruit-bearing trees, the seeds of this 'discontent' reached Barbados and took root in Errol Walton Barrow. The soon-to-be 'Father of Independence' was concluding his final push for an independent Barbados. I may have been new in my consciousness, but not so new that I couldn't appreciate the concerted effort he was making. He was determined to take Barbados from an island colony to a sovereign state.

CHAPTER 29

Move to Leytonstone

"By being grateful, a man makes himself deserving of yet another kindness."
MOZAMBICAN PROVERB

I remained at Finsbury Park from April 1963 to November 1965. The owner of the house was white but, because they could get substantially more rent for a room from a Black person than from a white tenant, they rented to Black people. Moving to Leytonstone in east London was a different move; I was going from a room to flat in a quiet residential, almost suburban, area. The house was very nice and I had three rooms: a living room, two bedrooms and my own kitchen and bathroom. I would live there for about eighteen months before moving back to Stoke Newington. I was still a bus conductor and I wish that I could say that I was able to avoid any major conflicts or altercations on the bus, but that would be wishful thinking. I had to endure racist and prejudiced behaviour from many of the white passengers. I think they behaved the way they did because they thought that, like most of the other conductors, I would endure their abuse and not retaliate. But I was both May Carter's son and a conscious, upstanding Black man. I was not going to look down at the floor and avoid eye-contact nor cower from anyone. I was more than willing to stand up and defend myself. One night, a white passenger discovered just how far I was willing to go.

To be honest, perhaps a combination of my political and social awareness (which had been growing since my arrival in London) and that first walk the morning after my arrival, were contributing factors in wanting to fight and, if need be, defend myself to the death. I remembered that I had intended to join the British Army and, in doing so, would have fought and perhaps died for a cause that had nothing to do with Black people. So I figured I was entitled to fight for *my rights* and defend myself at all costs.

Some might say that my actions prompted the fight, but my actions were as a direct result of the behaviour of the passenger. The bus on which I was working had already pulled out from the stop when I saw him. He was running for the bus and I did something that I seldom did: I waited for him. There wasn't anyone else on the bus but, rather than paying me the fare on the platform, he ran right up the stairs and sat all the way at the front of the bus. Remember, in those days the buses were double-deckers, which meant I now had to climb the stairs and walk all the way to the front to get his fare.

His lack of consideration made me angry: I'd had the decency to wait for him and I felt the least he could have done was to pay me on the platform, then go up the stairs. As I mounted the stairs I decided that if he gave me any coins that required change back, I was going to give him back all pennies. Just as I had guessed, he gave me a half-crown (which was two shillings and six pence). He wanted a six-pence ticket which meant I had to give him back two shillings change. I started to count out the two shillings in pennies and he said to me that he didn't want coppers. I told him that that was all I had. He said, "Let me see if I have six-pence." I said, "If you knew you had six-pence why did you give me a half-crown?" He didn't have the six-pence, so I pretended that I was making the change differently. When he held out his hand for the change, I dropped the coppers in it. As soon as I turned around to walk away, he threw the pennies at me, which struck the back of my head.

The pennies fell from my head like rain but didn't cool my mood. Instead, it lit my fuse and I spun around with anger in my eyes. I grabbed him, and during the scuffle we tumbled down the staircase. He tried to scramble off the bus but I was doing my best to prevent this from happening. Hearing all the commotion, the driver stopped the bus. By this time we were on the platform and the passenger jumped off the bus. I jumped after him, all the while swinging the ticket machine in my hand like the biblical tale of Sampson swinging the jawbone of the ass. I was mad with rage and hell-bent on bursting his head wide open. For the sake of us both, the driver held me back. The passenger ran off and I heeded the driver's warning that this incident could get me in trouble.

Getting back on the bus the next day wasn't easy. My now-lit fuse was still smouldering and I believe I stayed in this frame of mind for weeks. My state of mind did not improve when I heard that the man wrote to London Transport and complained about the incident.

I was now marked for dismissal based solely upon his complaint. I had a Union Representative but I didn't feel he was really 'representing' me, so I decided to represent myself. I told London Transport that, by throwing the coins at me (which he admitted to doing), the passenger had, in fact, assaulted me. Therefore, not only did I have the right to defend myself, but I would be taking legal action against him for the assault.

It was interesting to see the faces of the London Transport officials who had initially decided that they were 'my God and my judge'. But when I told them that I was going to take civil action, I showed them that I meant business. They looked at each other with concern, but what they didn't realise was that I was bluffing; I knew absolutely nothing about legal proceedings!

It was clear that they were thinking that if I took the matter to court it might get blown out of all proportion, so they decided not to sack me. Instead, they gave me a stern warning. But in their minds they had already decided that they *would* eventually sack me so they said: "This time, we're letting you off with a warning, but anytime there's a repeat of this same kind of behaviour, it will be the sack forthwith. We want 'you people' to know and understand that the equipment we give you is not supposed to be used as weapons; they are supposed to be used for the purpose for which they were intended and we won't tolerate this kind of behaviour." Of all that was said, what resonated with me most was the reference to 'you people'. To me, that said: "You

Black people; you niggers; you darkies." And, "You foreigners who are too stupid to tell the difference between a weapon and a precious piece of machinery that we've trained and entrusted you to use."

He, of course, knew that we knew what the machine was for. But if I had to use it as a weapon to defend myself, I was going to do so. This incident made me think that I had outstayed my welcome at London Transport. I knew that it could very well happen again and surely I wasn't going to allow anyone to take advantage of me, or to beat me up and then go home or to the pub and say: "I kicked a nigger's ass today!" I was going to put every one of them in their place. A kick-ass from any white man wasn't happening to May's last boy; and if I had to, I was going to kill somebody. My passion was hot and in my mind I was saying: "I gine kill some fucking body. I gine buss their ass. They can kill me or I kill them but I ent tekkin it and if I don't get off these buses I know I gine kill somebody." That was how I felt.

Feeling the way I did within three and a half years, I'd had enough but I had to work. I had already started the negotiation process to purchase a parcel of land back home in Barbados. I left my job as a conductor for new employment at Her Majesty's Royal Mint, but I continued my relationship with the London Transport as I kept my savings going through the London Transport Loan Club. This loan club was my way of paying for the land in Barbados.

SOAP BOXES IN HYDE PARK

I had started going to London's Hyde Park Corner, which isn't very far from Buckingham Palace. It was a place where anyone could 'get on their soapbox' and espouse whatever philosophies or opinions they wanted. People went there to be enlightened, entertained or just to listen. Some would cheer the speakers on and some would heckle them. At any time you could see a dozen or so soapbox orators. Somebody would be trying to save the world; some talking religion or a trade unionist talking about the trade unions, politics, or whatever. Hyde Park Corner on a Sunday afternoon was like an open university.

You could learn and hear about a lot of things that you probably wouldn't have read in the newspapers. This intrigued me. But I have to say that very few of my Caribbean compatriots felt the same, and it was rare to see any of them here on Sundays. They were mostly preparing themselves for work the following day. Turning up to experience the oratory delights of Hyde Park Corner may have been deemed as an unnecessary interruption in their schedule. They may have preferred to watch TV, or be sleeping off a Sunday lunch of rice and peas and chicken. But, one of the most notable orators at Speakers' Corner was, indeed, one of my Caribbean compatriots. From the late 1950s, Guyanese-born Roy Sawh was a regular feature at this iconic venue. This eloquent, and firebrand, orator was also one of the UK's most prolific activists and fighters for the rights of Black people.

A STREET BRAWL…BUT NOT OF MY OWN MAKING

With the racial tensions surrounding me, and my willingness to defend myself against it, it was inevitable that, sooner or later, I would be involved in another fight. This came about in 1964. I had a Barbadian friend called Lionel Alleyne, who had taken evening classes with me in Barbados for employment with London Transport. One evening he paid me a visit; I also had a female friend visiting so we chatted a while. Soon after Lionel had left, I heard a person shouting: "Carter! Carter! Carter! Carter!" I recognised Lionel's cries for help, and I took up piece of iron and a knife because he sounded as if he was in real trouble. There were two Irishmen (Murphy and Noon), who lived in the same house as me. They, too, had heard the cries and they, along with my female friend, joined me as I ran outside. As we approached, we saw Lionel being attacked by three white men. He was on the ground and being kicked down every time he tried to get to his feet. Two of the men saw me coming and ran off, but the one who was doing the kicking had his back to me. I took a swing at his head; the blow caused a blood-spurting injury. I then pulled out the knife from my back pocket, at which point my female friend shouted at Murphy and Noon: "Hold him! Hold him! Don't let him bring himself in trouble!" The Irishmen did as they were ordered and the assailant ran off, leaving one of his shoes at the scene.

Lionel got to his feet, staggered to the pavement and sat down. His face was swollen and covered with blood; some of his teeth had been knocked out. Murphy and Noon now had me firmly restrained as they knew I had every intention of running after the fleeing attacker. I struggled to free myself, without success, screaming, "Lemme go! Lemme go, cos I gine kill de bitch!" But they both ignored my pleas for revenge.

Still restraining me, they dragged me back to the house. By this time the other (mainly white) residents had heard the commotion and had pushed up their windows to see what was going on. Some of them were shouting: "He's got a knife! The black bastard has got a knife!"

It is alarming that when the three white thugs were beating one Black man, not one of the white neighbours even raised an eyebrow.

We all returned to the house and by this time my anger had me trembling and shaking. Lionel cleaned himself up as best he could and we went to the local police station and told them most of what had happened. I managed to leave out the part where I burst open the man's head. I took the shoe with me as additional 'evidence' alongside Lionel's injuries. But even as we reported the incident we knew that the police were not going to do anything. They would only have been interested if it had been a Black man who had been the attacker.

After that traumatic night, I always carried a knife. I could not be sure that such an incident would never happen again. I was still working on the buses and would travel home at all hours of the day or night. I accepted that I could be killed on these streets, but I wasn't going to go down without a fight.

I also took the decision to shave off the large beard I had grown in an effort to look less conspicuous. I did this the same night of the incident.

Let's pause for a brief 'Sankofa' moment (an African word meaning to look back at your past in order to contemplate where you started, where you are currently and plan for the future with much thought). Note where I started: my village and school environment, the Pentecostal church, Boy Scouts, the Barbados Regiment and employed as a health inspector with some people you grew up with; this environment was conducive to the production of docile humans (easily controlled persons). Where was I now? In London there was no school, no church, no scouts, no regiment and a job seen by others with much trepidation. These new people knew nothing about me nor did they respect me, they were xenophobic to the core. I still wonder how African-Caribbean people of that distinctive period in time could remain as docile today as the day they left the Caribbean. *That*, I cannot understand.

CHAPTER 30

Twenty-one days aboard a passenger vessel

"Odo nnyew fie kwan"
LOVE NEVER LOSES ITS WAY HOME

Seven winters, but none as brutal as my first one. Seven springs, which were really just an 'ease' from winter, but not enough that it ever made a difference. Seven summers that went in a blink: they never stayed around long enough to matter, or make you miss them when they became autumn. And going from autumn to winter was never an ease…one day it was cool, but when you got up the following morning it was winter. I have to say that, to me, winters in England just seemed to be constant! In my island home Barbados there were only two seasons: sunshine or rain.

Anyway, I had survived seven years in England and I was dreadfully homesick. I wanted to go home and see Mammy, even if I had to walk. At the time I was working at the Royal Mint and was due two weeks' annual leave; I asked the Personnel Officer for an additional two weeks off without pay. He answered my question by asking another question: "What would happen if all workers came and asked for time off without pay?" I told him: "I finished work at 7.00 am. I've waited here until 8.30 am to see you, when you should in fact have started work at 8.00 am. If you were to go into the staff canteen at 11 am that morning, you will see workers who, like me, finished at 7.00 am, but are in the canteen playing cards and dominoes and drinking Guinness and tea." He replied: "That might very well be so, but the answer to your request is no." I told him "I agreed to sell the Royal Mint some of my labour and they in turn have promised to pay me for it. I'm giving you two weeks' notice and I'm telling you now that I will not be hanging around Her Majesty's Mint after the next two weeks."

I proceeded to book my passage to leave in October for Barbados. This was the day I'd lived for and I was excited. That night in November 1962 when I'd boarded that BOAC airline and headed into the unknown, my only certainty was this day, the day of my return home, would be foremost in my mind. I did what I had to do in London to ensure that this day would happen. If this day wasn't going to be part of my future then I could not even envisaged leaving Barbados.

Prior to leaving Barbados, I didn't know that I would have to endure any of the hardships that were going to come my way: the racism, bigotry, disdain, and so often being made to feel like an intruder. But once I got to London, I knew I wasn't going to have a love affair with it and somehow have it replace Barbados. I was in London to work, to make money, acquire all the further education I could, then return to Barbados. If I thought that there would be no returning to my beloved Barbados, then I probably would never had left. I will always love Barbados; she was where my mother and brothers were. She knew me, held my past, knew my secrets and my footprints were permanently on her soil. England was where I worked, but Barbados, she was home. As we Bajans would say: "My navel string buried in Barbados."

There was a lot to do before my departure: selecting, buying and packing the various items and then getting them to the dock. Due to the number of packages and cases that I had, I felt it better and cheaper to travel by boat. I was returning, not on a BOAC plane but in the style that was the most economical: in this instance Geest Line vessel. At the time, Geest was the premier shipping line between England and the Caribbean, and had started life shipping bananas between the two places. Essentially, I was returning to Barbados on a banana boat! I was one of three passengers on this cargo vessel and I'd chosen this method of transportation not just because it fitted in with my pioneering spirit, but also because it allowed me to take the maximum amount of goods for Mammy. The journey took about nine days and we set sail from Barry in South Wales. The first three to four days of the journey were spent trying to get my sea legs and stop my stomach (and myself) from going overboard! That being said, I enjoyed the trip and the treatment was good.

The vessel first stopped in Dominica and then I was to have taken a flight from there to Barbados. But on arrival in the country I had a row with the authorities at Melville Hall Airport (now known as Douglas-Charles Airport). Geest was supposed to send a ticket for me from Dominica to Barbados, which they did not do. The authorities insisted that I would have to pay for the ticket and I was even more adamant that I would do no such thing. At that time, flights to and from Dominica were restricted to only flying during daylight hours and during the course of the argument it had started to get dark. They kept pushing me to buy the ticket and I kept refusing. At the last moment, they agreed to let me on the plane.

I arrived in Barbados at 7:30 pm on that October night 1969. I can only compare my shoes touching Barbadian soil after seven long years to the day Nelson Mandela was released from prison. I took a taxi from the airport to Mammy's home; I recall I didn't tell her I was coming home. When the taxi arrived in the village it was like a spectacle, the strange car was now the centre of everyone's interests. I believe Mammy would have been more curious to know why this strange car was stationary outside of her home. I remember getting out of the car, Mammy was so happy to see me and I was ecstatic to see her. This encounter was followed by her praying and thanking God for bringing me back safely.

Next on Mammy's agenda was food, "what can I get you to eat?" she asked. I told her I was headed straight to Ruby's in Tweedside Road, Ruby was a street vendor who was well known by Mammy and all others in the district. Mammy also had a spot on Tweedside Road a few years prior. Ruby was famous for selling fried fish served with slices of breadfruit, sweet potato etc. on arrival she stated how Ruby remembered me very well, although she did not remember my name, she knew my lineage in the family and that I was my mother's last boy. She recalled not seeing me for many years and knew that meant I had to be 'over and away.' After the hugs and kisses she was surprised to learn that I'd arrived in Barbados three hours before I presented myself before her tray. This knowledge made her beam with joy and she wanted everyone around to know. Although I had enough money at the time to pay for everything that Ruby had on her tray, she refused to take any money from me after I placed my order. I'm not sure that the people of the village today, share and care as they once did.

By the time I returned home, Mammy made me the largest mug of tea ever, so much that I told her I could not drink it all. Followed by a stream of questions and Mammy reminiscing on how much food and drink I could consume in any single hour prior to going to England, we spoke about what had changed and what remained the same. Mammy and I spoke about everything she and I could remember until almost sunrise.

The Next day, I travelled to the Bridgetown Port and cleared the eight or so cases I shipped from London containing household items and personal effects. I hired a lorry and transported the shipment to Mammy's house. When the lorry stopped in front of the house and she saw the consignment, she expected one case but as the cases came off she questioned why we were taking off all the cases to have to put them back on. The lorry driver informed her that all of the packages were hers. I will never forget the expression on my mother's face; she was lost for words. I had taken all the things that she never expected to see in her house. Apart from china, glassware, cutlery and linens, there were also rugs, fridges, gas cooker (stove), a new kitchen sink and washing machine. The memory of this makes me smile up to this day. The fridge and stove she could understand, but a washing machine? It was 1969 and here I was giving my mother a washing machine. Did I really expect my mother to accept a washing machine? Yes! Did she ever use it? NO! She said to me "you can sell it or give it away, whatever you care to do with it, 'cause I'm not going use it;

that would never be able to wash my clothes clean." Mammy meant what she said and I eventually gave it away. I must state here that by 1969 Mammy had developed what was known then as a peddling shop from home. Apart from her bread, she sold crackers, homemade pepper sauce, matches, cigarettes and kerosene oil, just to name a few.

A juking board was a staple in every Barbadian household. It was made from wood and would have carved ridges on it. The person doing the wash had a big galvanised wash pan where the clothes were soaked, then blue soap was rubbed against the garment being washed. The wet garment was then rubbed vigorously up and down the juking board until the washer it satisfied that it was clean enough to be dropped into the rinse bucket. This process was not as easy as it sounded; we must remember that in those days people worked harder, therefore clothes were much more soiled. Also, there was nothing to 'spot treat' clothes to remove stains. The only stain remover was the person standing or sitting in front of that juking board, putting in the muscle and elbow-grease. The bottom line to this is that my mother continued to wash clothes her way and stayed satisfied in her soul that she was doing a better job than the washing machine.

That same night, my first night in seven years on Bajan soil, at about ten o'clock I found myself at Ruby's tray. After going home, this was my first stop. Ruby was a street vendor who fried fish served with a slice of sweet potato or breadfruit. She had not seen me for several years and was so surprised and delighted that she didn't charge me for my dinner that night.

I noticed that Mammy's house needed some repairs and decided to do as much as I could. I'd done some of the repairs before going to England and, during the seven years I was away in London, I'd sent her money. I subsequently discovered that my mother had managed to save over $400 out of the money I had sent. But Mammy didn't save it in a bank; she didn't trust them with her son's hard earned money. I want you to imagine how Mammy had this money secured. She had it wrapped in several pieces of paper, pushed into a ballerina slipper, stuffed into a cardboard shoe box and then she had the box hidden under her bed. Feeling now she could relieve herself of the burden of keeping that money safe, she returned it to me.

I was determined to help in any way I could and when I saw her sacrifice I felt that the best way to use this money would be to make the necessary repairs to the house. I just hoped that she wouldn't refuse my help, and give the money to someone else. When I was nineteen I had taken out a life insurance policy and was able to use a loan secured against that policy to finance the repair the house. Of course, it took longer than four weeks but, as I'd already handed in my notice at the Royal Mint, I did not have a job to return to. However long it took, I was determined not to leave until the repairs were as close to completion as possible. But I knew that my time was limited so I set forth in earnest to get as much completed as possible.

Mammy was still bathing in the yard and we still had an outhouse. I felt she should have a proper bathroom and I would incorporate a tub. Unlike the washing machine, I believed that Mammy would use the bathtub as it would be more convenient.

As I mentioned in a previous chapter, Mammy's house had been moved to rented land, so I should have asked the landlord's permission before I built the bathroom. But I did not. I saw the need and I did what I had to do to get my mother a proper kitchen and bathroom. But I *would* need the landlord's permission to sink a well, as the land wasn't ours. But I'm not sure now if I waited for it, as time was against me. My one certainty was, I need to build this bathroom for Mammy. Plus, somewhere in the back of my mind, I felt that Mammy had been on the land so long, there would be no reason why she shouldn't have this very necessary thing.

Whilst in Barbados I wanted to continue expanding my Black consciousness, and I was very fortunate to meet group of conscious young people. I say 'fortunate' because we were in 1960s Barbados, where the white man still very much ruled. We met on Saturdays at a little bar and restaurant called the Fish Net located in Tudor Street in St Michael. We would meet on Saturdays and during these meetings we would try to put the world to rights and exchange ideas.

Three Sundays after my return in 1959, Mammy was on her way to church and, at the time, I was still lying in bed. She felt annoyed that after three Sundays, I made no attempt to go to church with her. "Do you go to church in England?" she asked me. "No," I replied. "Did I bring you up in church?" she asked. "Yes" was my answer. "Have you rejected God?" "No," was my reply. "Then tell me why you don't go to church?" My answers were many and fast. I told her that many of our ancestors did not arrive on the shores of Barbados as Christians in the way that people of Barbados accepted and practiced Christianity.

In the best way that I could explain, in a language she could understand, I went on to outline the role that black people had played in the Bible that was never talked about nor preached in the churches. I reminded her that all the overseers and superintendents of the New Testament Church of God (her church) were given to the church goers by people in the southern states of America, who whilst in America didn't care much for the black people in their churches. I reminded her that Pastor Marcus Prettijohn, one of her former pastors, was castigated by some members of the church because he dared to ask if the black people in Barbados were not good enough to be pastors and overseers.

I knew that the memory of that incident would have struck a chord and she argued that, in the late fifties, Pastor Prettijohn was right to ask such a question. For whatever reason, I am unsure, her interrogation stopped with the words, "I have taught all of you the way, if you all now are men and choose your own way, I cannot be responsible."

I knew how much my presence in church meant to her, so the following Sunday I went to church with Mammy. This was also a good experience for me; being in church and hearing the congregation congratulating her and welcoming me back into the fold. I could see the joy in Mammy's eyes as everyone greeted us. That alone made me happy as it took nothing out of me to go to church for her benefit. I was confident that my actions meant that Mammy would get a few more stars in her crown and I was very happy to do that for her.

Continuing on my path of conscious awakening, I made a move that my mother would (and did!) call foolishness. But by this time I believed myself to be man enough to ignore her threat of beating me "til the ambulance come and turn 'round". Mass demonstrations were being held on a daily basis on the twin-island state of Trinidad and Tobago: this revolutionary spirit was very much part and parcel of my aspirations and I went to join the protests, demonstrate with trade union workers and 'revolutionaries' and show solidarity with my Brothers and Sisters.

As a result of these protests, the government imposed a dusk-to-dawn curfew, intended to ban further protest and demonstrations being led by Black power leaders and the Black population against the government. It was bad enough that the government imposed a curfew on its citizens, but it seems to have turned a blind eye to the deteriorating conditions that had caused the demonstrations in the first place. Although Trinidad and Tobago had gained independence in 1962, the promised 'benefits' had not trickled down to the wider population. As was then the practice in many other Caribbean countries, job opportunities still favoured those with fairer complexions, and further education was available only to the very bright or the wealthy. By early 1970, unemployment stood at around 12 per cent, but among young people the figure had more than doubled to 25 per cent. To add to their frustrations, Trinidad's young people had a front-row seat to global generational upheaval. There was the Sir George Williams Computer Protest in Canada. In the USA, Blacks and radical whites rose up against racism and inequality. They were able to hear and read the revolutionary rhetoric of icons like Martin Luther King Jr, Malcolm X, Che Guevara and Stokely Carmichael. There was a growing resistance to the escalation of America's war in Vietnam and mass protests against it. They knew about the often violent liberation struggles in most of Africa and Asia.

In a surprising counter-strike to the curfew, two young lieutenants, along with more than 300 troops of the 600-strong Trinidad Regiment, mutinied and seized control of the army's headquarters. Despite interventions by the Coast Guard and Venezuelan and United States armed forces, the rebels took hostages and remained in control of the barracks for ten days. Although this was against the 'grain' of being an obedient soldier, I felt proud knowing that my fellow soldiers understood the plight of their brothers and sisters. They made the decision to join forces to fight *with* instead of against them. I knew if I was a soldier and I was asked to join in the mutiny I would have, without a moment's hesitation. The leaders eventually allowed themselves to be arrested and charged with mutiny and treason. In total nearly 100 soldiers were charged with various offences and faced four courts martial. The State of Emergency lasted for six months.

By the time I left Barbados and Trinidad, the four weeks had stretched into three months. The bathroom was built and functional and I was pleased to see the transformation of Mammy's kitchen as well. I had brought in a stainless steel sink and a family member had built new kitchen cabinets. My mother had gone from a kitchen with an old kitchen sink and a kerosene oil burning stove, to a newer kitchen with a modern sink and a gas stove that she did not object to using as it was more practical, especially when she started using it to bake her bread.

FOOTNOTE

1. Tubal Uriah "Buzz" Butler (21 January 1897 – 20 February 1977), was a Grenadian-born Spiritual Baptist preacher and labour leader in Trinidad and Tobago. He is best known for leading a series of labour riots between 19 June and 6 July 1937 and for forming a series of personalist political parties (the British Empire Citizens' and Workers' Home Rule Party, the Butler Home Rule Party, and finally the Butler Party) that focused its platform on the improvement of the working class.

BOOK V

1970 – 1980
Self-Sufficiency

Adinkra symbol, Fawohodie

Freedom / Independence
Fawohodie ene obre na enam
Independence comes with its responsibilities

**Symbols of African harvest celebration
And the reward of productive and collective labour**

CHAPTER 31

Got to find a way to do for self

*Nia: a sense of purpose. Setting goals
that benefit the community*

Whilst in Barbados I had had another important task to undertake, which was to look at the piece of land I'd been paying for since my arrival in London. The land was in Atlantic Shores in Christ Church; I didn't know the lot number so I went to see the real estate agent, a man called Clyde Barrow, a retired ex-head teacher who had gone into real estate after his retirement. Barrow showed me where the plot was, and after we returned to his office I asked him who was doing the development. He told me it was a Jewish white man called Oscar Pillersdorf. Let me remind you that back then I was a hot-headed young man and, in my "wanting-to-put-the-world-right" thinking, I was concerned that very good agricultural land, land that once would have produced the food to feed us, was being chopped up by non-Barbadians and being sold off, at exorbitant prices, as 'development' land. I berated Barrow, chastising him for being a Black man selling Barbadian land for a white man. To his credit, he let me finish my 'tirade' and, when I was done raging he said: "Young man, I'll put this scenario to you. You are ranting and raging about whom I'm selling the land for. I'll give you the opportunity to do the same thing that this white man has done. There are a significant number of acres to be sold at Green Point in St Philip. Permission has been given to cut it up, divide it into house lots and to develop it. I'm almost sure that once you can raise the deposit I can get the funding for you to develop it and among you and your young colleagues who are ranting and raging, you all could be doing the same thing that other people are doing."

[Now here I need to 'jump forward' a bit, if only to tell you what eventually happened. When I returned to London, I called together a group that I had previously worked with. I wanted to discuss the possibility of raising the funds to buy and develop this land at Green Point. Some months later Barrow came to England and we held a meeting in my home (which at that time consisted of two small rooms and a pigeon-hole kitchen) Twenty-four people squeezed into that small space to discuss the venture and everyone agreed it was worthy of action. Barrow returned to Barbados; once the group had a 'follow-up' meeting to see what funds could be accumulated, Barrow would make another trip to London. About a fortnight later we had another meeting: of the twenty-four people who were present when Barrow came, only three showed up. To say that I was extremely disappointed would be an understatement; however, I was encouraged by two of the other three attendees, who felt that we should still try to see what we could do. We knew that between us we couldn't raise enough money to do the development, but we would have to embark on some business project.]

After my 'revolutionary activities' in Trinidad, I returned to England. I returned the same way I went; by boat, but this time the trip took twenty-one days. I didn't mind as I had a lot of time to think and a lot of things to think about. I was convinced that the way forward for Black people wasn't just political. Up until that point I'd been involved in political activism, and with a limited mind-set I felt that if we could solve our political problems, we would have done very well. But I came to realise that, as a people, we *need* to be TOTALLY self-sufficient. We *need* to be able to feed ourselves. We *need* to be able to supply our needs. Most importantly, we *need* to be able to *defend* ourselves, aggressively if need be. Overall, we need to 'do' for ourselves; this was an essential and integral part of the liberation struggle. Hard work. Determination. Total and continuous commitment. Working assiduously in everything we have to do.

I was anxious to get on the road to doing for self or (better yet) explaining these concepts to like-minded people and seeing how many of them would come on board. I was evolving into a man who had a stronger African-centred sense of self, and without realising it I was applying one of the principles of Kwanzaa: "Nia" which means a sense of purpose and the action is to set goals that benefit the community. Kwanzaa is a week-long celebration held in the United States and in other nations of the Western African diaspora in the Americas. Although it was only about three years old at this time, it was having an impact. The celebration honours African heritage in African-American culture, and is observed from 26 December to 1 January, culminating in a feast and gift-giving. It was created by Maulana Karenga and was first celebrated in 1966-67. It has seven core principles (Nguzo Saba):

Umoja (Unity): To strive for and to maintain unity in the family, community, nation, and race.

Kujichagulia (Self-Determination): To define and name ourselves, as well as to create and speak for ourselves.

Ujima (Collective Work and Responsibility): To build and maintain our community together and make our brothers' and sisters' problems our problems and to solve them together.

Ujamaa (Cooperative Economics): To build and maintain our own stores, shops, and other businesses and to profit from them together.

Nia (Purpose): To make our collective vocation the building and developing of our community in order to restore our people to their traditional greatness.

Kuumba (Creativity): To do always as much as we can, in the way we can, in order to leave our community more beautiful and beneficial than we inherited it.

Imani (Faith): To believe with all our hearts in our people, our parents, our teachers, our leaders, and the righteousness and victory of our struggle.

CHAPTER 32

Forced into Independence

"If you think education is expensive try ignorance." AFRICAN PROVERB

For many people, when they think of independence they may think of reaching the legal age in their respective countries: in other words, they are independent and free of parental control. They can stay out late; drink as much alcohol as they want or have a smoke. For some, it might be a more nostalgic thought: for example, if they witnessed their sovereign nation achieve independence from the country that ruled over it. For these people, there would be an immense sense of pride and accomplishment if they had an active role in bringing their nation's independence. For me, however, my independence hinged on different factors; most (if not all) having to do with my arrival in England.

As I have stated before in this book, I wasn't prepared for life in Britain, on many levels. I had, and left, jobs at London Transport and the Royal Mint. My planned four-week stay in Barbados had turned into a three-month one (which included a 'revolutionary' foray into Trinidad). When I returned to London, I was unemployed but, like so many others, I still had bills to pay. So I took the first job I could get and became a factory labourer. This was out of sheer desperation as I wasn't contented doing nothing. I wasn't a labourer for very long, but the manner in which I acquired the job still makes me smile.

On my return from the Caribbean I went to the Employment Exchange to see about unemployment benefits (what was called "the dole"). I was informed that I wasn't entitled to any as I'd left my job at the Royal Mint. Even though I thought it humiliating to line up for benefits, I told the Exchange Agent (the person responsible for finding me a job) that I would take the first job she pulled out of the hat. As my luck would have it, the first job she selected was... you've guessed it... a labourer in a sweatshop! But I'd committed myself, so I took the details and presented myself at the relevant address.

I rang the bell; of course the man who answered the door said there were no vacancies. But I wasn't prepared to take no for an answer; not only because the job was so important to me but because I wanted to challenge the notion that a job wasn't available. So of course, being Collin Carter and May's Last Boy, I created a commotion. The business owner came out to see what all the fuss was. I told him that I'd been sent by the Employment Exchange to apply for a job. He gave me an application form, although after he saw my qualifications it was clear he had his doubts. But within three days I was made a storeroom keeper and in six months I had been promoted to Dispatch Manager responsible for the knitting factory. In this capacity I purchased yarn that was made into cloth; some of the cloth was made into clothing which the company then sold. As Dispatch Manager I was responsible for filling those orders. I stayed there for about a year. There was no room for further growth and, as the company was very small, there wasn't going to be a wage increase.

My journey to employment independence continued with my next job, which was as a proof-reader at Derwin Publications. The company published a quarterly document on insecticides and pesticides. I only stayed there four months: one day the office manager asked me to take a bag of mail to the post office. I told him that if I wanted to carry mail I would have worked at the Post Office. He didn't care for my answer and after that started to give me a hard time. But, true to my form of being Collin Carter and May's Last Boy, I didn't stand for any foolishness. I decided to leave before I had to show him how foolish I could be!

My next job was with the Greater London Council, where I worked as a Clerical Officer. Once again, I lasted four months. That was followed by a year working as a press operator at Gestetner, a duplicating machine manufacturer. That was my last job working for anyone. Now it was time to step away from working for someone else. Living in England, and with my increasing sense of Black-consciousness, I had to stop working for white people. I had to put all my efforts into working for Collin Leroy Carter. It was time to assert my independence.

CHAPTER 33

My foray into tertiary education

I came from an environment where people thought that the more letters (such as B.A., PhD.) you had after your name, the more intelligent you were. In my lifetime I have met numerous people with many letters after their names, all of whom have spent decades being educated. You could be forgiven for thinking that these people should be both very brilliant and very intelligent. But I found that this was not the case. As the ole Bajan adage goes: "Book sense isn't common sense."

Even today, if you were to go for a job interview, one of the most likely questions would be: "What qualifications do you have?" It's not that I wouldn't recommend tertiary education to my offspring, but very often too much emphasis is placed on the piece of paper we call a degree, and not enough emphasis is placed on teaching people how to think outside of the proverbial box. There is not enough teaching to prepare them for the world of work and the world of living.

When I left Barbados to come to England, tertiary education and obtaining a degree was of paramount importance, not just to me, but also to many other Barbadians. When we signed up to work for London Transport we were told that we would be allowed time to go to evening classes. However, this turned out not to be the case. The first bus left the garage at 3.20 am and the last bus returned at 1.30

am. There was never a 'set shift' and so you could be working at any time between 3.20 am and 1.30 am. London Transport did not allow us any time for studies, nor would it assign you a set shift to accommodate going to evening classes.

This was one of the many reasons I left London Transport: after being told that "London Transport customers come first," I realised I needed a job with a more stable work schedule, one that would allow me to go to evening classes. With this in mind, and after leaving London Transport and the Royal Mint, I enrolled for a degree course with Morley College which was located in Westminster in South London. I thought an easy subject would be what I call 'a pen and paper' subject and so I chose Sociology. I sailed through the first year of study. In the second year, most of the syllabus revolved around the British Industrial Revolution. Don't forget, between 1963 and 1966 I had been "fired up" on a cultural level: I had experienced the racism of the British working-classes, I was a member of the Black Panther movement and considered myself a revolutionary activist and all that went with it in those days. So I was well aware of both the birth and the history of the British Industrial Revolution but, as I read through the syllabus, I saw no mention of the trans-Atlantic Slave Trade.

I told my principal lecturer that the syllabus was incomplete and he questioned why I thought so. I explained to him that there was no way one could write about the British Industrial Revolution and its development, but not mention the critical role that slavery had played. I pointed out to him that to start the Industrial Revolution and to sustain it, the funds had been procured through slavery; People who were scattered across plantations and worked mercilessly from sun up to sundown and, if the moon was bright, they were forced to continue working. People who did all this work for no pay, absolutely nothing, and whose only 'rewards' were to be raped, beaten, maimed and murdered. It was the billions of pounds accrued over the years from the abduction, blood, sweat, tears of millions of Black people that financed and fuelled the British Industrial Revolution.

I also told him that there was a demand on the West Coast of Africa for certain commodities such as copper-bottomed pots. British industry had to mechanise in order to meet this demand. (It's ironic that we were thought of as 'savages' but even centuries ago our Ancestors know the benefits of cooking with copper-bottomed pots, which are so expensively popular today!)

I think he understood and agreed with me, but he could not voice his agreement publicly, especially not after giving the class a syllabus in which I had scathingly detailed such an obvious and glaring omission. His reply to me was: "When you get a PhD you can write down what you like. But if you submit any essays with any mention of the slave trade, or any essays that do not conform to the syllabus, I will fail you."

I told him in no uncertain terms (and in my own unique way!) that I didn't think that the degree was important enough for me to study for three years *knowing* that whatever I was being taught and studying was fictitious and false. With that, I packed my books into my bag, bade them all farewell and left the class.

From that day to this, I never again saw the need for structured, tertiary education. What I have always felt (and this is a personal belief) was that there was a greater need for me to educate myself. I embarked on that programme of self-education. Part of that self-education also meant that I had to de-educate myself. Retrospectively, I came to realise that a lot of the things I was taught at school and/or Sunday School did not make sense. A lot of the 'teaching' was done through the prejudiced views and perceptions of a people who were alien to Africans, who had no concept or recognition of the contributions that Black people had made to the development of human civilisation. Once that process was complete, I then had to re-educate myself and discover the true stories of my Ancestors.

CHAPTER 34

Getting started: Forging ahead and starting over... and over

To try and to fail is not laziness AFRICAN PROVERB

My foray into business began with my growth as a Black conscious man who now had a better idea as to why we, as a people, had to 'do' for ourselves. I realised that we, as a people, had to look inwardly and see how we can supply all of our needs. Those were the ideas that occupied most of my mind on the way back to London after leaving Trinidad. I also recognised that a lot of our problems were economic ones. In other words, we needed to supply our needs in every sphere. We wear clothes so we need be our own designers and manufacturers. We need to own the clothing factories. We eat food so we need to be the planters and producers of the food we eat. We live in houses, drive cars: whatever we used, we need to be able to supply these things for ourselves. This has to be a long-term plan for some semblance of true independence and liberation. That was the motivating factor.

With all of this in mind, I was still unsure as to what I would do or where I would go, but one thing was certain: I intended to create a job for myself rather than being dependent on anyone for creating a job for me. That motivation, that burning desire, was the driving force behind both my accomplishments and my failures. As a result of unstinting hard work, determination and some failures, I now own a number of relatively profitable businesses. To some people, the things I own and the things I am financial able to do, makes me a 'success'. But to me, success means one thing and one thing only: being able not only to dream but to bring that dream into realisation. My dream was that I would work for myself, create a job (and ultimately a business) for myself and, if at all possible, create one or more for someone else as well. The fact that I have managed to achieve this is my success.

By this time, my personal affairs can best be described as 'turbulent'. Between 1964 and 1966 I had had the first of my three children: my first daughter Josie and son Leroy with my then-partner Noreen. My second daughter Kay was born in 1965 and her mother Joan and I got married in 1966. The marriage ended in divorce; during my separation from Joan I fathered another son, Collin Jr, with my partner Misca. My present wife Ethlyn (Lynne) and I have a daughter Abenyamekye (Abe).

There are those who might say: "He thinks he's successful in business but he wasn't successful in his relationships. He wasn't successful in raising his children; he wasn't successful in being a good father to them, so how successful a human being was he?" I'm stating what *I* consider to be a success. That is what I perceived and what I intended. How are you going to tell me I wasn't a successful father? My response will be: "I never said I was." How are you going to tell me I wasn't successful in my relationships? Again, my answer will be: "I never said I was." When they say: "You weren't a success as a husband." again I will ask: "Show me where I said I was."

Some time back I read a quote along the lines of: "People will ask a successful person how they became a success, but no one will ask a failure how they became a failure." The implication is that it would make no sense to ask a perceived failure how he/she failed, as no one wants to follow that path. I found that to be profound and I think both questions should be asked. You can stand to learn from both, as one will perhaps teach you what to do whilst the other will teach you what not to do.

I have been asked many times: "Collin/Mr Carter how did you manage to do..." My answer is never a short one, as I make it clear to the person asking the question that I've experience both successes and failures. In fact, it was some of my failures that taught me the biggest lessons, and it was those lessons that drove me to stay focused on accomplishing my dream. I devised what I call the STAR approach to success. STAR is an acronym:

S SEE that thing you desire/need to accomplish.
T THINK of the best fit/approach to acquiring what you desire/need to accomplish.
A APPLY sound judgment.
R REASON with yourself through internal discussion/dialogue to live with your STAR decision.

Then, STAR. And STAR again! Do this continually until it is second nature. STAR!

CHAPTER 35

Friendship and business: Not always a good mix

"If you wish you move mountain tomorrow,
you must start by lifting stones today."
AFRICAN PROVERB

Between 1970 and 1971 three of my colleagues and I decided that we would embark on a business venture. These were the three colleagues who attended the follow-up meeting for the unsuccessful Clyde Barrow/Green Point development plan. As I've said, we couldn't raise enough money to do the development, but we had to embark on some business project. It was during this time that I met MacDonald Stanley and, based on our business determination, he was able to advise us on a number of subjects, such as the formation of companies and things that we would need to do.

As we were Bajans, we decided to base the business in our home country. The company we formed was called ECCY Limited (ExCee). ECCY stood for the surnames of the company directors: Elder, Carter, Callender and Yearwood.

But the primary reason for forming ECCY was to design and produce calcium silicate blocks. In our estimation, since no one else in Barbados was producing these blocks, we would have a niche market and therefore success. We discovered it would be most cost-effective to produce these blocks in Barbados; it wasn't going to be easy but it was still very doable. Once we sourced the machinery in London, we then had to confer with a manufacturer who would be willing to produce the machines for us. One of the main ingredients in the blocks was sand. Barbados produced the right type of sand for this venture we had in mind; so we started there.

This block would primarily use sand and white lime to make a building component, since the main (and the most costly) ingredient in the manufacture of a concrete block was cement which, at the time, we were not manufacturing in Barbados. We felt that this would have been a better product than the concrete block, especially since the materials would be sourced locally.

Getting these blocks manufactured in Barbados meant I had to get stone and sand to London, then get it to the machine manufacturer who would make these blocks. The manufacturer explained in detail the process that would be employed. They would burn the stones so to dehydrate them; they would then be turned into powder which would produce white lime. This white lime is similar to that found in kettles. This combination of lime, sand and water would be passed through an autoclave, pressed together then moulded into a block which would then be used for building.

The plant and equipment for manufacturing these blocks was very costly (about £150,000) so in order to finance the venture we 'segued' into a number of smaller 'offshoot' business ventures, in Barbados. We established a trading, wholesale and retail business and set up an office to produce technical and architectural drawings. We sold stationary and provided photocopying services. We also opened a driving school. We shipped a car to the island and fitted it with dual controls. One of the group members volunteered to go to Barbados to run the driving school business, another volunteered to give driving lessons. Things were looking positive and within eighteen months we had added three cars to our driving school.

Within eighteen months the businesses of ECCY Limited had failed. The biggest factor contributing to its demise was the lack of concentrated attention on *all* parts of the business. When the company was formed we were cognisant that all the company's managing body lived in London, so we saw the need to assign an individual to be the figure-head/manager in our absence. Two of the partners volunteered to go to Barbados, one to teach driving lessons and another to run the driving school and other businesses. Unfortunately (and without informing the rest of us), the director who was managing the businesses made an 'executive decision' to hand over the management to someone else. That individual had no managerial skills nor the level of interest the business needed and required.

It wasn't long before word reached me in London that there were some very shady business practices going on at ECCY Barbados. I was hearing allegations that the driving instructors were using the cars to do their own private lessons and pocketing all the proceeds. Nothing was going through the company books. The onus was on me to go to Barbados as I was, de facto, the Senior Director, so I went post haste. I conducted an investigation and discovered that the allegations were indeed correct. ECCY Limited was being defrauded. We restricted the business with new staff and tried to have a greater hand in all the business dealings but that was very difficult to do, Within three or four months of 'restructuring', the business in Barbados collapsed. We accepted this setback but we were still very keen to get things going with our calcium-blocks idea. Our next business venture was a freight-forwarding company, also based in London.

The freight-forwarding company was my first foray into the self-employment arena. As is my nature, I jumped in with both feet and hit the ground running. I was pouring myself into this venture because I wanted to see it become a success – after all the development and production of those blocks were dependent on it. Unfortunately, within two and a half years of ECCY's formation we had to initiate winding up procedures. There were various personality clashes, which resulted in strains on both me and the business. Shortly before the winding-up proceedings were concluded,

After the failure of ECCY, I decided to purchase and start my own business: Jetload Trading Limited, a shipping and freight forwarding company. I started the company with a limited knowledge of shipping and freight forwarding and whilst still being employed by Gestetner Limited. I was trying to run it part-time and it became evident that I couldn't run a successful business this way. I also thought that the guarantee of wages being handed to me every Friday would cause my focus to be divided. Jetload would suffer and perhaps ultimately go the way of ECCY. So I resigned from that job and committed myself to the full-time running of Jetload Limited.

The company was based in my home; by this time I was married so it was not an ideal situation. My wife, Joan, worked nights which meant that she slept during the day. At least she tried to, but the constant ringing of the telephones disrupted her sleep. She complained about the physical hardship this was causing her, but at the time I had no other alternative but to run the business from home. In an attempt to enhance marital harmony and lessen disruption, I tried to limit the number of calls. However, this didn't help and over time the situation got worse. I had no choice but to move the business out of the marital home.

My dear friend, Arif Ali, came to my aid. At the time, he ran *West Indian World*, a weekly African-Caribbean newspaper. Arif allowed me to operate from a corner of his office until I was able to get space to rent. He then offered further assistance by offering to place ads for Jetload in the newspaper. Instead of clients calling my home, Arif would provide the newspaper's number where clients could call and leave messages. I was still not wholly self-sufficient and so worked wherever I could find work, but in the evenings I would go to the office and return all calls.

It was during this time that I became involved in the UK Caribbean Chamber of Commerce (henceforth called the "Chamber"). I got involved with the organisation through Russell Pierre, who at that time was the Deputy Editor at *West Indian World*. He was a member and had asked me on several occasions to join the Chamber but I wasn't interested. He ignored my protestations, filled in an application form for the Chamber, signed my name to the form and paid my joining fee. So, by this 'fait accompli' I became a member of the organisation.

At the first meeting I attended of the Chamber, I was critical of the manner in which the organisation was handling their finances. When the Treasurer presented the financial report, the membership ripped it (and him!) to shreds. I suggested that, whatever the cost, the membership should pay to have the finances properly audited. This would not only be an impartial process but it would also erase any suspicion that the Treasurer was in any way dishonest. In my opinion, too often there is the suggestion/belief that if a Black man handles 10p, he will keep 5p for himself. Our development in whatever we do is so fragile that we need to look at these pitfalls and put checks and balances in place to hold the organisation together.

Soon after I spoke and my recommendation was taken on board, the Chamber held its General Election and I was asked to stand for office. I felt that I had to put my effort where my mouth was, so I stood and was elected Secretary of the Chamber. The organisation had no 'official space', indeed we were not in a financial position to rent a space, so I ran the organisation from whichever premises I was operating my businesses from.

Whilst I greatly appreciated Arif's assistance in letting my business operate out of the offices of *West Indian World*, I needed more space for business storage and my paperwork. I found another premises at 144 Stoke Newington Church Street and shared it with a man who was also just setting up in business. We had been sharing these premises for about eighteen months to two years; I was responsible for the premises but he was doing a lot more business than I was. I had a period of financial difficulty when I could not pay the rates (rent); he suggested that if I couldn't pay the rates/rent I should transfer the responsibility of the property to him and let him rent it. So I took him to the landlord and did that. After it was finalised and he was the one now responsible for the office, I asked him if he could extend to me the same courtesy I had extended, in that he would give me business accommodation in the same way I had done for him. His reply was that the space was not big enough for the two of us, so I was forced to leave.

Whilst vacating the office premises a friend of mine introduced me to a man who was moving to America and needed his personal effects shipped. I met with him and gave him a quote for the contents of his three-bedroom accommodation. He was satisfied with the quote and gave me the business. On visiting him on another occasion, I asked him about the flat he was leaving; he told me he had lived there for thirty years but didn't own it. He was what was called a 'Controlled Tenant'[1]. The landlord was a company based outside London. I asked him if, when he relocated to America, I could move in to the property and continue to pay the rent in his name; he said yes. Everything was set for me to move into the flat. Before he emigrated I visited him again and, during this conversation, he asked me about the friend who had initially referred me. He asked me if I considered the man to be my friend and I said that I did. He replied: "I don't think so." I asked why he would say that and he said, "I told him (calling the man by name) that I was letting you have the flat after I move out. He asked if I were charging you and I told him no. He then said that he didn't see any reason why we shouldn't both make some money out of it; he had a friend who was willing to pay handsomely for the flat and he could bring the friend around."

After he told me that, I asked him what he would like as compensation for the flat. He quoted me a price, I negotiated, we agreed on a sum and I moved in. My friend (the one who had referred me) died and I never told him that I knew he'd tried to double-cross me. As soon as I moved into the flat I started running Jetload from the premises. Both legally and illegally at the same time: I had 'balls': running my business from a property for which I had no tenure. Not only that, but I was an illegal tenant that was bold enough to sub-let to two other persons! The combined rent they were paying me paid for the whole apartment, so I was effectively living rent-free. Say what you will but a dollar (in this case a pound) is a dollar. Since this was a controlled rental unit the rent was very low, so my 'tenants' were quite happy. It was nowhere close to what the market rate demanded for the space.

By this time, my marriage had all but ended and I had moved out of the marital home. The flat was no different to the one in which I had the business and the circumstances were the same. I was in possession of two flats, neither of which was legally mine. With my current flat, I was sharing with another lodger and he was helping me with the rent.

But this 'arrangement' came to a sudden halt. I had gone to Barbados and while I was there the 'lodger' moved his entire family in to the flat! That meant that when I returned from Barbados I had to move. So I moved into the space from where I was running Jetload Trading. It was a tight squeeze, because I was also accommodating the two other tenants as well as the Chamber.

Everything was going very well until the agent for the first landlord's property came on site. They owned a number of properties on the block, a number of which were vacant, so they came to inspect them. Because of the relationship they had with the previous tenant, they rang the doorbell assuming that he would answer. Don't forget, that I was not only illegally occupying their property, but sub-letting without their knowledge. I was not in the office, but my assistant answered the door. When they asked for the previous tenant by name, she replied that there was no one by that name there. The agents asked if they could enter the property and she allowed them in. When they entered they saw that the flat was being used as a commercial property, so they asked her to get me to call them as soon as I could.

When I called, they asked me to explain the situation. I told them that the tenant had gone away for six months and had left me to look after the flat. They asked me when he was expected back and, always being a quick thinker, I said: "He's been away four weeks now and should be back in about five months." I doubt that they believed me, but they 'played along' and said that they would wait for five months before returning to speak to the original tenant. Of course he wasn't coming back, so they gave me another three months grace. They asked me to get the original tenant to write to them, but of course that wasn't possible. I was eventually given two months to vacate the premises with the warning that, if I hadn't left by then, they were going to take me to court to regain possession of the property.

A BUILDING FOR JETLOAD TRADING

Once again, I had to look for somewhere to rent from which to operate Jetload Trading. In my search I discovered that the rents were astronomical. I turned to a realtor/estate agent and asked what it would cost for me to buy a place and how much the mortgage would be, assuming that I could get one. I discovered that there was a thirty-three percent difference between what people were asking for rent, and what the mortgage repayment would be. The realtor then suggested that I consider buying a place: they had a place that was in bad condition that I could buy at a reduced price cheap. I considered that option and went to view the property. The realtor was right: it WAS in a bad state, but this didn't concern me too much. As its owner, in time I could get it repaired.

The next step was to approach the bank to see if they would give me a mortgage. The bank manager refused. I told him that I knew he would do so. He then said to me: "If you knew I was going to tell you no, why did you come?" I replied: "I came because I wear two hats. I'm not only the owner of Jetload Trading, I'm also the Secretary of the UK Caribbean Chamber of Commerce. We've just done a survey which showed that bank managers are unsympathetic in lending to Black people in business. We've taken this report to the Home Office Elect Committee and I've given evidence to that effect." I then showed him copies of the correspondence between the Home Office and myself as secretary. He somehow had a change of heart and decided he would, after all, give me the mortgage. But in order to get the mortgage I would have to use my domestic property (i.e. my marital home) as collateral.

Here, I was once again, looking at acquiring a property. "Not to worry", I told myself (this is my own personal mantra). I approached this acquisition in the same way as I'd approached buying my domestic (marital) property occupied with my wife. And I was in possession of another property: in addition to the land I had bought in Christ Church, Barbados, I had also bought a house in St James. Neither property was easy to acquire. Buying the St James property came about by what I can only call 'happenstance'.

I was still married at this time; on a visit to Barbados I became aware that a company called East Caribbean was developing properties and these was being handled by a company called Ideal Homes. The properties that were being built were lower and middle income houses. I was interested in buying one so I made an enquiry and was told that I would need 500 Barbadian dollars as a deposit to secure a mortgage. I had a few dollars with me but not enough to make up the deposit, so I borrowed the rest from a friend. I was then told that it would be six months before the house would be ready; on my return to London I borrowed £1,000 (at that time it was the equivalent of 5,000 Barbadian dollars. By the time I was told that the house was ready and that 10 per cent of the purchase price would be needed, I had the money.

I had made the application for two loans on the same day because I knew I would be asked if I had any loans outstanding or if I owed any finance companies. By applying for the loans on the same day, I could honestly answer truthfully: no. When both banks made inquiries they would have found I was telling the truth.

Once I got the house in Barbados I decided to let the property to holiday makers/tourists. This would produce a much greater rental income than if I had let it to one or two families. I had every intention of renting the place furnished but was short on funds to acquire the furniture. So, I came up with what I thought was a bright idea. I would ship the London household furniture to the rental house in Barbados.

As I mentioned previously, my wife worked nights, so I was able to pack up the furniture with no fuss. However, it was a different story when my wife came home in the morning and found the furniture was gone. She was absolutely livid. She didn't see it as I did – that the furniture was going from one home to another. She thought I was the most ignorant and crazy person ever and asked me how I could do such an outrageous thing. Despite her losing her temper with me, the gamble paid off.

About a year after this incident, the people who lived in the flat above bought a place of their own and moved out. I asked the landlord if he would sell me the flat they were vacating, as it had four rooms. You will probably think I was crazy because I'd just taken out a mortgage for the house in Barbados.

When the landlord went to inspect the vacant flat, the former tenants had left it in a bad state. He then looked at my flat and when he saw how much money I'd spent on his property to make my flat more like a home he was very impressed. He told me to give him a few days to think about it and he would be back in touch with me. Within a week he got back to me and he said that the property I was living in was worth about £7,000 but that he would sell it to me for £6,000.

I thought to myself: "I've got to get this building." I needed £700 or so as a deposit; the rest would be mortgaged. I had a friend who was running a small credit union. I explained my dilemma; he suggested that I deposit £100 into the credit union and on the back of that deposit he would lend me £400. I did this and I managed to raise the rest of the deposit. The credit union duly issued its cheque, which I deposited and then wrote a cheque to the solicitor. My cheque got to the bank before the credit union's cheque had cleared. The solicitor wrote to me, informing me that my cheque had been returned and suggested that it should be re-deposited. This letter was sent to my (marital) home and, as it was addressed to Mr and Mrs Carter, my wife Joan opened it. She was unaware that I was seeking to purchase the house and was less than enthusiastic; she saw it as another one of my foolhardy ventures into which she did not want to be drawn. She was even less optimistic as she was now holding a letter which indicated that the same cheque I had written to acquire the property had bounced. I listened to her concerns but forged ahead nonetheless. Within a week the cheque had cleared and I was on my way. I now had two properties under my belt. I also had to find money for two mortgages.

While working on establishing Jetload Trading I was involved in many organisations: In addition to the UK Caribbean Chamber of Commerce, I was also involved in the Hackney and Tower Hamlets Chambers of Commerce: Hackney was the borough in which I lived and Tower Hamlets is a neighbouring borough. The HTHCCC was primarily an all-white organisation. I was also an Executive Member of the Newlon Housing Trust Association, which provided accommodations for working class people. I gave all of these organisations as much of my time and undivided attention as possible.

So here was I, a husband and father, doing a lot of community work and trying to run a business. Under the circumstances, I was sharing my life with everything and everybody. You can't do this and *not* have your family/personal family not suffer to some degree. Mine did, and by the time all of this culminated, Joan and I had separated. Our daughter Kay remained with her; I left the marital home and, once again, was looking for someplace to live.

Success never comes easily and there are many pitfalls, especially when the business is owned by a Caribbean or African person: then those problems are compounded. You have problems with your friends, who are working standard-hours jobs whereas you are working any and all hours of the day and night. Your family and your relationships with them will suffer because sacrifices have to be made: for example, you may have to miss celebrations or important social events.

Another major demand will be access to finance or the lack thereof. There will be demands from your client base: your friends will likely demand "friends and family" discounts without wanting to pay. People will make demands on your business that they would not ask of a white business and, should you get it wrong, you are castigated and are likely to hear: "I will never again do business with a Black business."

In the meantime, my situation as a 'sub-letter' had not gone away. The landlord's agents had instigated court proceedings against me. I had two choices that could, at best, be sized up to pride or foolishness. On the pride side, l could decide to go to court and somehow try to convince a judge that I didn't know that the original tenant sub-letting the flat to me, and my further sub-letting the flat was illegal, or I could face facts and recognise that to make this gesture was akin to foolishness. As we say in Barbados, you can't be wrong and strong. Not only was I wrong, but I didn't have a legal leg to stand on. Recognising the futility of going to engaging in a court battle over something that wasn't mine, I decided to focus my energies on acquiring a new property – something that would be wholly mine.

MABLE CARTER HOUSE

By the time the case came to court I had acquired the property the realtor and I had discussed at 99 Stoke Newington Church Street (where my main businesses are located today). The realtor was not lying: at that time the property could best be described as 'derelict'. I called on a friend who was in the building trade and asked him to give me a quote on how much it would cost to repair. After he had looked at the property he said: "All I can tell you is that it's going to cost you a lot of money." He wasn't telling me anything that I didn't already know, so I decided to call on another man I knew, who had done some work for me while I lived in the matrimonial home. At that time the toilet was in the backyard, so he built an extension to bring the bathroom into the main building. He looked at the rest of the property and asked how much money I had. I told him the truth: I had none, as I'd used all my available funds to make the deposit on the properties, plus I was paying two mortgages. I was even indebted to Jetload, as I was using money from the line of credit the shipping company had extended to me. I had also used the money that people had paid me. The shipping line threatened to withdraw my line of credit but luckily for the business (and me) work came in, so they decided against it.

My friend was sympathetic and offered a very viable solution. He said: "I saw how you worked with me when I did that little extension on your home. If you can afford the materials, the first thing we must do is keep the water out. It needs a new roof. I can only give you Saturdays and Sundays. You buy the material, work with me, we put a new roof on and when you get money you can pay me for my labour." We did that and got the roof on. During this time, the Chamber got word that a local authority grant would be awarded, which would be enough to pay the rent and employ four people. The Executive members of the Chambers then said to me: "Since you've been giving the Chambers accommodations for free, now that you have this place we will rent from you. When we get the grant we will give you a lump sum that will help you do some of the repairs."

When the funds became available I was able to make repairs to the first and second floors and the Chambers moved in. However, the ground floor took me a longer time to renovate and it was here that I wanted my offices. In the meantime I moved in and, when money became available, I made the necessary repairs.

It was around this time that I would meet and start dating Lyn, the lady who became my current wife. She understood the business challenges I faced and was willing to do whatever she could to assist me. When it was time to repair Mable Carter House, she made a personal sacrifice that enabled us to move forward. We moved into the unfinished basement, slept on the floor and I focused my energies on keeping Jetload Trading going. It was due to this collaborative effort of living in the basement and renting to the Chamber that I was able to pay off the mortgage for the property I was now calling Mable Carter House.

I maintained my links and activities with organisations like the Black Power Movement, the Hackney Black People's Association, and other associations. Notwithstanding the stresses of ending my marriage, I was directing my energies towards the growth of my business. This hard work paid off and, as the business continued to grow, I continued to make my annual pilgrimage to Barbados. I refer to those trips as 'pilgrimages' because, after 1969, I vowed that I would never again let another year go by and Barbados not feel my feet upon her shores. In addition, Mammy was getting on in age and I felt two years should be the longest I should not set my eyes on her. But I never had to wait that long as I would sometimes make it to Barbados two or three times a year. During this time and through my travels I never gave up on the idea of establishing a business in Barbados.

JESSBANKS LIMITED ACQUIRES 97 STOKE NEWINGTON CHURCH STREET

With the growth of Jetload Trading in 1981, I acquired my first commercial freehold trading company, Mable Carter House in Stoke

Newington Church Street, and later my second commercial freehold trading company.

In June 1984, I started another company called Jessbank Limited, which was for the purpose of property management. Jessbank Limited acquired its first commercial/domestic property.

FOOTNOTE

1. A controlled tenant is one who pays below market rent for a property; this rent cannot be increased by beyond a certain level.

CHAPTER 36

The U.K. Caribbean Chamber
of Commerce

Apart from becoming a father and being the first Black man in the United Kingdom to become a funeral director and own an independent funeral business, I would have to say that one of my greatest achievements, and certainly one of my greatest challenges, was becoming General Secretary of the United Kingdom Caribbean Chamber of Commerce (which for the purposes of this book I shall refer to as "the Chamber").

The organisation was formed around 1978 by a group of West Indian businessmen who saw the need for a chamber of commerce that would address the unique needs of the West Indian business community. As I mentioned previously, Russell Pierre 'encouraged' me to join the organisation, which I did in 1979. I became the General Secretary in 1980.

The Chamber had a number of major aims and objectives. Firstly, we sought to create an organisation that reflected the true makeup of the Caricom Islands; hence the principal officers were Tony Wade (Monserrat), Caudley George (Antigua), Genny Cooper (Grenada), Blair Greaves (Jamaica), Collin Carter (Barbados), Samuel Holder (Guyana) and Vernon King (Trinidad). This approach was thought necessary to demonstrate that it was possible for us to work together as one people, for the common good of all. We managed to make significant inroads with this kind of arrangement; we also expected every member to 'pull their weight' and we depended on each other financially and otherwise.

The Chamber sought to enlist the support and active help from many Caribbean people, either professionally or in business, and utilise their range of skills and experience, in order to build a viable, economic Caribbean community in the United Kingdom. We developed fundraising initiatives and felt it necessary to develop contacts that the organisation would have with our respective Caribbean governments. We liased with like-minded people and business organisations in the Caribbean, the United Kingdom, the United States and Canada and solicited their cooperation to hammer out our policies of actions.

The Chamber's membership was wide-ranging, and included: builders, travel agents, financial consultants, publishers, clothing retailers, French polishers, accountants, upholsterers, clothing manufacturers, shipping agents, community organisations, photographers, carpenters, joiners, motor mechanics and bankers.

The Chamber also wanted to provide a number of services for their membership, some of which would include:

- A business information service;
- A members classified yearly handbook;
- The provision of specialist services, such as VAT and legal advice and representation;
- The Chamber's insignia as a responsible organisation (such as ties for men and brooches for women);
- The introduction to members of potential suppliers/buyers from various parts of the world;
- A financial advice panel;
- The willingness to mediate in disputes with customers;
- The promotion of new business ventures;
- The ownership of property for the use and benefit of the members

The Chamber organised several conferences to highlight the problems faced by Black businesspersons and those desirous of becoming entrepreneurs in the United Kingdom. The Managing Committee organised plans of action and, based on those actions, we invited key people to be part of that action, to make sure that, one way or another, they knew who we were and what we wanted to do. We organised a number of Black business conferences and extended invitations to dignitaries such as Britain's then Prime Minister Margaret Thatcher, various relevant government ministers, Michael Manley (who, at the time, was Prime Minister of Jamaica), key speakers and renowned civil rights leader, Dr Jesse Jackson.

We also conducted research to highlight the problems that Black businesspersons were facing: one of the greatest problems we identified was access to capital, either for start-up businesses or the working capital necessary for the continuation and expansion of existing businesses. We felt that the difficulties faced by Black business people were unique and particular, to the extent that business persons of other races did not face these problems with the same severity. The major problems we identified were:

- Access to commercial capital from credit giving institutions;
- Trading/business premises; and
- Lack of management skills, which stems from a lack of equal access to equal employment opportunities in both public and private sector industries, and a lack of formal education in this area. However, although management skills were important, they should not be elevated to the point where they were regarded as the principal problem, because it was not as fundamental a problem as the lack of commercial capital.

In December 1980, four of the Executive Officers of the Chamber and Council of Management were invited to give sworn testimony to the House of Commons Home Affairs Select Committee. During this testimony I stated unequivocally that Barclays Bank was the 'biggest offender' when it came to denying finance to Black businesses. Let me state here that I had no personal animus to Barclays but, at that time, Barclays Bank was the last of the major banking institutions to cease doing business in South Africa. The irony is that up until 2002, Barclays Bank had a significant presence in the Caribbean and thus had a substantial African-Caribbean customer base, but we felt that Barclays only viewed this customer base as a source from which to obtain money. At no point in time did they consider returning the favour (so to speak) and lend us that money. However, when the report on our testimony to the House of Commons was released, Barclays Bank was the first of the UK banking institutions to contact us to find out how it could best redress the situation and assist us with our efforts.

As Secretary of the Chamber, I, along with Mr Pal Ganguli (who was then the outgoing Chairman of the Chamber), held discussions with Barclays to see how the lending policies of Barclays could be improved to permit West Indians increased access to its financial services. Similar meetings were held with what was then Midland Bank (now HSBC), Lloyds and National Westminster Bank (now NatWest).

Discussions were held at the highest level with the Hackney Community Relations and the Commission for Racial Equality (CRE) regarding the follow up to Mr Martin Kazuka's report, *Why So Few Black Businessmen?* It was agreed that meetings should be sought at ministerial level with the Department of Industry. As a result of this, the Chamber, in conjunction with Hackney Council and the CRE, sent a joint delegation to see John MacGregor, the then Parliamentary Under-secretary of State for Industry, to discuss with and urge him to initiate positive measures to help West Indian businessmen/women and those intending to go into business by making loans easily accessible. In view of the difficulties which West Indians faced in securing loans for business start-up/expansion from the major credit-giving institutions, the Chamber asked the Minister to consider establishing an Ethnic Minority Enterprise Loan Fund which would meet the demand left unserved. Mr MacGregor said that the Government had just launched the Business Opportunities Programme and the Loan Guarantee Scheme, which were designed to help and promote the growth of small businesses. He said anyone could apply for loan finance and, in the circumstance, it was unlikely that the Government would specifically set up a loan fund for ethnic minorities. He suggested that the scheme would be given time to see how it operated.

At the time, many small businesses created by West Indians were funded through their own meagre savings and supplemented by loans from family and friends. The Government Loans Guarantee Scheme was then being operated by the clearing banks and ICFC (Industrial and Commercial Finance Corporation), but the Chamber felt that the Scheme was neither responsive enough nor sensitive to Black business people and prospective entrepreneurs with regards to their capital needs for business start-ups or development. For example, our own research showed that many potential Black entrepreneurs who wanted to start their own businesses and needed capital of less than £5,000 would be completely excluded from benefiting from the Loans Guarantee Scheme. As a matter of fact, we discovered that knowledge of the Scheme was limited, as the banks did not even publicise the Loans Guarantee Scheme in the West Indian press (such as the West Indian World newspaper). We also discovered that oftentimes the bank managers either didn't know about the Scheme or preferred to promote their own commercial lending ahead of the Scheme.

It is true to say that after the Chamber's Evidence and Recommendation to the House of Commons Home Affairs Select Committee in December 1980, the following year (1981) was the most eventful and promising year in the history of the UK Caribbean Chamber of Commerce. This was because many initiatives were taken by the Executive Officers of the Chamber and Council of Management to publicise and promote the Chamber so as to make it known to those in authority at Central and Local Government level. This awareness campaign succeeded to the extent that a series of meetings and discussions took place between the Chamber, Greater London Council (GLC) Officers, elected Councillors and Members of Parliament.

I believe that, to that point, the Chamber was doing good work and had made a substantial number of achievements. This was the background against which the GLC agreed to give us a grant to further the exceptional work that the Chamber was doing. The first grant was in excess of £80,000: the funds were earmarked for the procurement of a building to rent and to pay for said rent and to employ full-time staff to administer an African-Caribbean business advice service.

The conditions for the procurement of the grant stipulated the following:

- The funds received from the Funding Agency should only be used for the purpose(s) for which it was earmarked;
- A member of the Funding Agency would join the Management Committee of the United Kingdom Caribbean Chamber of Commerce; and
- The Principal Officer of the United Kingdom Caribbean Chamber of Commerce would be held responsible should there be a misappropriation of any of the grant funds.

We decided that it would be unfair for only one Principal Officer to be held responsible, so three Principal Officers agreed to accept joint and individual responsibility.

I believe there is a great deal of truth in that old saying: "The road to hell is paved with good intentions." For all the sterling work that had been done by the Chamber, in my opinion the crucial error we made was in accepting the grant funding to run our affairs. What I am about to say may sound contrary, but I would strongly advise Black organisations to try as best they can to be self-funding and as financially independent as possible. I know of a number of Black organisations that were created and functioned without grants, but once they received grants from various funding agencies, within three or four years they ceased to exist. They became dependant on the grant funding and once that ceased they were unable to continue; even though they had viable organisations prior to receiving the grants. I believe this is an issue we *must* accept and take into consideration;

even though the process may be hard (and at times painful) in my experience, I think we must be as financially independent as possible. I don't think this point can be stressed enough.

The GLC capitalised on the fact that it had given us the grant; the press were informed and people in the Black community automatically assumed that we were given money to hand out to all and sundry who came up with the idea that they wanted to start a business. That concept could not have been further from the truth and trying to explain this to the persons seeking financial assistance from the Chamber was like fighting an uphill battle.

Within the Chamber of itself, there was one 'particular member' who felt that, because of his indifference, greed and a profound 'slave mentality', it would have been a good opportunity for him, personally, to appropriate the funds. Purely for this reason, he encouraged a number of people to join the Chamber. The rest of the Chamber were encouraged by the increase in membership, without knowing or realising that this new membership was all part of a plan to oust the sitting administrative committee at the upcoming general election.

To this end, the plan was successful: the Executive was voted out and this 'particular member' became the Chairman of the organisation. The first thing that he did was to demand that I hand over the cheque book of the Chamber of Commerce. As General Secretary and thus 'custodian' of the chequebook, I told him that I would not do so until the Greater London Council (GLC), who had given us two years' funding, would absolve the principal guarantors of their original obligations.

The new Chairman rejected my position and, within 48 hours, the four former Executive Board Members of the Chamber (four Principals including myself) were dragged before the law courts. An injunction was taken out to demand that the cheque book be handed over; however, the court ruled in favour of the former Executive Board. It recognised that, as we were held jointly and individually responsible for the funds, it would be right for us to retain the cheque book and administer all payments until such time as the incoming Executive had assumed the responsibility and its associated liability.

Until that time, the court ruled that the existing ousted Executive was within legal rights to continue to make payments whilst retaining custody of the cheque book.

Arrangements were made to relinquish the principal former Officers from that responsibility and all the financial documents were released to the new Executive. They were now responsible should any funds be misappropriated.

One of the first things this 'new administration' did was to create a private company with an almost identical name to the Chamber: UK Caribbean Chamber of Commerce [and Trade Limited] So people who *thought* they were dealing with the Chamber (as they knew it) were actually dealing with this new entity. This new company was VAT-registered but of course it never paid VAT. Funds were siphoned off; there was gross mis-appropriation of funds. They were subjected to investigation by Her Majesty's Customs for the non-payment of VAT; they were also investigated by the Funding Agency (GLC) for the mis-appropriation of funds.

The Principal Officers disappeared overnight. Two returned to Guyana; I know for a fact that one went back to Barbados and opened a financial services company.

That was the end of the noble organisation known as the United Kingdom Caribbean Chamber of Commerce. Now, even after nearly three decades since the shocking demise of this venerable African-Caribbean organisation, it both saddens and angers me to tell the story. But it is important for me to tell you the story, and for you to know that we are indeed capable of creating and maintaining (to a fashion) such an organisation. I would like all those who have an interest in Black development to understand, from this experience, the pitfalls they are likely to encounter in the future and the sort of pitfalls organisations have been plagued with for decades. "Post-Traumatic Slave Syndrome" (as described in Chapter 1) was a factor in the demise of the UK Chamber of Commerce then, and today, in spite of what we may think of ourselves, many people of African descent are still in the strong, tenacious grip of the Syndrome.

CHAPTER 37

African-Caribbean Funeral Services (May 1992)

As I contemplate on my journey into funeral services in the UK, what comes to mind is the old maxim: "no man is an island, entire of itself". In other words, we are ALL connected to each other, in one way or another. Our success and accomplishments, personal and otherwise, cannot take place in isolation. "Hence, I AM because WE are."

There are some things you never imagine yourself doing. If someone was to say to you, "In ten years you are going to be doing [this] or [that] ..." depending on how utterly outrageous it sounds, you may laugh or tell the person they are crazy. Well, my road to being a funeral director took such a path. It was a question posed to me by my friend Thelma Bailey and it was a simple enough question: "Mr Carter, do you ship bodies?" I believe I simply replied: "No". But Thelma was determined and sometime later she returned asking the same question. When I gave the same answer, she simply asked me another question: "Why not?"

This "why not?" became a turning point in my life and set me on a career path I would never have imagined: me, Collin Leroy Carter, a funeral director. I started to think about it and, when I couldn't come up with a good "why not", I started to formulate a plan that would lead me to a road where, if I were asked this question again, this time my answer would be "yes". After all, we Black people were losing loved ones like everyone else and, like everyone else, we should have dignity in death. There weren't any funeral homes being operated by Black people, which meant that we had to rely on other races during our time of bereavement.

At first, our journey to get this far was steeped in racial bias that betrayed all notions of our ability to be engaged in funeral services. The history of funerary, dating back at least 4,000 years, clearly shows that the art of embalming, the marking of graves with stones, pre-paid funerals and the stately and ceremonial display at funerals has not only been an integral part of African culture, but many others outside of Africa have benefited from these most ancient African contributions to human development. This is the battle we fought to be here, as we continue to make our contribution and positively impact on the lives of those in our community, whilst serving, sharing and caring.

The negative perception strengthened my resolve to build a funeral business that would not only just undertake funerals, but would also use its abilities to highlight and fight against some of the socio-cultural bias we first encountered.

For those who only know *HIStory* and for those who know *no* story the following incident testifies to OUR story which is generally unknown by us.

African festivals and mortuary rights were continuously fought for by slaves in the Caribbean. One of the biggest and most well-known fights came about in the parish of St Peter on the island of Barbados in the year 1763. It revolved around an acrimonious union between a slave master and his enslaved African mistress. As a result of this most hostile union, the African woman poisoned her master; sadly without a fatal outcome.

The woman was convicted of the attempted murder of her master and was sentenced to death by hanging. After she had been hung the slaves on the plantation, who knew the deceased very well, took her body from the legal authorities and proceeded to give her a mass African funeral. The militia was called out and, in trying to stop the funeral and recover her body, they killed twenty-four slaves. The militia took the body and buried it at sea. These acts were commonplace; many slaves were buried at sea, not as a way of honouring them, but to curtail slaves from engaging in their traditional funerary. However, the slaves on the plantation continued to give their heroine a 'mock' African funeral.

Today, we must remember that the rights we think we have, those rights that we hold so dear, were all fought for by our ancestors, who paid the ultimate price. THEY GAVE THEIR LIVES. In the words of Sir William Ewart Gladstone:

"Show me the manner in which a nation cares for its dead, and I will measure with mathematical exactness, the tender mercies of its people, their respect for the laws of the land, and their loyalty to high ideals."

On reflection, it would seem like only a decade ago that I was encouraged by Thelma Bailey to start a funeral service. At that time, it was really only a dream until I discussed my dream with Mary Embrack and Barry Birdsall. With their input, the process began to make the dream a reality.

I went to those persons I respected and 'bounced' the idea off them. Some, who were supportive of me in other business ventures, were not as supportive as I'd hoped they should or would have been. But I was not deterred. On a visit to Barbados I had a discussion with a friend of mine who was a funeral director, Owen Sealy of Belmont Funeral Home. I told Owen what I was considering. He assuaged my fears and persuaded me to look beyond the criticisms of those who had tried to discourage me from entering what they saw as a morbid line of work. Owen went a step further and told me that if I needed any assistance, advice or anything, he would be there for me.

That was it. I was even more determined to establish myself as a funeral director. As you can imagine one doesn't just get up one morning and decide that they will be a funeral director and hang a sign on a door saying, "I'm Open For Business – Bring Your Dearly Departed To Me." There is the requisite training. Now you may wonder how one goes from packing and shipping one day to being a funeral director the next. I will say this much (without providing more information that you might be ready, willing or able to accept.) The answer is really easy: Hard work. Hard work. And more hard work.

In June 1992, I started African-Caribbean Funeral Services (ACFS) and, soon after this, my very own mantra of "Hard work. Hard work. And more hard work" came back to test me. We were asked to undertake (pardon the pun!) our most nationally controversial funeral to date, the funeral of Joy Gardner.

For those of you who may be unfamiliar with the case, Joy was a forty-year-old Jamaican who had entered the UK legally on a six-month visitor's visa, but overstayed when the visa elapsed. At the time of her death, Joy was separated from her husband, living in north London with her five-year-old son and studying Media Studies at what was then the London Guildhall University (now called London Metropolitan University).

At 7.40 am on the morning of 28 July 1993, three officers from the ADG (Aliens Deportation Group, a division of the Metropolitan Police Service) along with two officers and an official from the UK Immigration Service, raided Joy's home in Crouch End, north London, with orders to "detain and remove" her and her five-year-old son for immediate deportation to Jamaica. The officers took a four-inch wide restraint belt with attached handcuffs, and leather straps and rolls of adhesive tape to restrain her thighs and ankles. Sadly, Joy's son witnessed everything. He watched the officers' attempts to place his mother in the restraint belt; Joy initially resisted these attempts and she was handcuffed and gagged. A 13-foot length of adhesive 'Elastoplast' tape was wrapped around her head.

She was unable to breathe and almost immediately suffered respiratory failure. She

Joy Gardner

was taken to the Whittington Hospital in north London. She had suffered brain damage due to asphyxia and cardiac arrest. Although she was placed on life support, she died on 1 August 1993, without regaining consciousness.

In 1995, three of the police officers involved stood trial for Gardner's manslaughter, but were acquitted. Despite continuing pressure by campaigners, no coroner's inquest or public inquiry into the circumstances of her death has been held. In February 1999, Joy Gardner's family brought a civil suit against the police for compensation.

Joy's death was extremely controversial. People demonstrated and her body was held for months before it was released for burial. Her death became a *cause célèbre* for civil rights and justice campaigners, and for the first time the public was made aware of what the Modern Law Review called "the inhumanity of the methods used routinely in the execution of deportation orders".

At the time, African-Caribbean Funeral Services was the only Black-owned funeral service in the United Kingdom, but we had to compete with a well-known white funeral home for the business. As is often the case in these situations, there were the inevitable 'hangers-on': in particular there were two high-profile individuals who, whilst being extremely vocal in their outrage at the circumstances leading to Joy's death and being 'front-and-centre' at the demonstrations, were using these events (and the pursuant publicity) to enhance their public profile and capitalise on their own personal interests. These were the people who argued that the other, more well-known, white-run funeral home should conduct Joy's funeral.

The Joy Gardner Committee was totally against this. In their minds, it was inconceivable that Joy should have died at the hands of white people and now white people were set to bury her. They felt that a Black funeral home should take care of Joy; to see her on her final journey to the Ancestors. So, although it had already been 'suggested' to the Committee which funeral home they should use, they contacted me and invited me to a meeting.

At the meeting, the Committee told me that they had been given a quote of £1,600 for Joy's funeral, and asked me what my fee would

The funeral of Joy Gardner

be. I told them that I would not make a charge. They looked at me in disbelief, and I also told them that there was no 'catch'. I said just because the funeral would cost them nothing, did not mean that it would be badly done. I said that African-Caribbean Funeral Services was a unique funeral home; at that time it was the only one of its kind in England; it was Black-owned and run. By conducting this funeral, my good name, my business and the future of my business would be at stake. But the main reason I was willing to do the funeral for free was because of the controversy. I knew that every section of the press was going to attend that funeral. I was only too aware of the high profile of the event. The exposure that African-Caribbean Funeral Services would get, especially the image of a Black funeral director conducting the funeral, was good publicity. When I had finished speaking, they agreed that I had been fair and honest in my discussions, and decided that African-Caribbean Funeral Services should take care of Joy. They agreed to pay me the £1,600 that another firm had quoted them.

The pressure to arrange and direct this funeral was overwhelming. In addition to the public furore and microscopic scrutiny surrounding

Joy's death and the role played by the authorities, I had undergone major surgery just four weeks prior to Joy's death and was recuperating after the removal of a cancerous kidney. I was told in no uncertain terms that I was in no fit physical state to direct Joy's funeral. But, as you will have gathered by now, I am not in the habit of doing as I am told.

We put a great deal of thought into Joy's funeral. Against the strongest of my physician's objections, I went ahead with the arrangements and direction. I carefully selected the pallbearers; none of the six was less than 6 feet tall. For several nights before the funeral, we rehearsed the entire event and used a weighted casket to ensure we were 'comfortable' with the process. I used my knowledge of military funerals to ensure that Joy's final journey befitted her passage to greet the Ancestors. On 17 December 1993, we buried Joy Gardner. As I predicted, the media was out in full force, as were Joy's family, friends, acquaintances and supporters. That evening, the work done by African-Caribbean Funeral Services was a feature story on the evening news of all the major TV stations. The following day, most of the broadsheets carried the story on either the front or first pages.

I have a deep commitment to the community in which we live and work, and to my race as a whole. As I reflect on the 25 years of African-Caribbean Funeral Services in the United Kingdom, I am proud of the contributions I have made to the cultural funeral landscape not only in the UK but also in Ghana, West Africa, Jamaica and my native Barbados.

FOOTNOTES

1. Source: https://en.wikipedia.org/wiki/Death_of_Joy_Gardner;
2. Source:https://www.theguardian.com/celldeaths/article/ 0,2763,195387,00.html. (Author: Heather Mills, Sunday 7 March 1999
3. Source: http://www.blackpresence.co.uk/the-joy-gardner-death/

CHAPTER 38

When days stretch into years

"We should talk while we are still alive."
KENYAN PROVERB

For a number of years Mammy had complained about what she referred to as, "the burning stomach." When it started getting worse she automatically assumed that it was ulcers. She went to the doctor and it's my feeling, given that it was thirty-eight years ago, they probably won't have shown much interest in a seemingly poor Black woman going to the doctor. So, when she said she had ulcers, the doctor would treat her for just that. The pain got worse but she never told anyone. My brother Rudolph was living with her at this time. He went home one evening at about 6.00 pm and she wasn't home. He discovered a note that she'd left saying: "If when you come home and I'm not here, I gone cross by the hospital." He assumed that she'd gone to the hospital to visit someone, but by 8.30 pm she still wasn't back. Rudolph started to wonder if she wasn't feeling well or if she had been involved in some sort of accident and was now in the emergency ward, so he went to the hospital. When he inquired, he was told that she was indeed and told him which ward she was on. They allowed him on to the ward and when he saw her he asked: "What's the matter? What's gone wrong?" What happened? Why are you here?" She replied: "This stomach thing was getting worse so I decided to come to hospital to speak to the doctor. The doctor says he might have to operate. They are going to operate tomorrow. It's going to be alright so you don't have to tell Collin. If you tell him then he's going to be down here in a hurry. If you want to tell him, then tell him when I come out of the hospital."

When he got back home from the hospital it was almost midnight in Barbados (5.00 am or 6.00 am in London) He phoned me and when I answered he said: "Mammy is in the hospital." I asked: "What's wrong with her?" He gave me the story and he further explained that she'd instructed him not to tell me. I told him that it was OK and to call me every evening and let me know what's happening. He agreed. When I went to work that morning (I believe it was a Tuesday,) the first thing I did was to book a flight to Barbados scheduled to leave that Saturday. I continued speaking with Rudolph each day, but I never told him that I was coming home. I spoke with him the Friday night and told him that I'd speak with him the following (Saturday) evening, but by that time, I knew I'd be in Barbados.

When I arrived home in Barbados, I got a taxi and told the driver to take me straight to the hospital. On the way to the hospital I thought: "Here I am with a big suitcase going to the hospital; am I going to ask the taxi driver to wait and if I do what am I going to do with the suitcase?" So I told the driver to take a detour and take me to the Old Lady's place, let me put the suitcase down and then take me to the hospital. Once I was done visiting Mammy I would make my way back.

When I approached the house I heard Mammy's voice, plus the voices of two of her friends. The door was open: as I entered one of her friends said: "Lord have mercy May, you know your child Collin is here?!" Mammy then looked at Rudolph and said: "What's wrong with you? Why did you tell him? I thought I told you not to tell him."

In her excitement one of her friends (known to me as Mother Moor) gave me a bear hug (as only those women that spend a lot of time in the church can do). She said, "It's Collin! Boy I just asked your mother if you know and she told me that she told Rudolph not to tell you anything 'cause you goin' be on the first flight and look! You here!"

I discovered that she'd been discharged from the hospital earlier that day. They had performed the surgery that Tuesday and on the following Monday she was scheduled to return to the hospital to have the stitches removed. I told her that I would go with her. Rudolph was prepared to go but since it would involve him taking a day off I said to him, "You go to work. I'm here now, I'll take her to the doctor."

On the following Monday, I took Mammy to the hospital to have her stitches removed. I asked to speak with the doctor in charge of her case after he'd finished treating her. I expressed how much she meant to me, so much that as soon as I got word of her situation I took the first opportunity to fly in from London to take care of her. I explained to him that Mammy told me she had the operation and she believed she had an ulcer. Here I was, standing in front of the doctor who performed the procedure. "Level with me," I said, "and leave no stone unturned. What exactly is wrong with my mother?" I pleaded. The doctor said, "After performing the procedure we saw that she had cancer of the stomach. Given her age and the advancement of the tumour, we were unable to treat it."

The doctors never told Mammy she had cancer. Instead, she believed she had stomach ulcers and I never told her otherwise. The reality of Mammy having cancer set in. I asked the doctor how long Mammy had with us, to which he couldn't give a definitive answer. Maybe a day, maybe a year, but he said Mammy was a strong woman and what we could do as her family is give her the tender love and care that she needed.

When I came out of the consultation with the doctor, Mammy asked me what we were discussing. I told her that I was trying to ascertain if there was a cost associated with the operation. She looked at me squarely in the eyes and said: "I thought I told you not to tell lies? You think that I'm an idiot?" She then turned to the doctor and asked: "What were you and my son discussing?" I didn't hear the doctor's response but then she said: "Both of you are liars and you think you can fool me but you all can't fool me."

Mammy lived for about two years after that day. A few weeks after surgery she went about life doing the things she had always done. Although she was old, Mammy still acted as Rudolph's 'alarm clock' waking him for work every morning. She retained her faculties and only lost her 'senses' about two days before she died because by that time she was heavily sedated with morphine

If Mammy felt that she'd had ulcers, and that they'd been removed during the surgery, then psychologically it was a good thing. It wasn't till about four months before she died that the cancer started to affect her aggressively and she started going downhill. Sometimes I struggle with the fact that cancer was left to spread, untreated, over my mother's body. However, I am mindful that it was a different era: it was over thirty-six years ago and I'm not sure how many people who were diagnosed with cancer were being treated with chemotherapy or radiotherapy. Nor am I sure what technology or medicine was available. So, thinking in the context of thirty-eight years ago, I want to believe that her care, or perceived lack thereof, was simply in alignment with the times.

One day, Mammy and I were talking. She looked at me and out of the blue said: "There were times when I asked myself why did I have to get pregnant a fifth time? At that time, I already had four mouths to feed. It was during the war, you could hardly get the things you needed to cook. People had to line up, get coupons to get a pint of rice of a pound of flour. I asked myself what would I be doing with another child? There were times when I was down to my last three pairs of panties: one standing by, one on the line and the last one on my backside! But look at you today! You are a dutiful son and you have done me proud. May God richly bless you."

It was only during Mammy's latter days that I suspected that she knew it wasn't ulcers and we'd tried to tell her it was something else. She said that she'd nursed her cousin and her cousin's daughter, and she had the same symptoms that they too had exhibited. They had cancer, so therefore she figured out that she too had cancer and not ulcers. To her credit, once she knew that she didn't have ulcers, Mammy wasn't angry. I have to point out here that, even though I have a problem with 'established religion, I don't knock it: sometimes it's better to have or believe in something than nothing at all. The reason I say that is because I saw how Mammy held on to her religion in her last days. When she was experiencing excruciating pains she would say something like: "I rebuke you Satan! I rebuke you! You can take my body, do whatever you like with my body but you'll never get my soul. I'm going to be just like Job."

She had her religion and her faith, right up to the end. Before she went into the hospital she would always say: "I'm holding onto my faith and I know where I am going. When I'm gone and if you all live right, you will see me. I've brought you up and I've taught you the right way. If you all stray from it and you find yourself in hell it is not my fault, but if you live right you going to see me."

CHAPTER 39

Oh! That you would bless me indeed

The Prayer of Jabez: 1 Chronicles 4:10: "And Jabez called on the God of Israel, saying, 'Oh that you would bless me indeed, and enlarge my coast, and that your hand might be with me, and that you would keep me from evil, that it may not grieve me!' And God granted him that which he requested."

Genesis 27: 26-28 (New International Version (NIV): [26] "Then his father Isaac said to him, "Come here, my son, and kiss me." [27] So he went to him and kissed him. When Isaac caught the smell of his clothes, he blessed him and said, "Ah, the smell of my son is like the smell of a field that the Lord has blessed. [28] May God give you heaven's dew and earth's richness – an abundance of grain and new wine."

I am sure that seeing those two scripture verses (or any scripture verse) in a book by Collin Carter will garner much criticism. There will be those who will be quick to espouse, "Collin Carter is a hypocrite. I thought he didn't believe in this…"; or "he had me fool, why is he pretending in the pages of this book to be so religious?"

Well, I'll tell you. There is a reason for the two aforementioned scriptures. I am not by any means a religious man and no one who knows me would ever say that Collin Carter is a Christian or that Collin Carter is a religious man. However, what they *can* say is that Collin Carter aspires to respects people's beliefs that differ from his own, regardless of how greatly. I do not always succeed in keeping my opinions to myself, but if you know me then at least you know how I feel.

This particular narrative is a continuation of my mother's beliefs. Even though I had a difference of opinion with her as I got older, I always stayed respectful of my mother and her beliefs. As I stated some chapters back, on many a day I religiously followed my mother to church, church meetings, and camp meetings, so it is very possible that not all of what I heard went into one ear and came out the other. I may not espouse the virtues (or lack thereof) of Christianity, but that does not mean I don't know what it is. That is why I will never tease or harass a person for what they believe in. I know better. The Christian religion (in whatever guise: Catholic, Church of England) offers me no spiritual relief, but my African centric/centred spirituality comforts me in the same way as I believe that Christianity does for its followers, and in the same way that I know it did for Mammy. We both have something, something different, to hold to.

At one point during the four months when the cancer was progressing, Mammy was in her bed and called me. I knew how sick Mammy was and not going to her would never have entered my mind. I was respectful to my mother when she was young and strong (as the Bajans would say) and I saw no reason for that to change now that she was dying. When I got to her bedside she said: "Kneel down there." I did as she asked. She put her hand on my head and prayed for me. When she was done praying for me she wished me well. Then she said, "You've been a dutiful son and I pray that you would be dutifully blessed. I hope that you'll come back to Barbados and not spend all your time in England, because you've worked hard and you deserve to come back and enjoy your life. Stop working like a Joe Heath mare[1]."

It's not my intent to speculate as to why Mammy did this, I can only state the facts as they occurred. I Googled "the purpose of blessing of children" during the writing of this book, Years after my blessing I now have a better understanding why she did what she did and it is in this context that I chose the scriptures that I believe she was familiar with. It is my feeling that she was familiar with Jacob, Issac, Esau and Jabez, and she was fulfilling the work according to the scripture as she knew it.

There is an even stranger irony to all of this: at this time, all four of Mammy's living sons were living in Barbados. My three brothers were permanently ensconced and I spent about six or seven months out of the year there. Mammy would be pleased to know that 'Joe Heath's mare' had indeed slowed down.

FOOTNOTE

1. 'Joe Heath mare' is a Barbadian colloquialism that means a proverbial work horse.

CHAPTER 40

The longest wait: Waiting on Lemuel

"The heart that truly loves has not time for grudges" GHANAIAN PROVERB

Mammy was dying. She knew it, she accepted it. Like any other mother in this situation, she wanted to see her first-born son. Lemuel. What she couldn't accept was that Lemuel had not yet arrived like her other four sons. She knew that we'd sent word to him of her condition. I think what was worse for her was the wait, which seemed to stretch on longer than the eternity that she was getting ready to spend at the feet of Jesus. I had no doubt that Mammy was sure about where she would end up. It was just the wait on Lemuel that was simultaneously keeping her hands on and off the Pearly Gates. She was ready to go to her heavenly home but didn't want to leave this one without blessing her eyes on her first born.

I could see that Mammy felt for sure that he was coming. He had to be coming. How could he not? After all, in 1948 she had made the sacrifice to see him safely ensconced in Guyana. That had to have been a most difficult decision for her; well, for both of them. For her, it meant not seeing her son until God knew when and, for him, it meant leaving behind his mother, brothers, beloved Barbados and perhaps even a sweetheart. But whatever the reason behind his leaving for Guyana, Mammy was now waiting on him to do the right thing and come to her. I wanted to hear (almost as badly as Mammy, I'd venture to say) "Lemuel is here! Lemuel is here!"

The much waited announcement never came. The message sent to him was not mixed or convoluted, it was brief and to the point: "Mammy has cancer. She's dying. She wants to see you one more time. Please come." We waited in all stages of anticipation. The only thing not waiting on anyone of us was the cancer. As each day went by, it was evident that it was consuming Mammy, and with a voracious appetite. Time, of which she had so little, was ticking by. We waited right along with her for news of Lemuel and his arrival but as the days ticked by slowly it became evident that he wasn't coming. As it became clearer that the end was near, but neither he nor news of his imminent arrival came, we couldn't figure out how to tell Mammy that he wasn't coming. We didn't have to tell her. She told us: in her matter-of-fact way she said: *"I guess he in coming."*

There was no answer that we could give her. How do you tell your dying mother that the son she's holding onto life for to see isn't coming? After Mammy said that, it was apparent that she'd resigned herself to the fact that her dying eyes will not have one last opportunity to behold her first born son. Mammy stopped waiting on Lemuel. As Mammy had done so often in our lives, she spoke straight from her heart. A heart that had accepted that her first born son didn't care enough to come and let her bless her old eyes on him. When she spoke for the last time about Lemuel, she stated simply in a matter-of-fact way: "I can't wait for him [Lemuel] any longer." She shifted her focus and instead prepared herself for the time her eyes would behold her beloved King Jesus. She didn't have long to wait. She was who let us know that her entry into the Pearly Gates wouldn't be long.

One day as we were sitting in wait with her, she said that her mother Dell, her father Pappy and her sister Eudora) were standing at the foot of the bed. She knew that none of us could see the Ancestors who had come to assist her on this last leg of her journey and she told us as much. A cousin that she was very close to was in the room and asked: "What are you saying May?" She said, "I'm not dotish. You all can't see them but they are standing at the foot of the bed."

None of us said anything. She then asked when the next moon phase was. When we told her she replied: "I can't wait for him any longer. I'll leave you all within the next three days."

The following narrative might seem heartless (if not cruel), but I will say to you that unless you've witnessed a loved one writhing in pain from cancer (or any other debilitating illness), then refrain from passing judgment. I was at that place. I was watching Mammy going through the throes of agonising pain and all any of us could do, at her request, was rub her stomach with rubbing alcohol. There was nothing else we could do for her. I felt extremely helpless. It was from that place of helplessness I made the decision I did. Although Mammy wanted to stay at home and make the transitioning from her bed in her bedroom, I went against her wishes and made a decision: We had nothing at home that could help alleviate her pain and suffering. I would take her back to the hospital. My thinking was that if she was in the hospital, at least they could give her morphine. It was paining us to see her suffering as she was.

When I got Mammy to the hospital I was 'confronted' by a doctor of Indian descent. He wanted to know why I'd brought her back to the hospital since I knew what the situation was. I told him that, whilst I knew what he was saying was true, what I also knew was that they couldn't give me the morphine so I could give it to her at home. I said to him: "Since you can't give it to me, then you keep her. She's in too much pain. No one should be subjected to so much pain. If she's going to die there's no reason why she should die in excruciating pain. So you give her the morphine and I'm not taking her back home." The nurse that admitted her said to me: "Don't worry Mr Carter, we'll look after her." With that, we left her at the hospital.

Once Mammy was admitted she was kept quite heavily sedated. There have been times when I've questioned if she might not have had assistance in her transition. I say that because of the way she was always so sedated. She had very brief moments of lucidity/consciousness (about two minutes each time) when we were there. I would say: "Mammy it's me." She would put up her hand and she would hold mine and give it a good squeeze. She would hold my hand like that until she fell back into the sedated/comatose state.

I wasn't there on the last day of Mammy's life. I had some business to do in New York and, although I knew that she wouldn't last long, I felt that I could conduct my business and return to Barbados before she passed. However, she died about twelve hours after I reached New York. Word came to me that she had died at about 2.00 am. Rudolph was with her when she transitioned, but he and I have never discussed what those final hours were like. My brother, Victor, wasn't there. He left Barbados about six hours prior to her death. He was well aware that she was dying but couldn't take it. He returned to his job at British Railways and did not return to Barbados for Mammy's funeral. My brother Carl was in Barbados two weeks prior to Mammy's death but, unlike Victor, he returned for the funeral.

Since it wasn't long after Mammy had seen her ancestors when she died, I've often wondered if they returned to assist her on her final journey home. I will never know if my grandparents or my aunt returned, but one thing I know for sure: Lemuel never came. He had denied her that last wish – to set her eyes upon him before she died. It has been over thirty-six years since that day and I still remember what it felt like to wait with her for him to come, and how powerless I felt that I couldn't do this one last thing for her.

I am not sure how long I stayed angry at Lemuel or if I have ever forgiven him. He, too, has transitioned, without ever seeing any of his brothers before he closed his eyes. Rudolph, my daughter Kay and I had no prior knowledge of his illness, or that he was near death's door. But once we learned of his death, this lack of knowledge didn't stop us from attending his funeral in Guyana.

CHAPTER 41

A seat at Jesus' feet

"God never dies, therefore, I cannot die."
NYAME NNWU NA MAWU

I was glad when I received word that the end had finally come for Mammy. Not glad in a 'celebratory' sense, but glad that my prayers had been answered. During the final weeks of her life, when all we could do to help ease her agonising pain was to gently massage rubbing alcohol onto her stomach, my prayers had been that she would be taken out of her misery. I'd wanted her free of the pain, even though I realised that once she was free of the pain, she would be absent to me. I would no longer be able to talk to her, hold her hand or have her hold mine. I would never feel the weight of her hand on my head the way I did on that day she blessed me. I would not hear her occasioned laughter, nor her words of advice or correction. I was willing to accept my loss to spare her pain. My love for her was that great.

I did not allow myself to break. I accepted that Mammy had crossed over to be with the Ancestors and was now on the way to becoming one herself. I was glad that her earthly body was now released from the chains of pain that held her steadfastly anchored to earth. I was glad that Mammy was now going to reap that reward she'd worked so hard for – her chance to sit at the feet of her King Jesus.

I returned to Barbados the day after Mammy's death. The days following were busy. For a start, there was a funeral to be planned. I wasn't yet a funeral director but I knew what I wanted: a funeral that was dignified and befitting a lady of her stature. Mammy had discussed with us what she wanted so she had the funeral she'd requested, down to her burial garment. No detail was left out. Her funeral was held at the Bank Hall New Testament Church of God, her 'other home', where she had dragged me…not kicking and screaming; because I had better sense! Her blood family, church family, friends from the villages, and friends to whom she'd sold her baked goods: they all came to pay their respects and say goodbye. They followed as the cortege made its way to Westbury Cemetery where we said our final goodbye. In Barbadians terms, she had a good send off.

All through the funeral, and in the days following, I remained stoic. I was being 'strong': it's what Mammy would have wanted. I felt I had to show all that we, her sons, were the men she'd wanted us to be.

I returned to London three days later, settled into my life and returned to my routine. She would have expected that of me. I thought of Mammy often and remained stoic and 'strong' throughout. Then, one particular evening, about three months after Mammy had died, I was driving home from work. The traffic lights turned red and, as I sat there waiting for the light to turn to green, my mind strayed to thoughts of Mammy. Right there at that red traffic light my heart broke. I started to weep. It was the kind of crying that, had I done it at her funeral, I might not have been able to stop as I would have lost all composure.

When the light changed I drove home crying all the while. When I reached home I pulled up in front of my house and wept for my mother and my friend. I cried at the knowledge that although I prayed she'd be released from her pain, I now missed her so much it felt like a physical pain, a gut-wrenching ache. I was almost writhing in the same kind of pain she experienced before her release.

I stayed in the car until the flow of tears stemmed. It was quite a cathartic cry. The man that was her child had finally cried for his mother. I accepted that she'd gone on to that place she'd longed, that she was with the Ancestors but, at that moment, I was simply a son missing his mother. I was missing this woman who had been a constant and stalwart presence in my life.

Although I was mourning the loss of the 'man in our house', the best example of a man I ever knew, the man that was her child pulled himself together as she would have wanted him to do. I got on with the business of doing those things that would make her proud of me.

CHAPTER 42

Reflections on Mammy

"Return to old watering holes for more than water; friends and dreams are there to meet you."
AFRICAN PROVERB

After all these years, the more I listen to people of all ages reflect on Mable Matilda Carter, the more it helped me get a better understanding of the woman that was my mother. My friend, Annette Smith, has been invaluable in the writing and researching of this book and, as I have done since I embarked on this work, I asked her to 'interview' those persons that knew Mammy and all of her children. I had no idea whom I would speak with next; who I might meet; where I was going to meet this individual or when the interview will take place. What I found interesting and amazing was the respective individual's ability to just let Annette interview them.

More often than not, and often without forewarning, I would arrive at someone's house and say: "It's me, Collin, I have a friend with me." Annette was surprised at the ease with which I was allowed into their homes and I could tell from the expression on her face that she was pleased to be allowed to share these glimpses into a by-gone world. I had previously thought that I knew a great deal about this world but I realised that, in the telling of these stories, that there was a lot I didn't understand and I didn't have as first-hand a knowledge as I had thought.

One such visit took place with Mrs Greene. She was younger than Mammy but that did not stop them from forming a friendship that would last until Mammy's death. About two years after we moved to Deane's Village in 1948, Mrs Green moved there with her two children, a boy and a girl. There's no clear recollection on how the two met, but what was clearly evident was that once they met, a 'til-death-do-us-part' friendship was forged, and an unbreakable bond held these two women and their children together.

When Mrs Greene saw me her eyes immediately filled with memories. When I told her I was writing this book, she became very excited. She was more than happy and willing to speak of her friend Mammy. To hear her tell it, she called Mammy "Mamma Carter". Mrs Greene's daughter was also happy to join in and share her memories, not just of Mammy but of myself also. As I spoke with Mrs Greene I was transported to another place and time. Mammy was no longer gone; she was alive, vibrant and being very much Mable Matilda Carter.

My mother was an attractive woman; she wasn't very tall but she carried herself with such poise that she appeared much taller than her five foot six frame. She had what the Bajans called a 'good size'; she was glamorous and loved to dress. She was also a Lead Walker at funerals[1]; they had to have a dignified walk and good posture, carry her head with the right lilt to it and she had to have a good 'carriage'. She also had to know how to step properly and make it look easy.

It was once said that there was a local church lady who wanted to join the rank of the Lead Walkers. When the idea was brought to my mother she simply said: "I'm not going to walk with her. She doesn't know how to step." That was it, this lady's dreams were deferred and were going to stay that way as long as Mable Matilda Carter was an Official Walker. Being a Lead Walker was one of the duties Mammy undertook as part of her community and civic duties. In later years, when people no longer walked at funerals, a car was hired and, through her relationship with the hired car company, she was able to assist those persons who were not in a position to hire a car on their own. Similar to carpooling today, a sitting was arranged, and in this way the person could be present at, and have transportation to and from the funeral. Being at the cemetery/grave-side was very important, since that was the ultimate 'farewell'. You had to go and see that individual 'down'.

However, the responsibility that was most important to her would have been the one that brought food into the household and help her feed her boys. That job was being a hawker. This was not a job that could be characterised as glamorous on any level. It was hard and laborious work. It wasn't as hard as working in the cane or potato fields but it was hard. A hawker had to be physically and mentally strong and find a good spot that would have good pedestrian traffic, as this would determine how much money she made. She had to make things people liked and think up new creations. She had to be one step ahead of the game.

FOOTNOTE

1. A Lead Walker walked in front of the funeral cortege.

BOOK VI

1980 – 1990
Planning and Planting

Adinkra symbol, Akoma (The Heart)

Patience and Tolerance

CHAPTER 43

On becoming and being a father

"A family tie is like a tree, it can bend but it does not break" AFRICAN PROVERB

There are some truths that, despite your best intentions, you know deep in your heart will carry far-reaching consequences when told. Feelings may sometimes be hurt, judgments may be made and someone may feel miffed or slighted. Yet, despite this knowledge, sometimes these truths have to be told. Even now, I smile when I think of the fall-out of what I'm writing. I'm smiling because I'm seeing the young man of twenty-three years who made a decision that, once it started to germinate in his soul, couldn't be changed. At twenty-three, I decided I wanted a child. It's true that I had only been in England for about two years and there were many things I was uncertain of, but I was absolutely certain that I wanted this child.

This was my first child. After Josie, who was born in 1964, the blessings and pride continued when Kay, my second daughter, was born in 1965. In 1966 I experienced the joy of becoming a father to my son; Leroy. The three of them would remain my only children for the next fourteen years; when I became a father again it was to another son Collin, Jr. A few years later I had my final child, another daughter, Abi.

What I have not thus far stated is that my five children are with four different women. My mother had five children for five different men and I have five children with four different women. That is where the similarities end. All of my mother's children had her surname: Carter. My children do not, but as far as I'm concerned, *all* of them are Carters. I believe that if you ask any of them if they are Carters they will all say, "Yes. I am a Carter." What is fundamentally important here is the same way my mother never made a difference between my brothers and me; neither do I make one between my children. My brothers and I were not allowed to call or think of each other as 'half-brothers'. We were all Mable Carter's sons and, as so, we were 'whole' brothers.

That is how I view my children. They are not 'half' siblings. I don't know, nor can I say, how my children view themselves in relation to each other, but I can tell you that they are Collin Carter's children and to me that makes them wholly mine. My children are not as close as I would like them to be but that is something I must live with. I have to take more than a share of responsibility for their relationships being the way they are. Even though they have different mothers, I do not know if their relationships would have been different if they were raised under the same roof. I can only speculate. I can't even look to the African culture or tradition, in which my life is firmly rooted, where the man has many wives and children and he, along with his wives, co-parent the children. This is not part of our societal norm.

The circumstance surrounding my children and their parentage is what it is. However I can say that, like my mother, I favour none of my children over the other. I love all my children and they are all equal in my eyes and heart. Having said that (and having been married twice) I would be the first to say I wasn't a good father or a good husband. Don't get me wrong, being married twice (or more) does not dictate the goodness of a person by any means; it is that I don't believe that I was a good husband in either marriage. I am not sure what either of my wives would say but I have no doubt that my children will agree with this. On that score, they will get no argument from me.

However, I am now addressing my 'failures' as a father. I truly believe feeling that, when taken in its full context, some of my parenting decisions can or might be understood. I am not asking that any of my children change whatever views they now hold of me, but that all factors and circumstances be considered in arriving at their verdict.

Here is what must be understood: I was parenting from the place I knew. I am Barbadian and from a Barbados where being a strict parent was expected. A child's so-called failings or failures were not just that child's; the parents held a share of that failure. I brought that belief to my parenting approach, as well as an African-centric way of doing things.

My commitment to self-employment and empowerment in the late 1960s, demanded working assiduously most days and nights of a week. The social conditions of the time demanded that commitment from those of us who were pioneers. Judge me as an African, Barbadian and a man who tried to make a positive difference as far as our liberation is concerned. Making these decisions to be a torch-bearer for the cause, affected my ability to parent my children as I would have liked. But, because of my dedication to a cause, I failed; I accept that.

At the time, I made choices that I felt were best; if some of these choices impacted my family negatively then I take full responsibility for them. My choice to put my energies behind the business may be construed by some as selfish, but I didn't see it that way. As a Black man, I was doing what I could to raise my consciousness and the standard of living that surrounded me and my family. I wanted better. I wasn't chasing an English dream of a house and picket fence, but I was going after liberation and self-sufficiency. Part of that consciousness-raising meant being self-employed and, if being self-employed meant the end of my first marriage (and sadly enough it did) then I accepted that. Again, I take the responsibility for the decision I made that meant I wasn't around my daughter from this marriage on a daily basis.

Once I was no longer in the household, I redoubled my energies and threw myself into developing my business. I could not allow myself to lose sight of the vision, which was the liberation of my people. I had already sacrificed my marriage and family for this effort and, therefore, felt my only option was to stay the course and continue

Left to right: Leroy Robertson, Kay Carter, Collin (Junior) Radix-Carter, Kemet Robertson and Abi Lee-Carter

to focus on the uplifting of my Black consciousness and the betterment of my people.

I will also say that, despite my perceived short-comings as a father, I was determined that no child of mine would experience what I did, namely, not knowing their father. I realise that 'knowing' me was no replacement for my absence, but if putting my energies into a growing business meant that my children saw less of me, then that is something I will have to live with. In retrospect, I cannot say if I would have done it any other way. Once again, I realise that this could be perceived as selfishness but, at that time, I was a man driven. I would not accept hand-outs. I had set my sights on pulling myself up from the poverty that I had experienced as a child. I was determined to never again face my near emasculation just to gain employment. The man that I was could not see himself going through life with another person making decisions about how or what I would do to keep a roof over my head. The awakened man that I was knew this *could not be* and I would *not let it be*. It is my hope that, one day, my children will understand what drove their father to do the best he could to control his own destiny. Do I think that the sacrifice of not being more available to my children was worth it? It is for them to decide.

BOOK VII

1990 – 2000
A True Pan-Africanist

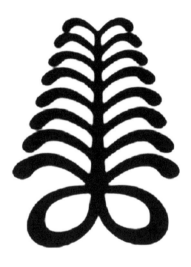

Adinkra symbol, Aya (The Fern)

Endurance / Resourcefulness

CHAPTER 44

Tears for the Ancestors

"A people without the knowledge of their past history, origin and culture is like a tree without roots." MARCUS GARVEY

There are times when people who are overcome by a particular emotion, might say that words fail them or that they simply don't know what to say. I have experienced such a feeling many times, but I want to share what was the most profound experience I have had in my 'three-score-and-ten' years. But in order to recall the experience, and to convey the enormity of its impact, I cannot afford to be 'lost for words'. I not only need words, I need the right ones, and many of them. I need to transport you, figuratively, to a place and time that defies logic or reason; a place that has been indelibly altered by circumstances and human emotions. I want to take you to what was once the hellhole of Elmina Castle in Ghana.

Whether an African was born on the continent or is a child of the African Diaspora, they should never forget the tragic hand that fate dealt to the people of that continent. The facts and the history of the enslavement and slaughter of our Ancestors by Arabs and Europeans must never be forgotten. None was spared this fate: men, women, children, babies, elders.

It is said that those who forget the past are doomed to repeat it. We must do all we can to ensure that this can never happen again. We must never forget the suffering endured by millions of our Ancestors.

Elmina Castle, above and below

I, therefore, urge everyone, whatever their colour, race or creed, to visit Elmina Castle.

From the first time you set eyes on it, a change starts to occur deep in your core. An internal, emotional reaction begins to unfold and there is nothing you can do to stop it. This feeling was among the myriad of emotions I experienced as I stood, barefoot and 'bare-soul', in the place where my Ancestors stood, or cowered, or fell,

never again to rise. They were stolen, chained, beaten, lost, afraid, desperate, some defiant, some defeated, many dying. The very essence of all these emotions has stayed with me ever since. You 'feel' Elmina Castle from the moment you enter. Wave after wave of emotions overwhelm you. The experience is haunting and you are haunted by the experience for ever more. It engulfs you and becomes part of you; and

you become part of it. It is now part of your soul.

History comes alive as it seeps into your every pore; layer upon layer of history is peeled away. You *are* an Ancestor. Their fears becomes yours. Their anxieties; their degradation; their humiliation, their anguish, their torment and pain; they all become yours. Emotions run deep, deeper than you ever thought possible. You cry. You cry some more. Then you want to cry out.

In the bowels of the castle the atmosphere is heavy, and there is a smell; it is dank; it is musty. Because your emotions are running so high, it is also the smell of loss, of sadness, of sorrow; it is the smell of pain, if there could ever be such an aroma.

From this wretched place, our Ancestors were shipped in chains across the Atlantic like cargo, or slaughtered where they stood in defiance, powerless to defend themselves against their captors.

Before the European enslavers arrived, our Ancestors' lives were full and promising. From the ordinary man or woman, to the visionary leaders, the Africans were shaping their region and, in turn, shaping their continent. But in an instant, these people were deemed as chattel; as domestic animals; good for nothing but labour; expendable; disposable; and available from an inexhaustible source.

There is an energy in this former hellhole; this castle of catastrophe; this fortress of unimaginable fear. The energy is felt in every crevice, every brick, every grain of sand.

Collin in the slave pen

Our Ancestors had no idea of the fate that awaited them. The trauma of capture was hell enough, but what was next? History gave us the answers to this and many other questions. And this is why you cry. But are we doomed to one day ask similar questions? What next for the African? What next for the African continent?

This is why Elmina Castle should be a place of pilgrimage for *every* child of Africa. And for everyone else, it should stand as a beacon of remembrance; a symbol of the depths to which humanity can sink both in the interests of commerce but, more importantly, how one race can consider itself to be superior to another. We must never forget.

I remember sitting in one of the slave dungeons at Elmina Castle and reflected on the horrors that awaited our Ancestors. They didn't know of the horrors, but I am sure they knew that nothing good awaited them. History certainly told us. It told us that after we experienced all their imagined cruelties and hardships, we are here. The fact that we are still here is a testament to our tenacity and courage to survive.

I know that as long as this body has breath I will never forget my pilgrimage there, or the sister (Christine Boyce) who invited me to come home again. A brother of Barbadian heritage had transitioned in order to take his place among the elders. He had the good fortune to be married to a sister from the Mother Land. She sought me out to ensure that he would have the funeral of their heritage. After her husband's funeral she extended the invitation for me to come home. I accepted and so a few weeks later I was flying over the vast expanse of desert known as the Sahara.

I had heard of other people's experience upon setting foot on the continent, but I wasn't prepared for the sudden and immediate impact it had on me. It's not a choice factor. You do not decide if or what you will feel. The ancestors take that away from you. The spirits of the millions and millions that went through that gate shackled and bound are still there. They are still longing for those they had to leave behind. They are longing for the freedom that was denied them. They are longing for the way of life they had before the Portuguese. It is this silent cry that engulfs you. I sincerely believe that no one leaves the way they came. I certainly didn't.

BOOK VIII

2000 – 2014
Still Pressing On

Hye wonhye
"That which cannot be burnt"

Imperishability / endurance

CHAPTER 45

Bakes and fishcakes for lunch

"If you can walk, you can dance. If you can talk, you can sing." ZIMBABWEAN PROVERB

In early March 2014, I was invited to participate in two African History programmes in two different primary schools in Barbados and of course I readily accepted. The programme entailed the children performing African dances and songs. They were joined by a cultural group which performed drumming and dancing. We, the Elders from PACO (Pan-African Coalition of Organisations), performed the libation and explained to the children the reason for so. We also sang a song and interacted with the children. Being there and interacting with the students and the teachers took me back to my days at St Giles.

I was pleased to see that most of the children were dressed in their African garments, but was curious to find out why some of the other children were not. I asked one young boy why he wasn't wearing African dress; he said it was because his grandmother had forgotten. It was at that moment that I had an inspiration: I wanted to demonstrate to all the children the importance of making more than a slight effort to be attired as requested. After consulting with the headmistress and getting her permission, I announced that I would give a grand prize of one hundred Barbados dollars each to the boy and girl who were wearing the best African garments. The children would select the judges, but only if they were themselves wearing African garments.

I was aware of the impact my sudden generosity would have on the children who were not wearing African dress, but I wanted it to be that way. I wanted those children to think about why he/she didn't make a greater effort to wear an African outfit. I also told those assembled that the following year there would be prize as well as a trophy. I'm sure that on next African History Celebration Day, each child will be attired, hoping to be the Best Dressed and claim their prize.

At the conclusion of the programmes, lunch was served. There were traditional Barbadian as well as African dishes: macaroni pie, cou cou, jollof rice and yam pie. I found it both amusing and amazing to be back in that setting, as I watched the children make their way towards the lunch. I noticed that they didn't want the jollof rice, nor any of the other traditional foods being offered. The children were making a 'B' line for the bakes and fishcakes that were being served. I kept waiting to see at least one of the students with a plate of jollof rice and yam pie, but I was disappointed. Plate after plate had bakes and fishcakes.

All in all I had a wonderful time and felt very light in my spirit when I left the school. I had enjoyed a fantastic programme and I had also instituted a new tradition of awarding a monetary prize and a trophy to the boy and girl who were the Best Dressed in their African attire. The teachers made a sterling effort to emphasise the importance of African consciousness and the contribution that Africans have made to human civilisation. I could not have been more pleased.

BOOK IX

Historical Reflections and Tributes

Adinkra symbol, Akofena, "Sword of War"

Symbol of courage, valour and heroism

CHAPTER 46

A tribute to Miss Riley

"He who learns, teaches" AFRICAN PROVERB

Ms Iris Riley was a very attractive teacher in every way. She was the cub (scout) Mistress and, in her khaki uniform and green beret, she was the best looking and most charming teacher at St Giles. All the boys thought so. Without equivocation, she could get any boy to do whatever she wanted. By the time I was eleven years old, Mrs Riley had also suggested that I join the Boys Scout and so, as I mentioned before, I started to show an interest from a distance. All because Mrs Riley had made the suggestion. All the boys wanted to please her and I was no exception.

These sentiments towards Mrs Riley never changed. I was four years old when I first said hello to Mrs Riley (who at that time was unmarried and called Miss Mullin) and seventy-one years old when I said my final farewell. This was on the afternoon of 12 July, 2012 and I, along with her family, friends, former and present students and former cub scout representatives all stood in St Barnabas Church yard in St Michael Barbados; not only to mourn her passing, but to reflect on the life of this amazing woman who helped to shape not only my life but, judging by the accolades being bestowed upon her; the lives of many.

I don't know how many of you have seen the film To Sir, With Love[1], starring Sidney Poitier and Lulu. Well, to me, this phenomenal woman, Iris Jeanetha Riley, was like "Sir" in the film. In a scene at the end, the actress Lulu sings these words:

Those schoolgirl days of telling tales and biting nails are gone
But in my mind I know they will still live on and on
But how do you thank someone who has taken you from crayons to
*   perfume?*
It isn't easy, but I'll try
If you wanted the sky I would write across the sky in letters
That would soar a thousand feet high 'To Sir, With Love'
The time has come for closing books and long last looks must end
And as I leave I know that I am leaving my best friend
A friend who taught me right from wrong and weak from strong
That's a lot to learn, but what can I give you in return?
If you wanted the moon I would try to make a start
But I would rather you let me give my heart 'To Sir, With Love'

Lulu sings this song as a tribute to her teacher: ironically, in Lulu's case the teacher was a male West Indian teacher in London! I find the song touching, to say the least, and I readily identified with her

The Late Iris Jeanetha Riley
(My Teacher and Mentor)

sentiments. The first line of the song goes: "Those schoolgirl days of telling tales and biting nails are gone..."

I am today where Lulu was then: schoolboy days of talking, sharing and yes, even biting nails are gone, and have been for many years. Yet even after all these years, I can still relate to the emotions expressed in that song, because in my most formative years there was such a "someone" for me: Miss Mullin.

When I became a young adult I returned to thank her and to let her know that I was making 'something' of my life. I'd continue to assist her with the St Giles Cub Scout years after I left St Giles. In those additional years I had the benefit of her continued tutelage, from which I gained additional knowledge.

Standing there in that church I wished I'd had another opportunity to let her see that none of her teaching had gone by the wayside. I'd listened and applied her instructions and even made one of her expressions another one of my mantras: "You Must Think!" Sitting there amongst those gathered, I couldn't help but think how do you thank someone who saw you through your childhood storms? Who was right there, physically, mentally and emotionally present that first frightening day of school. Someone who challenged you when you didn't even know what a challenge was? Someone who said to you, "I won't provide the answers for you, you must think. If, however, you've exhausted all the avenues available to you and you're still unable to get it, then and only then will I help you."

She was born on 16 November 1923 making her a Scorpio like myself with many of the attendant characteristics. On that September day in 1945, my first day of school, she was all of twenty-two: a very young adult lady, yet to us she was an old teacher. As was the custom we called her "Miss", a term used by us young children to those we saw as 'older' than us. Miss Riley was our "Miss" or our "Miss Teacher". So many of us were there but unsure of what the day held.

Now, sixty-seven years later, I wonder about this extraordinary woman who took me from crayons (in my case slate and pencil, an abacus, match sticks and counting on my fingers) to pen, ink, paper, and learning to think, not merely on a physiological level but also a cognitive one. Mrs Riley was the epitome of an instructor/teacher because she loved learning and was willing to impart that trait to all she encountered.

She will be missed but will live on through her countless contributions. Miss Mullin/Mrs Riley you a truly "a beautiful Soul", for you have truly taught me how to care and to give back, touching the souls of those we meet along the way.

FOOTNOTE

1. 'To Sir, With Love' is a British film that was released in 1967. Based on E.R. Braithwaite's 1959 autobiographical novel of the same name, it deals with social and racial issues in an inner city school. The film stars Sidney Poitier and British singer Lulu. E.R. Braithwaite (Eustace Edward Ricardo Braithwaite) was a Guyanese-born British-American novelist, writer, teacher and diplomat, best known for his stories of social conditions and racial discrimination against Black people. He died in 2016, aged 104.

CHAPTER 47

Memoriam: Tribute to Comrades in the Struggle and the Ancestors

The late great Comrade George Joseph was an amazing soldier in the struggle that we, as Black people, faced in England. I would like to humbly thank him for the work that he did, and for being such an instrumental force in working for the liberation of our people. To you, my brother in the struggle, thank you for welcoming us into your home and heart. Thank you for each time you dipped into your vast storehouse of knowledge, brought out something that was both relevant and of vital importance to the race, and shared it with us. We, my dear Comrade George Joseph, are eternally grateful for the seeds you have planted. They have taken root and we, your soldiers and students of that by-gone era, are still on the battlefield. We have absorbed the knowledge you so freely gave and we are using it towards the ultimate procurement: the liberation of our people. The struggle continues but your work has not been in vain. It is my sincere hope that your rise to the seat of the elders was swift and, when you made it to their midst, they welcomed you with open arms saying: "Well done Comrade George; well done."

EPILOGUE

"All is never said" IBO PEOPLE

You have travelled with me from 1895 to present. You have read the highs and some of the lows of my life. There may have been things you read where you could have surmised that I felt a degree of embarrassment (or even regret), nevertheless, you have walked with me and we have made it to this point. Now, here we are in 2017, one hundred and twenty two years from where we started. It has been a long journey.

Now that we've reached this point, I want to say that when I came into my consciousness in the 1960s, I was eager to do what I could for my Brothers and my Sisters to bring them to a place of awareness, so we can be a more unified people. That has not changed within me: I'm still doing what I can to ensure that the knowledge of our story is well-known and that we learn to think. I pray every day that the fire is kept lit and the light shines within us for the benefit of all African and African-diaspora people.

A few months ago during February, to celebrate Black History Month one of the Bishops and one of the senior Sisters of the Spiritual Baptists in Barbados came to my home and asked if they may borrow some of the African artefacts that I keep there. They wanted to share them with the children and help to bring enlightenment about our

Ancestors and our history. I readily and happily agreed. It filled me with a sense of pride and I said to myself: "See Collin Carter, you are still working. You are still teaching, you are still sharing."

I was proud then, but now I am excited as I come to this end of this book. You have come this far with me, and for that I thank you.

The journey is not over. As this journey continues, with God's grace and the Ancestor's guidance, I will ask you to continue to... "Walk With Me."

"When an old man dies, a library burns to the ground" AFRICAN PROVERB

"If you don't like someone's story, write your own" CHINUA ACHOBE

AUTHOR
Collin Leroy Carter

Collin Leroy Carter is a citizen of Barbados. With the completion of this book he is seeing a dream fulfilled; he finally gets to see his words written in stone.

"Oh that my words were now written! Oh that they were printed in a book! That they were graven with an iron pen and lead in the rock forever!" (Job 19:23, 24)

RESEARCHER
Annette Ione Smith

Annette Ione Smith is a citizen of Barbados who lives in New York City. She is the author of two books: *Etched* and *Rend*. This collaboration is her first foray into the non-fiction world. With the completion of this book she has fulfilled a dream which was to assist a friend in seeing his dream realised.